D1569307

Murder at Harvard

Murder at Harvard

HELEN THOMSON

19 71

HOUGHTON MIFFLIN COMPANY BOSTON

For Harry

Acknowledgments

I wish to express my appreciation for the generous help I received with the research for this book. I am especially indebted to Carolyn E. Jakeman, The Houghton Library, Harvard University, Winifred V. Collins, Massachusetts Historical Society, Olive R. Carter, Amesbury Public Library, and Mrs. Margaret Bryning, Cambridge Public Library. Also, Richard J. Wolfe, librarian of The Francis A. Countway Library of Medicine, and Harley P. Holden, Harvard University Archives, both generously answered questions for me on a number of occasions. I am obliged for many kindnesses to staff members at Widener Library, Harvard University, the Library of Congress, and the New York Public Library.

The Office of Sheriff Thomas S. Eisenstadt, Suffolk County, Boston, Massachusetts, was most helpful. Deputy Morton L. Bardfield patiently supplied answers to many questions. Dr. Miriam R. Small kindly wrote to me concerning Oliver Wendell Holmes' reaction to the murder as reflected in her work on his letters. Also, I am much obliged to Mr. and Mrs. E. J. Brehaut, Danvers, Massachusetts, who helped in a major way by sharing their Webster-Parkman collection with me.

Finally, I want to express my thanks to my husband, Harry C. Thomson, for many kinds of help, patiently and thoughtfully given.

H.T.

Foreword

WHEN CHARLES DICKENS arrived in Boston in November, 1868, a half-dozen of his close friends were on the little tug that met the *Cuba* as she entered Boston harbor. Together they escorted Dickens to the Parker House where a celebration dinner was served in his rooms. More than a quarter of a century had elapsed since Dickens' first visit to Boston, his friends reminded him. Now that he was back, what did he want to see in the old town? What Boston events of the past twenty-five years interested him most?

Dickens did not hesitate. He said he had long looked forward to visiting the room where Dr. Parkman was murdered by Professor Webster. He remembered that Dr. Holmes was Dean of the Medical College at the time of the tragedy and he meant to ask Holmes to give him a tour of the Medical College building. Consequently, when Dr. Oliver Wendell Holmes called at the Parker House the following afternoon, Dickens made his request and on January 5 the two men paid a visit to the red brick building on North Grove Street in Boston's West End. Dickens enjoyed himself immensely. "I saw the identical furnace smelling fearfully as if the body were still there," he told the friends assembled at a dinner party that evening.

For reasons that will be apparent as the story of the murder unfolds, Dr. Holmes found that visit to the Medical College

anything but enjoyable. In fact, many Bostonians were upset
over Dickens' visit to the room where Dr. Parkman was murdered. They were indignant that Dickens could be so insensitive as to reawaken public interest in an event Boston was very
eager to forget. Indeed, during the eighteen years that had intervened between the date of the murder and the occasion of
Dickens' visit, those closest to the tragedy pretended they *had*
forgotten. The biographies of contemporaries such as Oliver
Wendell Holmes, William Hickling Prescott, Edward Everett,
and President Jared Sparks of Harvard do not so much as acknowledge the fact that a murder took place. Furthermore, this
reticence extended to the following generation. Henry Cabot
Lodge wrote *Early Memories* in 1913. His family had lived
next door to the Parkmans for forty years. Yet he mentions
neither the tragedy nor the George Parkman family.

Bostonians were unwavering in their refusal to discuss in
public what Edward Everett called "the most disgraceful event
in our domestic history." But in private those who knew both
men — a list of their names reads like a Beacon Hill Blue Book
— speculated for a long, long time on how such a murder could
possibly have taken place. The famous American historian,
Albert Bushnell Hart, said that the subject was discussed when
he was a student at Harvard in the 1880's. Bostonians asked
each other how two men who had been friends for fifty years,
men who had gone to Harvard together and shared many interests and many, many friends — how could two such men become involved in *murder?* How could it happen in Boston,
where the proper handling of one's feelings was a condition of
Beacon Hill culture, if not a characteristic of Beacon Hill genes?

One objective of this book is to suggest answers to these questions. This means understanding what life was like in New
England after the Revolution, the period when Charles Bulfinch's architecture and the men from Essex County converted
Boston from a country town that delighted in public suppers on

the Common to a sophisticated city with the flavor of London during the Regency. It means understanding the economic and social changes that came about when Massachusetts began to look inland, and not to England, as a consequence of the War of 1812. And to understand the murder of Dr. George Parkman it is necessary to assess the impact of those forces on two men. John Webster was the son of an apothecary who grew rich during the Revolution, rich enough to live next door to Governor Hutchinson. For him, life was a desperate struggle to maintain a hold on the way of life enjoyed by his friends, relatives, and most of his professional colleagues. George Parkman was the scion of a wealthy Federalist family whose sons were at Harvard two generations before the Revolution. For this man life was a series of makeshift, second-choice satisfactions because the opportunity to do the work for which he had so eagerly prepared was denied him. An act that grew out of the deepest feelings of both these men resulted in a tragedy which Edmund Pearson, the historian of homicide, has labeled America's most celebrated murder.

Helen Thomson

Evanston, Illinois
May, 1971

Contents

Illustrations

following page 152

Sketch of Dr. Parkman

Sketch of Dr. Webster

Bowdoin Square in 1822 showing the Parkman mansion, the Blake-Tuckerman house built by Samuel Parkman for two of his daughters, and Charles Bulfinch's birthplace

Massachusetts Medical College, Harvard University

Map showing the location of the Medical College in the West End

Floor plan of the basement of the Medical College where Dr. Webster's lower laboratory was located and a drawing of the foundation of the building

The Massachusetts General Hospital and the Medical College across the street

Facsimiles of a note Marshal Tukey received after Dr. Webster's arrest

Dr. Keep's plaster casts of Dr. Parkman's jaws and the drawing Dr. Wyman made from pieces of bone found in the furnace in Dr. Webster's lower laboratory

Rufus Choate

Lemuel Shaw

Murder at Harvard

CHAPTER I

November 23, 1849

ON FRIDAY, November 23, 1849, Boston was busy with preparations for the most prosperous Thanksgiving in the city's history. The harbor was crowded with every kind of craft afloat
— sloops, schooners, barques, brigantines — all loaded with
provisions for Thanksgiving dinner. There were melons up
from the Azores, peaches from Italy, Madeira that had been
twice around the Horn, and plenty of choice old London Particular. Quincy Market and Faneuil Hall were enmeshed in
a tangle of tipcarts and barrows, sledges and wagons. Por-
tuguese sailors jostled oystermen from Gloucester; farmers from
Jamaica Plain bargained with housewives from Cambridge.
Business was transacted in half a dozen languages but most
often in the accents of County Clare and County Cork, for by
1849 Boston's North End was populated by the Irish.

The Irish not only built railroads and mansions and worked
in the tailor shops on Ann Street; they also solved housekeep-
ing problems for many a Boston lady. Now for the first time
there were plenty of willing Bridgets and Marys to shine the
silver and help the cook. No longer were Boston hostesses de-
pendent on the uncertain services of stiff-necked Massachusetts
farm girls who resented being "in service" and who left as soon
as they found a husband. With plenty of money and plenty of
help, Boston hostesses were relaxed and happy. At long last they

could give big parties and plenty of them. And they did.
Young William Prescott, son of the famous historian, was traveling in Europe with George Parkman, Jr., and heard about the
Thanksgiving parties in a letter from his father. The Prescotts
themselves were giving a dance the Wednesday before Thanksgiving; Lizzie and Amory had received cards for a ball at the
George Peabodys'; the Sam Eliots were having a dinner; and
the Charles Cunninghams were entertaining on Thanksgiving
evening. All very enjoyable, William Hickling Prescott wrote,
but he had to confess he couldn't report much progress on his
biography of Philip II.

Around the corner from the Prescott mansion at 55 Beacon
Street was Number 8 Walnut, the residence of Dr. George
Parkman, a handsome four-story house of red brick with a
spread eagle in bronze embedded in the fanlight above the
door. On this Friday before Thanksgiving, the last day of his
life, Dr. Parkman emerged from his house about noon. It was
a fine day, unseasonably warm for November in Boston, and
Dr. Parkman, a thin, homely man in his late fifties, was comfortable without a greatcoat. He wore a dark frock coat, dark
trousers, a purple satin vest, and, as always, a stovepipe hat.

The elms were bare now and from the steps of his house Dr.
Parkman could look down over the Common and see that
Tremont Street was even busier than it had been when he was
out earlier that morning. There was an unending stream of
chaises, broughams, and wagons, of women hurrying in the
direction of Quincy Market, of men on horseback, and little
boys trying to sell roasted chestnuts. Well, anybody who knew
Boston would expect this hustle and bustle on the Friday before
Thanksgiving. Old Fisher Ames had had a point when he told
those Jeffersonian Democrats in Washington: "In Boston, gentlemen, Thanksgiving is far more important than the Louisiana
Purchase."

Dr. Parkman started down his steps. Certainly he shared

few convictions with Fisher Ames, whom he recalled as an acid little man in small clothes and a tie-wig. Yet nobody could argue the importance of Thanksgiving to Bostonians. He was sure that for many others, as for him, Thanksgiving stirred memories in a way that was true of no other day on the calendar. He was on Beacon Street now and he glanced over at the old Hancock mansion, its huge clump of lilacs a great bundle of brown canes in winter. How many times had he visited that house with his father? And it was in his father's house that he had talked with John Adams, second President of the United States, and through his father's influence that he had been presented to Lafayette and entertained at Count Rumford's beautiful estate on the outskirts of Paris. Invariably at Thanksgiving he had a renewed sense of belonging to an old and distinguished family. At such times his bitterness over his own limitations and his failures was bearable only because of his confidence in his stewardship of his family's name and its fortune.

Dr. Parkman hurried along Beacon Street with his customary short, rapid stride. He walked with his body bent forward from the waist, a mannerism that accentuated his distinguishing feature, his protruding chin. (At the trial Mrs. Philena Hatch testified that during the evening of November 23 she said to her sister, "I saw Old Chin in Cambridge Street today.") As he turned into Park Street, Dr. Parkman passed George Ticknor's* home, once the site of the town almshouse. Across fifty years he remembered the ragged arms that reached out through the holes in the old wooden wall and the children's hands under the huge, ancient gates. Across fifty years he could still hear their crying. Long ago he had decided that he owed much to those miserable wretches, for they had awakened an interest that led to the most rewarding experience of his life. Nothing in after years matched those days in Paris when

---

* George Ticknor (1791-1871), former professor of languages at Harvard, author of a fine history of Spanish literature published in 1849.

in the dark of early morning he had hurried through the
groves of lime trees in the Luxembourg Gardens to La
Salpêtrière, to follow Dr. Pinel on his rounds through wards
lit by candlelight. It was Dr. Pinel who had taught him that
the insane should not be treated with stripes and starvation. He
said they needed decent physical care and the services of a
compassionate physician.

As Dr. Parkman arrived at the corner of Park and Tremont
by the Park Street Church, a brougham bore down on him
from the north and Sam Eliot bowed imperiously from its
window. Amused, he returned the bow. Samuel Atkins Eliot,
erstwhile mayor of Boston and treasurer of Harvard College.
In less than forty years Eliot's father had translated a shop on
Dock Square into a fortune that enabled his son to live like a
prince, better than most of them, in fact. The Ticknors had
been storekeepers, too, but that was something else nobody
mentioned these days. Not that there was anything wrong with
humble beginnings. Sam Appleton said he arrived in Boston
with his total capital the four pence he had earned helping
a stranger drive a herd of cattle, and Harry Otis himself
was the son of a bucket maker from Hingham. Maybe
jealousy explained the fact that a good many Boston people
were pretty hard on old Sam Eliot. When folks couldn't
think of any other basis for criticism, they shook their heads at
Sam for standing during church service, turning his back on
the pulpit when he disagreed with the minister. Well, he could
do worse. How about the January Sunday in 1720 when the
Reverend Peter Thatcher was installed at the North Church?
On that occasion the opposition gathered on the balcony and
expressed their displeasure by urinating on the congregation
below. How many times had he heard his father tell that
story?

Dodging tipcarts traveling in the direction of the Arlington
Street dump, watching out for ladies' carriages, farm wagons,
omnibuses, and an assortment of men on horseback, Dr. Park-

man crossed Tremont and went down School Street, past King's Chapel, along Washington into Cornhill Street. Old Cornhill, the only street in Boston that had a sidewalk when he was a child. The closer he got to Faneuil Hall, the denser the crowd became. There were a dozen times as many women as there had been in his youth when Federalist merchants in three-corner hats and scarlet cloaks did the family marketing with a servant close behind to carry home the purchases. They had all carried long Majorca walking sticks of a kind nobody but Daniel Webster used anymore. He thought of the chimney sweeps who used to frighten him far more than he ever admitted to anyone, certainly not to his father. What had become of those swarms of little Negro boys with their brooms and the pieces of dirty, ragged blanket they hauled the soot in?

The area from the foot of Cornhill to Quincy Market was alive with people and noise. Carts rattled over the cobblestones. Fish peddlers bellowed about cod and haddock; oystermen sang out their age-old chants; Irish women haggled with hucksters and yelled at their children. And as an obbligato to the din was the hollering of the men unloading cargo onto the wharves. Dr. Parkman decided to leave as soon as he had bought Harriette's lettuce. He would stop at Holland's out by the Medical College for the other things the family needed.

He clutched his hat and ducked to avoid a tray of rolls a baker held overhead and at that moment saw a familiar bonnet and shawl.

It was Mrs. Duggan arguing with a farmer guarding a huge pile of squash. She had a bill in her hand.

"Mrs. Duggan!" Dr. Parkman shouted.

Mrs. Duggan was a thin, red-haired woman in her thirties. When she saw Dr. Parkman, her look grew suddenly apprehensive.

Dr. Parkman had got to her now and was reaching for the bill.

Mrs. Duggan jerked it away.

"Mrs. Duggan, that money belongs to me! Have you forgotten you still owe me a dollar on this month's rent?"

Mrs. Duggan tried to turn away but the press of the crowd defeated her.

"Did you hear me, Mrs. Duggan?" Dr. Parkman's high, thin voice was sharp.

Mrs. Duggan looked frightened. "I need it for food! Eliza needs something to eat, don't she?"

Dr. Parkman's tone did not change. "Madam, you made an agreement with me and I expect you to live up to it. I *require* you to live up to it. Give me that money!"

He extended his hand and, sobbing, Mrs. Duggan gave him the money. After Dr. Parkman had smoothed the bill and put it into his black purse, he said in a different voice, "Now, then, Mrs. Duggan, you have honored your obligation to me. We have transacted our business and that matter is taken care of. Now let us consider the entirely separate problem of why you have no money. Did you lose your job at the hotel?"

Mrs. Duggan shook her head. When she spoke, her voice was blurred with crying. "It's Eliza. I haven't been to work since you and Dr. Shattuck was in on Thursday. She's too sick for the little ones to take care of. I couldn't leave her! She'd die!"

"Come over here by the building," Dr. Parkman said. "This man has to sell his produce." His tone was sharp again. He was not prepared for the hurt he felt to see Mrs. Duggan looking up at him as though he were the personification of greed and evil, Mrs. Duggan whom he had helped through many, many crises these past ten years. He knew people said he was hard, and maybe he was sometimes. It was his responsibility to manage wisely and at a profit the land he had inherited. He had no quarter deck and no counting house. He had no pulpit, as his brother, Francis, had. He was not the hospital superintendent he had prepared himself to be. He was a landlord, that was his business. But he was not *only* a landlord. In that moment he thought of the unknown hack writer — unknown to him, at least — who wrote the book in which all the rich men in Boston were listed and characterized with a sentence or two. In the light of recent events, including the experience at hand, it was a comfort to remember the description of him as a just man who unostentatiously dispensed many charities to Boston's poor.

His manner toward Mrs. Duggan did not soften. The more she trembled and cowered, the angrier he grew.

"Has Eliza taken the medicine Dr. Shattuck prescribed?" he demanded.

"How can she take it when we don't have it?" Mrs. Duggan cried at him. "How can I have the money for the apothecary when I'm not working? You expect her to get well if she don't have no medicine and nothing to eat!"

Mrs. Duggan's manner was belligerent as she thrust her tear-stained face up at him.

Well, he would rather have her belligerent than cringing, Dr. Parkman thought, but his tone did not change. He said coldly, "Speaking as a physician, I would expect little progress in such a situation." He reached for his pocketbook and counted out three dollars. "Have the prescription refilled and get her to take beef broth. Dr. Shattuck and I will be around to see her in the morning."

He turned away without waiting for her to speak.

He stopped at Quincy Market and got Harriette's lettuce. The price was murderous but the money would be well spent if only Harriette's appetite improved. It was hard to see her barely able to walk at a time of life when most young people were robust. He thought again of taking her to New York, but who there was any more skilled in diagnoses than the Boston men? Young Francis, his nephew, was back in Boston after

almost two years' treatment in New York and seemed little improved, if he was improved at all.* Harriette was twenty-eight
now. She had been in bad health all her life, but maybe
one day she would be well. Every day they found new ways to
help patients. Think of the advances they'd made in surgery
now that patients could be anesthetized.

Dr. Parkman consulted his watch and made a sudden decision
to go out to the West End by way of Bowdoin Square. Maybe it
was his worry over Harriette or maybe it was the memories
Thanksgiving stirred in him. In any event, he felt an urge to
see the Square again. Crossing over to Court Street, he thought
back to the days when so many Parkmans lived in the neighborhood of Green Street, when Elizabeth and Sally were young
brides living in the Bowdoin Square houses their father had
given them as wedding presents. Francis had moved back to
the old house long ago and for years he himself had lived next
to Kirk Boott's home. But fond as he was of Bowdoin Square,
he could not live next door to a hotel — the Revere House,
they called the remodeled Boott mansion — even a hotel fine
enough for President Polk.

Standing in front of the hotel, Dr. Parkman wondered who
had designed that high, narrow old house. It had none of the
Bulfinch touch of the other houses in Bowdoin Square.† He
looked across the street to the spot where Charles Bulfinch's
home had stood behind a row of poplars. Charles had watched
the Battle of Bunker Hill from the roof of that house and had
returned to it at the end of a harder life than any man should
have to bear. But Charles had had his triumphs, too, and that
was a comfort to remember. His first big success was the house
he had built for his brother-in-law, Joseph Coolidge, right

---

* Francis Parkman (1823-1893), later to win fame as the author of *The Oregon
Trail* and other historical works. He was the son of Dr. Parkman's brother, the
Reverend Francis Parkman.
† Charles Bulfinch (1763-1844), first professional United States architect.

here in Bowdoin Square. Joseph was gone now and so was his
house with its fine oval dining room, but Bostonians still told
a story about another Coolidge, Cornelius. For years Cornelius
had fretted about the row of State House privies that bordered
his Beacon Hill property. It was Charles Bulfinch who suggested that Cornelius might be rid of the privies if he offered
to build vaults in the basement of the State House. The Massachusetts legislature greeted that proposal with some hesi-
tancy. Finally they accepted Mr. Coolidge's offer for a trial
period of three years with the stipulation that he post a $5000
bond and agree to remove the vaults if they proved "inadequate." *Inadequate?*

Dr. Parkman walked on up Green Street to the house his
father had enjoyed so much, the house where his brother, Francis, still lived. In his father's time the house had fine gardens
shaded by chestnut trees. He remembered his father's pride in
the pears he raised, a hobby he shared with President Kirkland
of Harvard. Many an afternoon they spent discussing pear culture over a dinner of roast goose and claret. President Kirkland
enjoyed himself so much he wanted to change the chapel hour at
Harvard so he could get over to Boston in plenty of time for two
o'clock dinner with his friends. His request brought down the
wrath of the righteous in both Boston and Cambridge, a fore-
seeable development that bothered him not at all. What *did*
bother him was the Overseers' unwillingness to do as he asked.

Samuel Parkman had enjoyed the hullabaloo. Dr. Parkman
envied his father his talent for enjoying life. The old man enjoyed his silver plate and his fine furniture and Spanish wine.
He enjoyed the portrait Stuart had done of him. That portrait
still hung in the old house. There he was, a ruddy-com-
plexioned man with the glow of good health and good spirits,
resplendent in a blue velvet suit.

As he hurried out Cambridge Street, Dr. Parkman thought
about his father's warmth and his generosity. His own failure

to get the appointment as superintendent of the McLean
Asylum was a blow his father felt deeply. Yet he did not with-
hold his contribution toward the building of the Massachusetts
General Hospital — and a handsome contribution it was,
$200,000 — even though the men who were responsible for
Dr. Wyman's appointment to McLean were the men who im-
plemented the plans for Massachusetts General.

His father had been a staunch Federalist who had attended
the Hartford Convention in 1814 but he had a sense of humor
that had been denied to such dour characters as Fisher Ames and
Timothy Pickering. Glancing back at Harrison Otis' big house
at the corner of Lynde Street, he thought that of all his friends,
his father enjoyed none more than Harry Otis, another old
Federalist who lived a life in which there was no place for
homespun and raspberry tea. He gave wonderful parties in
the second-floor drawing room of his Beacon Street house.
And for those who found the climb up the stairs enervating,
there was a ten-gallon Lowestoft punch bowl on the landing.

Harry Otis was good-natured and easygoing but he had a
temper. His friends enjoyed telling the story about the
Federalist with the unlikely name of Salem Towne who voted
for a piece of legislation that was a trap set by the Democrats
in the Massachusetts legislature for just such Federalists as
Mr. Towne. Otis was furious at such stupidity.

"Your parents were four miles out of the way when they
named you!" he thundered at the hapless Salem Towne. "They
should have called you Marble Head!"

Dr. Parkman was not aware that he had laughed aloud over
that old story until the two little boys standing by a
wagon looked at him questioningly.

"It's a fine warm day for Thanksgiving time, isn't it, boys?"
he said as he passed them.

One of them — was he Calvin Moore's boy? — answered
respectfully, "Yes, it is, Doctor."

Dr. Parkman was surprised at the pleasure the youngster's greeting gave him. Why was he so eager for reassurance that he was respected? Did he feel in his heart that to be betrayed by a lifelong friend implied that a man was a weakling anybody could take advantage of?

To the boys he said, "My, those horses have a load." He gestured toward the Marsh and Barrett's wagon. "What have they got there, pig iron for the foundry?"

Before the boys could answer, a woman leaned out of a window in the house behind them.

"Good day, Dr. Parkman. You must be enjoying your walk on a day like this." She spoke pleasantly and again Dr. Parkman responded to the respectful way in which he was greeted.

The woman addressed the two boys. "You two get along to school. It's already ten minutes to one. Are you planning to *fly* from here to Pinckney Street?"

Dr. Parkman had reached Paul Holland's grocery store at the corner of Blossom Street at Vine. He enjoyed the old wooden building with its smells of molasses and sweet wood smoke, of cheese and pickles and fish.

Calvin Moore was talking to Mr. Holland as Dr. Parkman entered the store.

"Good day to you both," he said. "We could never ask for finer Thanksgiving weather than this, now could we?"

As the men returned his greeting, he said to Mr. Moore, "Just had a word with your boy as I came in. Fine-looking little chap. What is he, about ten?"

"He'll be ten next month, Dr. Parkman, and thank you. His mother and I think he's a fine youngster but that's to be expected, I guess."

When their laughter had died, Dr. Parkman said to Mr. Holland: "I've got a few things I want sent up to the house. Can you do that this afternoon?"

When Mr. Holland nodded, he said, "Send over six pounds

of butter. And sugar. I could use thirty pounds of sugar."

Mr. Holland got a wooden bucket. "This holds thirty-two pounds, sir."

"Fill it and send it over," Dr. Parkman told him. "And I'd best be moving along if I'm to be home by dinner time. A good Thanksgiving to you both if I don't see you before Thursday, which I probably will." From the doorway he added, "Could I leave this package with you for a few minutes, Mr. Holland?" He set the bag of lettuce on the counter behind a round of cheese. "I'll pick it up very shortly."

Mr. Holland said, "I'll be pleased to keep an eye on it for you, Dr. Parkman."

Dr. Parkman walked rapidly along Vine Street. He looked over at the Massachusetts General Hospital standing on land that had once been old Sam Prince's pasture. He wondered how many winter afternoons of his childhood had been spent in Sam Prince's dusty sail loft on India Wharf. What fun it had been to go next door from the cold, shadowy loft to his father's place, to a crackling hickory fire and plenty of hot toddy for a chilled youngster. After half a century he could still feel his surreptitious pleasure in the clerks' deferential manner and his pride in being his father's son. He never met another man who radiated success and security in the unostentatious manner that had added so much to his father's charm.

Elias Fuller bowed from the doorway of the iron foundry and Dr. Parkman returned his greeting perfunctorily. Absently he looked out beyond the foundry to the Charles River and across the Charles to the old Joseph Barrell mansion. Charles Bulfinch had drawn the plans for that house and once it was the showplace of the whole Boston area. In those days there were imported plants in the gardens, marble fountains stocked with goldfish, and a stable of fine horses. When Joseph Barrell entertained at dinner, which was often, his guests were not subjected to the long drive home. A barge with boatmen in livery carried them back to Boston by way of the Charles. Then in the twinkling of an eye the Barrell fortune was swept away. Joseph Barrell saw the day when he was penniless and deeply in debt. After his bankruptcy he never left his house. When he died, he was buried after dark as he had directed. On a windy October night he was taken over the Charlestown Bridge, the long drive he had always spared his guests, to the family vault in King's Chapel. Now his mansion was the McLean Asylum and the superintendent was Rufus Wyman, not George Parkman. Standing there, looking at the old house with its fine Doric columns, Dr. Parkman could understand how Joseph Barrell felt about failure.

As he crossed North Grove Street to the Medical College, Dr. Parkman felt sudden, hot anger. He knew how to deal with a man who betrayed his old friends, a man who repaid generosity with trickery! He would teach John Webster that George Parkman was nobody's dupe!

Dr. Parkman took the brick steps two at a time. As he opened the wide door that led into the first-floor hall, he heard students' laughter from Dr. Holmes' lecture room overhead. He closed the door behind him for the last time. Dr. George Parkman was never seen alive after about one o'clock on Friday, November 23, 1849.

CHAPTER II

Saturday Morning

BEFORE EIGHT O'CLOCK the following morning, Saturday, the Parkmans' manservant, Patrick McGowan, was on his way to Summer Street to the home of Dr. Parkman's brother-in-law, Robert Gould Shaw. A thin, red-haired Irishman in his early twenties, Patrick was a touch apprehensive under the best of circumstances. This morning his anxiety was almost more than he could bear. Hurrying through the Common, preoccupied with the message he carried, he had no time to speak to Molly, the apple woman, or to the little boys selling chestnuts, or even to Tim, the Prescotts' coachman, whom he had known all his life. Crossing Tremont Street he dodged drays and wagons so recklessly that the drivers yelled at him.

Patrick went down Winter Street at a run. As he entered Summer Street from Washington, he saw the Reverend Mr. Gardiner emerge from Trinity Church with three men in tall black hats. Out of respect he slowed down to a fast walk. He picked up speed again as he hurried along the porcelain wall that surrounded the Cushing mansion. On any other morning he would have tried for a glimpse of the Chinese servants Mr. Cushing had brought from Canton along with his porcelain wall, but not today.

Now Patrick had reached his destination, the big square brick house at 46 Summer Street. He seized the iron gate and let himself into Mr. Shaw's garden with its fine boxwood hedge

and the statue of a mermaid playing with a fish. At the door
he said he brought an urgent message from Mrs. Parkman. He
was immediately admitted to the reception hall.

While he waited, Patrick struggled to keep down his nerv-
ousness by concentrating on the end of the parlor he could see
from where he stood, the heavy green draperies, the black wal-
nut bookcases between the windows, the flowered carpet.
Above the white mantel hung portraits of Mr. and Mrs. Shaw,
Mrs. Shaw's dark hair covered by a turban of figured silk.
Those portraits were probably painted by Mr. Gilbert Stuart,
Patrick thought. Long ago he had learned that everybody in
Boston who was anybody had his portrait painted by Mr. Stuart.

And the Shaws were certainly somebody. Everybody knew
Mr. Shaw's story, how after his father's death he had come to
Boston from Maine, an awkward, penniless thirteen-year-old,
to live with his uncle, William Shaw. Another of his uncles
was Samuel Parkman, whose first wife was a Shaw. Robert
Shaw was a frequent visitor in the Parkman home on Bowdoin
Square where there was plenty of room and plenty of money.
There were also plenty of children, nine when Mr. Shaw came
to Boston. George was born the following February, 1790, and
the two youngest children, Samuel and Daniel, within the next
four years. Young Shaw proved to be a smart, hard-working
lad so nobody was surprised when two of his Parkman relatives,
Edward Tuckerman and Samuel Rogers, offered him a part-
nership in their firm. What *did* surprise Boston was Shaw's
marriage to Elizabeth Parkman, Samuel Parkman's only
daughter by his second marriage. A beautiful, vivacious girl
sought after by the most eligible bachelors in town, Elizabeth
chose the shy boy with only a few months' formal schooling.
The wedding took place during George Parkman's senior year
at Harvard and it united two people he deeply loved.

Mr. Shaw appeared from the far end of the parlor. He had
the long, bony face of the man in the portrait, but now

at seventy-three he looked thinner and his light brown hair
was white. He wore a silk dressing gown. He listened in silence
while Patrick told his story.

Speaking rapidly, Patrick described how Dr. Parkman had left
his house the previous day about noon and had not returned.
Mrs. Parkman said that in the thirty-three years of their marriage, the Doctor had never before failed to come home to two
o'clock dinner. He had been late only three or four times in
all those years and even then he had always sent a message. Mrs. Parkman had stayed up all night, waiting. She had
taken nothing but a cup of tea since breakfast yesterday. She
said to tell Mr. Shaw she was in great distress and she wanted
him to come up to Walnut Street as soon as he could.

Mr. Shaw thought a moment. Then he asked whether Mrs.
Parkman knew of any possible explanation for the Doctor's
absence, any piece of business that might have taken him out
of town unexpectedly.

Patrick shook his head. Mrs. Parkman couldn't think of any
reason the Doctor would go away suddenly like that.

Who besides the family and the servants knew of Dr. Parkman's absence, Mr. Shaw asked.

Nobody but Mr. Kingsley, Patrick said. Mr. Kingsley had
called on business during the afternoon and the maids told him
Dr. Parkman hadn't come home.

Patrick hesitated and fidgeted. There was one thing more,
he stammered. About nine o'clock Friday morning Dr. Parkman had a caller. The Doctor himself was passing through
the hall as Patrick opened the door, so he greeted the visitor
himself. Patrick didn't get the man's name but he did hear
something about arrangements for a meeting at half-past one.
The caller was short and stocky. He was middle-aged and he
wore glasses. He had on a black coat, dark pantaloons and he
didn't have a hat. Patrick had gone over and over that description but Mrs. Parkman couldn't think who the man might be.

Patrick felt terrible. But, he pleaded, could he be expected to know all Dr. Parkman's friends and all his business acquaintances when he had worked for the family only a little more than two months?

Of course not, Mr. Shaw said reassuringly. And Patrick wasn't to worry. Doubtless the caller, whoever he was, would step forward when word got around that Dr. Parkman was missing, if he *was* missing. Mr. Shaw paused, frowning. Then he said Patrick was to go back to Mrs. Parkman and tell her Mr. Shaw would be with her within half an hour. He would say a word to Mrs. Shaw, who was not well this morning, and then leave for Walnut Street.

The news that something was amiss with the Parkmans had permeated the Shaw household by the time Patrick was halfway to the garden gate. He saw Henry, the Shaws' coachman, on his way to the carriage house. One of the maids came flying down the path, a pretty girl with red curls escaping her white cap. Hadn't Dr. Parkman come home *at all,* she asked Patrick, incredulous. Didn't *anybody* know where he was, not even *Mrs. Parkman?*

Before Patrick could answer, Henry opened the carriage house doors and at the sight of him, the girl flew back to the house, her black skirt billowing as she ran, the white ties of her apron a neat bow at her back.

Patrick stepped into Summer Street with a fine, exhilarating sense of relief. Mr. Shaw had not blamed him about the caller after all! Patrick sighed gustily. For the first time that morning he noticed the bright blue November sky and the graceful, arching elms of Summer Street. Directly ahead he saw a cluster of funeral carriages at Trinity and to avoid them he turned into Chauncy Place. As he passed the First Church, he glanced up at its new glass roof. Everybody in Boston teased Dr. Frothingham about trying to raise Christians under glass. Patrick laughed aloud — and immediately felt guilty. How could he enjoy himself like this when Mrs. Parkman and Harriette were so miserable? Sobered, he ran up Bedford Street, along Judge Jackson's gardens, into West Street. He saw Mr. John Gardner enter Miss Peabody's little bookshop and noted perfunctorily that he was wearing clothes. Folks said Mr. Gardner made money so fast you could set him down stark naked at the foot of State Street and by the time he got to the old State House, he would have a new suit, a tall hat, a cane, and money in his pockets.

Patrick heard somebody calling him and turned his head to see Mr. Kingsley beckoning from Tremont Street. Mr. Kingsley looked upset. Everything about him seemed to droop, his good-natured fat face, his old black coat, the brown paper bag he carried. Mr. Kingsley helped Dr. Parkman manage his property and the two men shared a close friendship. For years Mr. Kingsley had vehemently defended the Doctor against those who accused him of being greedy and mean.

Mr. Kingsley was speaking. He sounded tired and worried. "I was up at Parkman's after you left. He hasn't come home yet."

"How long ago were you there?" Patrick asked him.

"Half an hour, maybe less."

"What do you suppose could have happened to him?"

Mr. Kingsley shrugged his shoulders. "I traced him from School Street down Cornhill to the market and over to Bowdoin Square and on out Cambridge Street to the Medical College. Word is getting around that he's missing. I didn't have any trouble tracing him."

He held out the brown paper bag. "He stopped at Holland's and left this lettuce. Take it up to the house with you, will you?"

Patrick accepted the bag. "What time was he there?"

"About two o'clock. Elias Fuller was standing in the doorway of the foundry a few minutes before two and the Doctor passed by and spoke to him. Elias knows the time for sure because he was standing there waiting for his brother to get back from dinner so he could go and get his." Mr. Kingsley got out his watch. "I'll stop back up at the Parkmans' this afternoon. Right now I think I'll go around to the railroad stations again. If there's any news, send word over to my place, will you? I'll be home for dinner." He started off up Tremont Street then and looking after him, Patrick saw Mr. Shaw's brougham cross into Park Street, Henry on the box.

Mrs. Parkman opened the door the moment the Shaw carriage pulled into Walnut Street. She stood waiting while Henry let the step down for Mr. Shaw. A slight, dark-haired woman, Mrs. Parkman was a daughter of Thomas McDonough, for many years the British consul to Boston. Her British rearing was still apparent in a certain reserve in her manner. All the same, there was warmth in her greeting to Mr. Shaw, whom she had known for almost forty years.

Mrs. Parkman led the way into the small sitting room that overlooked the garden. She said that when she was in this room, George's favorite, she had the courage to believe that at any moment he would be there in his big green chair, leaning to look down into the garden he loved. Just this past spring he had sent to England for a special wooden handle for that old pump out there. Sometimes if he was very tired, he refreshed himself by taking down one of those old volumes of the *Medical Intelligence*. He loved to recall the days when Dr. Smith and he were its editors. It was a source of pride to him that the present editor, David Clapp, was an awkward, uneducated printer's boy when George offered to tutor him. And how often had she seen George fondle that little wooden box on the center table? She could see him now, peering in at the little wren on the twig. John Audubon had named that

species *The Parkman Wren* as a gesture of appreciation for
George's kindnesses to him. And George *was* kind to Mr.
Audubon, giving him money to finance his Labrador expedi-
tion, arranging to have his work published. George was kind
to so many people. Mrs. Parkman began to weep.

Gently Mr. Shaw said he understood from Patrick that she
had no knowledge of any business that might have taken
George out of town unexpectedly. Was that right?

Mrs. Parkman nodded and in answer to further questions
said she knew of no unusual worries troubling George at this
time. Harriette wasn't any better but she wasn't any worse,
either. George talked of taking her to Dr. Elliot's place on
Staten Island but he was uncertain since the New York doctors hadn't been able to help young Francis. As she tucked
her handkerchief into the cuff of her sleeve, she asked whether
Patrick had told about the caller whose name they didn't know.
At first she had been terribly upset about that and she knew
she had been hard on Patrick. But today she felt resigned.
Judging from Patrick's description of how George greeted the
man, he must be a close friend. All the same, she deeply regretted that they did not know more about the appointment
Patrick spoke of. George was away for two hours in the middle
of the morning. He came home about eleven and left again
at noon. He marketed sometime during the day. Holland's
delivered an order in the afternoon.

Mr. Shaw said he could account for George's whereabouts
for an hour and a half during the morning. He had come down
to Summer Street shortly after breakfast, around nine, and
together they walked over to State Street. George was in fine
spirits. They discussed the City Council's recommendation
about filling in Back Bay which, according to the Council, was
nothing but a smelly cesspool. They talked over the news that
California had adopted a constitution outlawing slavery. If anything, George was in better spirits than usual.

Abruptly Mrs. Parkman leaned forward. Wasn't it time they

went to the police, she asked urgently. Maybe George was lying someplace, seriously hurt, unable to get home. And shouldn't she try to get word to young George? He was somewhere in Germany. Maybe the Prescotts had heard more recently than they. And what about Harriette? What should she tell Harriette?

Mr. Shaw thought they should wait a little longer before they asked the police to begin a search. Granted it was not like him, it was possible George had made a sudden decision to go out of town. Mr. Shaw had heard him discuss the possibility of taking Harriette to New York. It was at least conceivable that he had gone there to arrange for her care. Had Elizabeth sent word of George's disappearance to Bowdoin Square?

Mrs. Parkman shook her head. She did not want to alarm Francis unnecessarily. It was only within the past few weeks that he had begun to recover from the news of Sam's death. As it was, he was depressed because young Francis' eyes were no better. If the day was bright, the boy still had to shut himself up in the dark of the garret to stave off a headache. It was the same thing all over again.

Patrick appeared in the doorway. When Mrs. Parkman looked over at him, he said he wanted to tell her that when he was on his way back from Summer Street, Mr. Kingsley gave him a bag of lettuce Dr. Parkman left at Holland's yesterday.

Mrs. Parkman's eyes filled. "For Harriette. He bought lettuce to tempt Harriette's appetite," she said.

Mr. Shaw rose. He thought he had better go over to Bowdoin Square and talk with Francis. One or the other of them would come over to Walnut Street by early afternoon at least. As for Harriette, he felt Elizabeth had no choice but to tell her they still had no word from her father but they hoped for news momentarily. In all probability he would come into town on one of the afternoon trains and all their worrying would be for nothing.

When Mrs. Parkman looked uncertain, he suggested that if

Harriette became seriously upset, it would be wise to send for
Dr. Bigelow. Certainly in time of trouble no family could turn
to a finer physician or a kinder friend than Jacob Bigelow. Mr.
Shaw paused. Then speaking gently and slowly he said he
knew the question he was about to ask would be upsetting.
Yet he felt he had to know about the clothes George wore yesterday. That information would be important if it was necessary for the police to publicize his disappearance.

Elizabeth Parkman burst into tears. When she was able to
control her crying, she said that when she last saw him, her
husband was wearing a dark coat and dark pantaloons, a black
figured stock, his purple waistcoat, and his tall black hat.

Standing at the corner of Walnut and Beacon streets, Mr.
Shaw fingered his watch. Twenty minutes past nine, almost
three hours until noon. Five hours until the two o'clock trains
came in. Should they wait that long before going to the police,
granted there was no word from George in the meantime? As
he put his own watch away, he thought of the watch George
treasured, the Lepine he had bought in London, in Adams
Street. Doubtless he had it with him now, wherever he was.

Walking slowly, considering what he would say to Francis,
Mr. Shaw started on out Beacon Street. As he crossed Belknap,
he thought of the Saturday nights of his childhood when the
barbers' boys streamed up the north side of Beacon Hill, each
of them with a mountain of wig boxes ready for Boston's Sunday morning. He saw Mr. Prescott coming up Park Street on
his big white horse. George Parkman, Jr., and young William
Prescott were somewhere in Europe together. Momentarily he
considered asking Mr. Prescott about the boys' address. It was
better to wait, he decided. No point in confiding the family's
fears unless it was necessary. He watched Mr. Prescott turn into
Beacon Street, a handsome man who knew how to sit his fine
horse, a man whose books won world acclaim despite the college
brawl that had blinded his left eye and seriously damaged the
other. Boston was justly proud of Mr. Prescott.

Mr. Shaw paused in front of Governor Hancock's mansion. The old house looked much as it had fifty years earlier when he had stood on the same spot and watched Governor Hancock's servants carry him out of his house in a sedan chair, the old man dressed in satin and lace, his ailing foot wrapped in bandages. George said it was no wonder Governor Hancock suffered with gout. The Governor had one solution for all his problems, personal and political: he gave a dinner. Well, that solution had one great merit, Mr. Shaw reflected as he turned into Bowdoin Square. It worked. For many years the anniversary of the Gunpowder Plot had been the signal for a bloody riot with the battle line drawn at the Mill Bridge in Hanover Street. For decades neither the resources of the law nor the length of the casualty lists diminished by one iota the town's enthusiasm for the fray. Then Governor Hancock invited everybody in both factions to a dinner at the Green Dragon Inn. The dinner cost $1000, which he paid out of his own pocket, but it did the trick. There was no more rioting on Guy Fawkes Day.

It was the year the Governor died that the town had a dinner celebrating the Revolution in France. And what a dinner. Mr. Shaw shook his head over the memory. The table stretched all the way from Kilby Street to the Old State House. The roast ox weighed 1000 pounds and they gilded his horns and hauled him through town on a wagon 20 feet high. The children were served cakes with *Liberty* and *Equality* stamped on them. And all this in January. Maybe one day Mr. Prescott would write about those times.

Well, Governor Hancock had been in his grave for fifty years and more, but he was very much alive when Samuel Parkman built his house at 5 Bowdoin Square. The big house with its Doric columns had the Bulfinch look. Doubtless Charles Bulfinch had a hand in designing it. The two families were close friends at the time it was built and for long afterward. Living across the Square from each other, they shared their gardens and many other interests. It was in the Bulfinch parlor that the *Columbia*'s owners planned the voyage that made her the first American vessel to circumnavigate the globe; it was Samuel Parkman who bought the cargo of tea she brought home from Canton. Earlier Charles had made the trip to England that shaped his own destiny and in so doing changed Boston from a village with three or four brick buildings to a town with the look of London during the Regency. His family never let him forget the letter he wrote from London when the Charles River Bridge was finished. "I hope the bridge is still standing when I get home," he said. "I should like to see it but I don't think I should venture to walk over it."

The Parkmans heard Charles Bulfinch's descriptions of London with the same interest with which they listened to his father's stories about Edinburgh during the days when he was in medical school there. Doubtless Dr. Bulfinch's influence was a major factor in the family's decision to send George and Francis to Scotland for their graduate work. And perhaps it was the memory of those happy years in Bowdoin Square that accounted for Francis Parkman's pleasure in his father's house. He had lived at 5 Bowdoin Square for the twenty-five years that had elapsed since the old man's death. He said the house was convenient to his church in the North End and it didn't bother him that the gardens were gone or that the Kirk Boott mansion was now a hotel they called the Revere House. Neither was he disturbed by the racket of the horse cars or the hullabaloo of Marshal Tukey's parades.

Mr. Shaw reflected that Francis and George Parkman were both high-strung men, but their nervousness was manifest in ways as different as their appearances. Francis, a small-boned, slender man with fine, regular features, was as handsome as George was homely. George had a reputation as a difficult, stingy, ill-natured man with a highly explosive temper. On the other hand, Francis was an urbane gentleman whose wit and polish made him successful in the pulpit of one of Boston's most fashionable churches. In him, tension was expressed in deep, terrible depressions.

Francis Parkman could rarely say what triggered those attacks of melancholia. Everyone knew, though, that his deepest sorrow was his troubled relationship with his son. Young Francis Parkman could not stomach urbanity, which he equated with superficiality, and this was the charge he leveled against the clergy, whom he characterized as "vermin." The father realized it was no coincidence that his son's *bete noire* had been the Reverend William Ellery Channing, the man he himself admired as he admired few other human beings.* Whatever else he was, the Reverend Mr. Channing had *not* been urbane. With his thin face lost under a wide-brimmed hat tied on with a scarf in winter, he was one of the funniest looking men who ever trod the streets of Boston. Francis Parkman recognized that the trouble in his relationship with his son went deeper than young Francis' distaste for urbanity. Was the boy reacting to what he saw as artificiality in both men, artificiality manifest in his father's polished manners on the one hand and on the other in William Channing's insistence in living in the cold garret of his rich wife's magnificent house? Whatever the explanation, Francis Parkman suffered deeply over his relationship with his son. The knowledge that young Francis' wide circle of friends found him a warm and charming person only added to his father's heartache.

When the two men were seated in the big parlor at 5 Bowdoin Square and he had told the story of George's disappearance, it did not surprise Mr. Shaw that Francis immediately suggested temporary insanity as the explanation. In all likelihood, he said, George was the victim of an "aberration of the mind" and in the grip of the attack had wandered

* William Ellery Channing (1780-1842), Unitarian clergyman noted for his humane and liberal philosophy.

off into the woods. Also, they could not disregard the possibility of suicide. As they both knew, George was a very highstrung man. Under the impact of some experience that upset him to the point of irrationality, he might have taken his own life. Yes, it was possible that George had made an impulsive decision to go off on a trip. Possible, but not probable, Francis thought. However, he agreed they should wait until the two o'clock trains were in before they went to the police.

Sitting there, looking into the fire, the Reverend Francis Parkman began to talk about the emotional instability that plagued the family. George with his explosive temperament, he with his depressions, and the other brother erratic, irresponsible Sam. Sam's divorce had been a scandal eclipsed only by the rumor that embezzlement was the real reason for his decision to spend the rest of his life abroad. Even in France Sam had continued to be a source of sorrow to the family. "Naughty Sam," Boston nicknamed him. Everybody knew he lived the life of a bon vivant in Paris, unrepentant for all the heartache he had caused. How many Boston mothers had warned their sons against associating with Samuel Parkman once they got to Paris? During these six months since Sam's death, Francis had thought much about the family strain of instability. He had a terrible premonition they were about to face another instance of their trouble.

Mr. Shaw said he was not ready — not yet, at least — to take such a grim view of the situation. In the first place, he could not believe George was the victim of an attack of insanity. He told about his Friday morning walk with him, described their conversation with friends, George's interest in the news from California and the rumor that Bronson Alcott planned to start one of his Conversation Series in a room next door to Miss Peabody's shop in West Street. You could buy a ticket from Miss Peabody for $5. $5! George was appalled at the price. When the discussion turned to Henry Clay's compromise efforts on the slavery question, somebody commented that Mr. Clay never did have any luck in New England. At that George recalled the old story about the time the Exchange Building burned, interrupting a poker game in which Clay held four aces. Mr. Shaw said he had rarely seen George in better spirits. He could not believe that the explanation of his disappearance lay in an upset that brought on an attack of insanity.

Francis Parkman rose suddenly. He crossed the room to a window that looked out on the route of the Bowdoin Square horse cars, across a street that was once the terraced garden where his father raised bergamot pears. Turning back to Mr. Shaw, he asked what could have happened to George if his absence was not explained by an emotional crisis. If he was off on a trip, *what* trip — to *where?* Then he paused. Come to think of it, George had talked a good deal about the Magee place recently. This past month he had spent many afternoons at the Lunatic Asylum arranging for the installation of the organ he had bought for the chapel, helping Dr. Brown plan the new wing. Could those visits have stirred memories so unsettling that he had gone to see the Magee place again and stayed in Roxbury for the night?

It was hard to believe that it was thirty-six years since George had come home from Paris determined to introduce Dr. Pinel's methods for the treatment of the insane into New England. How excited he was when he learned that the committee charged with soliciting funds for the Massachusetts General Hospital was also interested in establishing a hospital for the insane! He could hardly wait to apply for the post of superintendent of the asylum. He did everything he could think of to promote his candidacy. Remember how he wrote a treatise describing the treatment methods he believed in, had it printed, and distributed to the committee? Remember how he maneuvered to get himself an invitation to read a paper on insanity at a meeting of the Medical Society? And how happy

he was the day he found the old Shirley Mansion in Roxbury
was for sale for a modest $16,000. He had already rented the
place for the small private institution he planned to establish.
Built of brick with a layer of wood for extra warmth, the house
had a great center hall that served perfectly for the activities
George felt were indispensable in the treatment of the insane.
And he insisted that the fine view of the harbor had a calming
effect on patients.

But in the end Rufus Wyman was appointed superintendent
of the McLean Asylum and George suffered a bitter blow. Sitting there in the quiet of Samuel Parkman's parlor, looking
up at the portrait of him in his fine blue velvet suit, Robert
Shaw and Francis Parkman speculated, as they had speculated
many times before, on what went wrong. True, there was a
misunderstanding about money. George had said that if the
committee would be responsible for $5000 of the purchase
price of the Magee place, he would see that the remaining
$11,000 was contributed. The committee understood him to
mean that he would solicit additional contributions in the
amount of $11,000, but George's intention was to ask friends
to allow money already pledged to be earmarked for the hospital for the insane. When George's proposal was clarified, the
committee withdrew its interest in the Magee place and
initiated plans for the purchase of the Joseph Barrell estate.
It was hard to believe that a misunderstanding over money was
reason enough to deny a man an appointment for which he was
so well qualified.

Yet the appointment went to Dr. Rufus Wyman, a man
twelve years George's senior, a kind, conscientious physician
whose poor health had led him to leave Boston for a country
practice, a man with no special training or experience that
equipped him for the responsibility of managing an asylum for
the insane. When the committee questioned him, Dr. Wyman
said he shared Dr. Parkman's convictions concerning the

methods of Dr. Philippe Pinel, the French physician, where
the treatment of the insane was concerned. However, Dr. Wyman said he would give first place to the moral teaching of the
Reverend William Tuke, the English clergyman, whereas Dr.
Parkman would give precedence to Dr. Pinel's medical treatment. Was George the victim of remnants of the old
Federalist feeling that anything French smacked of mobs,
anarchy, and atheism? After all, wasn't it Louis XVI who took
special pleasure in bestowing gifts of Sèvres chamber pots with
Benjamin Franklin's picture painted on the bottom?

Some of the Parkmans' friends had a different explanation.
They were convinced that Dr. James Jackson, the motivating
force behind the establishment of the Massachusetts General
Hospital, had tipped the scales against George's appointment.
Dr. Jackson was New England's foremost physician. After his
graduation from Harvard, he had studied with Dr. Augustus
Holyoke of Salem, a man he idolized and to whom he referred
as "my glorious master." It happened that Benjamin Pick-
man, the man who sponsored Dr. Wyman for the position of
superintendent of the McLean Asylum, was a relative of Dr.
Holyoke's first wife. Those who knew him best thought that
Dr. Jackson would have been unable to deny a request from
any member of the Holyoke family. Years later Dr. Holmes
said the committee's choice of Rufus Wyman resulted from the
decision to make the asylum a part of Massachusetts General
Hospital. This explanation was hard for the Parkmans to accept since neither Rufus Wyman nor George Parkman had a
connection with the Massachusetts General Hospital.

Whatever the truth of the matter, it spelled heartbreak for
George. Yet he was never heard to say a word against Dr. Wyman. As his family knew, he persuaded his father to honor
his generous pledge to the hospital fund. Samuel Parkman knew
how deeply George was hurt. So did Dr. John Jeffries with
whom both Rufus Wyman and George had studied after their

graduation from Harvard during the year before George went
to Scotland. Dr. Jeffries and Samuel Parkman were close
friends. How many winter afternoons had the two old men
spent in this very room, before this blackened fireplace? Dr.
Jeffries loved to tell the old stories. His favorite was about the
day he searched the battlefield at Bunker Hill for the body of
General Warren. The General had got a bullet in his face so
making the identification was not easy. In the end Paul Revere
had to row over from Charlestown to see the body. He had
fitted two artificial teeth into the General's mouth shortly before Lexington and he recognized his silver wire. He said
there was no doubt whatsoever; Dr. Jeffries had found General Warren's body. Yes, Dr. Jeffries had dozens of stories to
tell but he never told the story behind George's failure to get
the appointment as superintendent of the McLean Asylum, although there was no doubt that he knew it.

Francis Parkman said that when he thought of George's troubles — Harriette's ill health, the death of that first little boy,
the McLean disappointment — it was a consolation to remember how happy George was during their school days.
George was an excellent student. He had given the Salutatory
Oration at his graduation from Harvard and he did equally
well at medical school. George felt the most valuable medical
training he received was in Paris. Ten years earlier John
Collins Warren had written home to Boston that the center of
medical training in Europe had shifted to Paris. George's
experience confirmed that opinion. In Paris he found physicians with a sensitivity for patients that George found truly
humbling. At Salpêtrière Dr. Pinel ordered the chains
removed from every patient in the hospital. Moreover,
he walked among his patients, showing them the same courtesy and consideration he showed his friends. And there was
gruff Dr. Boussais whose concern for his patients was manifest
in his indictment of the medical profession; he said his colleagues were far more interested in performing autopsies than

in preventing them. George also respected the American-born Philippe Ricord, a specialist in venereal disease. Warmth was not among Dr. Ricord's feelings for humanity, however. In the opinion of his students and his colleagues, he was cynical enough to order a course of blue pills for the vestal virgins.

During the seven months he spent studying with Dr. Pinel in Paris, George visited Count Rumford, the Benjamin Thompson his father had known when they were both apprentices in the same dry goods shop in Union Street. To most Bostonians Count Rumford was a scoundrel and a traitor but George found him a generous, thoughtful host. Autueil, his beautiful estate four miles from Paris, was once the home of Lavoisier, the celebrated French chemist. It was a small world, Francis said. Benjamin Thompson, the dry goods apprentice, became the Count Rumford who gave $1000 to endow a chair at the Medical College, a chair first occupied by Jacob Bigelow. Furthermore, the will in which the bequest was made was witnessed by a man whom both Count Rumford and Samuel Parkman had known in Boston during the Revolution, the Marquis de Lafayette. What a fine time they all had when Lafayette came to Boston in 1825, the fiftieth anniversary of his first visit. Remember the handsome reception Daniel Webster gave in his Summer Street house? Then Francis was silent for a moment. He said sadly that he knew all his evoking of the past was nothing more than a screen conjured up to protect them both from the ominous present.

Mr. Shaw got out his watch. Looking at it, he said he knew they had decided to wait until the two o'clock trains were in before they got in touch with the police. But as time went by and there was no word from Walnut Street, he felt a growing sense of urgency. He thought he would go down to Court Street and alert Marshal Tukey. It would do no harm to let the Marshal know of George's disappearance even though they did not want him to begin an official search just yet.

Francis nodded. To take some definite step toward finding

George would release some of the tension they both felt, he was sure. He would go up to Walnut Street to be with Elizabeth. What must this lengthening uncertainty mean to her?

When he got to Court Street, Mr. Shaw walked on down into Cornhill, the better to see the spars and the rigging that crowded the harbor, the better to smell the tar and the hemp and the cod. Francis was right. The old and the familiar made it easier to bear the ominous uncertainty of the moment. From where he stood he could see wagons loaded with stone from Salem and onions from Danvers and cheese and game from everywhere. How many hundreds of times had Francis and George and he run down this very street to the harbor to beg fireworks from the captain of a ship just in from Canton? And how many times had they licked the bung hole of a molasses barrel or spent their money to suck cider?

"Get away from there! You've had your pennyworth!" He could still hear the yells of those red-faced farmers.

Mr. Shaw was at 39 Court Street now and he made a sudden decision to talk with Edward Blake before he went to Marshal Tukey's office. Edward had a right to know about George's disappearance. His wife was a Parkman and it was their son, Parkman Blake, to whom George had recently turned for help in managing his property. Mr. Shaw frowned, remembering Francis' comments. Come to think of it, George had given his health as his reason for needing young Blake. Well, that was nothing to feel apprehensive about, he told himself. After all, George would be sixty in February. He went up the stairs. Passing Charles Loring's office he glanced in and saw Loring deep in conversation with Charles Sumner, Sumner's long homely face solemn with earnestness.* He went on down the hall, found Edward in his office, and told him about George.

* Charles Sumner (1811-1874), one of the founders of the Free Soil party in 1848 and later a United States senator.

Together they decided to ask Marshal Tukey to come to them for the reason that any discussion in the Marshal's office was likely to reach the ears of the newspaper reporters who divided their time between that office and the Bell in Hand tavern.

The Marshal arrived as requested albeit with a flavor of noblesse oblige in his manner, justified, perhaps, in a handsome man who was a Harvard graduate and a hero in a town that loved the jubilees, parades, and fireworks he staged for its pleasure.

As Mr. Shaw told the Marshal about George's disappearance, he found himself minimizing the situation. Doubtless George would come into town on one of the two o'clock trains. No doubt they would find that some little scalawag had neglected to deliver the message Dr. Parkman had entrusted to him. But the Marshal did not conceal his opinion as to the seriousness of the matter. Because the family so requested, he would not notify the entire police force of the Doctor's disappearance until after the afternoon trains were in. However, he would immediately call in the men assigned to the West End where Dr. Parkman owned so much property. He would direct them to make up excuses to get into the houses in that area to search basements. They could say they had orders to inspect all drains in that neighborhood. Marshal Tukey knew that both Mr. Shaw and Mr. Blake were well aware that although Dr. Parkman was a just man in his dealings with his tenants, he was sometimes a hard man. Consequently, it was logical to consider foul play as a possible explanation of his disappearance. If there was no news by two o'clock when the trains came in, would the family want a notice inserted in the evening papers? And if there was no word from the Doctor by the end of the day, would the family consider offering a reward for information as to his whereabouts?

Mr. Shaw nodded and the Marshal got a slip of paper from his pocket. Mr. Blake handed him a pen. Could Mr. Shaw and Mr. Blake give a description of the clothes Dr. Parkman was wearing when he left home Friday noon?

Mr. Shaw and Marshal Tukey separated outside Mr. Blake's building, the Marshal to go back to his office, Mr. Shaw to go up to Walnut Street. Mr. Shaw crossed Tremont Street and as he did, he saw Mr. Kingsley motioning to him from the steps of the Park Street Church. The man's face was taut with strain.

"There's a rumor that the Doctor was seen in the South End last night about five o'clock, down around Washington Street," he said.

He hesitated and Mr. Shaw urged him on. "Yes? Anything else?"

Mr. Kingsley's voice faltered. He said hoarsely. "I was on my way up to Walnut Street to find you. I've just come from talking with the tollkeeper at Craigie's Bridge. He said Mr. Westerman from the tin shop told him somebody saw Dr. Parkman in a carriage headed out toward Cambridge yesterday afternoon. His face was bloody and he was bent over as though he was hurt. There was somebody in the carriage with him."

Mr. Shaw put his hand on Kingsley's arm. "Go over to Marshal Tukey's office and tell him what you've just told me. He knows about Dr. Parkman's disappearance. I've just come from talking with him. Quick, now!" With a growing sense of foreboding he watched Mr. Kingsley hurrying across Tremont and into School Street toward City Hall.

CHAPTER III

The Search

BY EARLY CANDLELIGHT on Saturday evening all Boston was astir with the news of Dr. Parkman's disappearance. It was a cold night with a sharp east wind and a powdering of snow on the Common. Nevertheless, people clustered on street corners and crowded the newspaper offices on Court Street. Marshal Tukey's men were besieged with questions.

Was it true the Marshal had ordered the river dragged?

Yes, it was true.

And the harbor, too?

And the harbor, too.

Everybody knew that messengers were on their way to all towns within sixty miles of Boston, including both sides of the Cape. Police officers were dispatched to the West End, each man accompanied by a crowd of a dozen or more. Some of them concentrated on the houses Dr. Parkman owned, particularly those which were empty. Others went out to the marshy, wooded land beyond the hospital, the place where the new jail was to be built. At midnight the streets of the West End were still bright with the lanterns of the search parties.

By Sunday morning Marshal Tukey had the town plastered with handbills.

SPECIAL NOTICE

George Parkman, M.D., a well known, and highly respectable citizen of Boston, left his house in Walnut street, to meet an en-

gagement of business, on Friday last, November 23d, between
twelve and one o'clock, P.M., and was seen in the southerly part
of the city, in and near Washington street, in conversation with
some persons, at about five o'clock of the afternoon of the same
day.

Any person who can give information relative to him, that may
lead to his discovery, is earnestly requested to communicate the
same, immediately, to the City Marshal, for which he shall be
liberally rewarded.

Boston, November 25th, 1849

All day Sunday the search continued unabated despite the
cold and the intermittent rain. Cellars, sheds, vacant buildings,
woods — every foot was searched and searched again. Men in
small boats poked into the coves and inlets above and below
the city.

Sunday afternoon the Parkmans received calls from anxious
friends and relatives. Mrs. Abby Rhoades, one of the Reverend
Francis Parkman's parishioners, wanted him to know that she
and her daughter, Mary, had seen Dr. Parkman in Bowdoin
Square about a quarter to five Friday afternoon. He was going
toward Green Street. Mrs. Rhoades remembered the circumstances very clearly. Mary and she had just come from Hovey's
store in Winter Street where they had bought eleven yards of
muslin de laine. There was no doubt about the date. Mrs.
Rhoades had been back to the store to make sure of it.

Mrs. Sarah Greenough saw the Doctor on Cambridge Street
about three. She was on her way to tea in Temple Place. She
was late and it so happened that she had just looked at her
watch before she saw Dr. Parkman on the other side of Cambridge between Belknap and Russell. As the Reverend Mr.
Parkman knew, she had been a friend of the Parkmans for
many years. She remembered that Dr. Parkman always did the
marketing. Could she have the privilege of sending a servant to
help Mrs. Parkman in this way?

At about half-past four Patrick burst into the parlor in high excitement. "He's here!" he cried. "The man with the black hair and the glasses!"

The Parkmans rushed to the reception hall.

Mrs. Parkman showed the relief she felt. "So it was you, John! It was you who called on George early Friday morning!" she exclaimed.

Both Mrs. Parkman and the Reverend Mr. Parkman were delighted to see Dr. Webster. Did the family have a closer friend than he? Hadn't their fathers been friends long before the Revolution made Redford Webster a rich man as it made Andrew Craigie and John Joy and a dozen other apothecaries rich? Those were the days before the Websters bought the Franklin mansion and lived next door to Governor Hutchinson himself. For years John and George carried on a friendly rivalry about the respective merits of Aberdeen and London as centers of medical training.

Later that afternoon, when the Reverend Francis Parkman called on Mr. Shaw, he said that the memory of all that John Webster and George and he had shared made it hard for him to understand John's manner during that Sunday afternoon call. As John Webster sat there in the parlor, you would have thought he had no more than a nodding acquaintance with the family. He was businesslike, hardly more than civil. In a matter-of-fact tone he said he had read of George's disappearance in the Saturday evening papers. He said his purpose in calling was to dispel the mystery about the person who called on George Friday morning to arrange for an appointment later in the day. The caller was he and the appointment was for a meeting at the Medical College at 1:30 that afternoon. George arrived at approximately a quarter to two and John gave him $483.64, a payment on a loan. George took the money and, walking rapidly, as was his custom, hurried toward the door. When John called after him, he said he would go immediately

to Cambridge to see that the payment was properly recorded
with the city clerk. At that John rose abruptly, bowed, and left
without expressing either concern for George or sympathy for
his family. The Reverend Francis Parkman said that as he
stood at the reception hall window watching John hurrying
away from the house, it crossed his mind that John's dress was
as strange as his manner. Cold as it was, he wore no outer coat
and although it had been raining off and on all day, he carried
a cane, not an umbrella.

Immediately after John left, Elizabeth went up to Harriette
and Francis Parkman said he was glad to be alone with the
hurt he felt. Unbecoming as it may have been in a Christian,
to say nothing of a clergyman, he sat there in the twilight thinking of all the Parkmans had done for John Webster — and
then to have him act like this in their time of trouble. When
John came back from his year in the Azores with a new bride,
as well as the material for his book on geology, who used influence to get him an appointment at Harvard? George Parkman. And for thirty years the Websters had been members
of the New North Church. As the minister of that Church,
he had baptized John's four daughters, buried his little son,
and officiated when the eldest Webster girl married Charles
Dabney. Just this past autumn, in September, he had baptized
the first grandson at a ceremony at the Websters' home in Cambridge. Moreover, where in Boston were there three women
who enjoyed a closer relationship than Elizabeth Parkman,
Harriet Webster, and Catherine Prescott? The experience
of growing up in a consul's family in a foreign land was a bond
that held them very close. Furthermore, he was certain that
the Prescotts, as well as the Parkmans, had helped the Websters
financially.

At that point Mr. Shaw recalled a conversation George and
he had had on the subject of John's finances when they passed
him in Mt. Vernon Street on an afternoon early in November.
Mr. Shaw said he made some reference to John's financial strug-

gle, commenting that $1200 a year plus a few hundred in fees
from the students at the Medical College was nowhere near
enough income for a Harvard professor with a family, particularly a family accustomed to the Websters' standard of living.
How could John Webster deny his wife those delightful parties
she loved to give? Dr. Webster had tried to find the money to
meet his obligations, Mr. Shaw reminded George. He had asked
President Everett's permission to take the position of Inspector
of Drugs for the city of Boston. Predictably, Everett told him
such work was beneath the dignity of a Harvard professor. No
wonder John was irritable. His financial worries would ruin
the disposition of an angel. As everybody knew, the one way a
Harvard professor could insure himself of a life free of financial
strain was to marry a rich woman.

They were in State Street by this time. A coach pulled up to
the Devonshire Inn and George Bancroft alighted.* As they
exchanged bows, Mr. Shaw commented that Bancroft was a fine
example of a Harvard professor who honored the precept about
marrying money. Bancroft was put to the trouble of going all
the way to Springfield to find his wife, but great was his reward.
Jonathan Dwight's daughter was not only rich, she was good-
natured, so who noticed how plain she was? And there was
Edward Everett himself.† Who would argue that the best was
none too good for a man who looked like Apollo, according to
President Kirkland of Harvard College, and who was pastor of
the most fashionable church in Boston when he was nineteen?
Certainly not Edward Everett. He married Charlotte Brooks,
the daughter of Boston's richest citizen and that, Mr. Shaw said
with a smile, was an impressive statement, present company
considered. And Longfellow. Don't forget Longfellow, he
told George. Fanny Appleton was not only rich, she was beautiful. By the way, had George seen Tom Appleton wearing a

* George Bancroft (1800-1891), famous United States historian and diplomat,
United States Minister to Great Britain, 1846-49.
† Edward Everett (1794-1865), noted clergyman, statesman, and former president
of Harvard University.

mustache? Apparently he was content to remain a bachelor.

George said he had not seen Tom Appleton and his mustache but that morning he had seen Sam Eliot whose sisters had contributed measurably to the financial comfort of two Harvard professors in the persons of George Ticknor and Andrews Norton. George said he agreed that Harvard salaries were far below what they ought to be. But the meagerness of John Webster's salary did not alter the fact that he had squandered the substantial fortune, more than $50,000, he inherited from his father. For almost ten years he lived like a lord with his European trips and the fine house he built — and lost. He knew how much money he had. Where did he think it was all going to end? He lived in luxury for ten years and then came upon times when his family faced actual want.

But foolish as he was, John Webster was an old friend, George said. He thought it was generally known that by 1842 John had to resort to borrowing from his friends. He himself began to loan money to John that year. John did not keep up the interest, let alone making any payment on the principal. George said he could understand how a man simply could not find the money to meet a financial obligation. He could feel sympathetic toward an honest debtor. But for the blackguard who through trickery tried to slide out from under an obligation he had nothing but contempt. Such a fellow George would prosecute to the full extent of the law. Well, John sank deeper and deeper into debt. From time to time all his close friends — the Prescotts, the Cunninghams, the Bigelows — loaned him money. In fact, in January of 1847 a group of them got together and made him a loan of $2432, a sum that included the balance of John's debt to him, $343.83. The loan was secured by mortgage on all John's property including his household furniture and his treasured mineral cabinet. George thought it was a measure of John's desperation that he tried to sell his mineral collection to Harvard College. In George's opinion the College was shortsighted in not buying it for the $10,000 John asked. Benjamin Silliman had persuaded Yale to pay $25,000 for a collection that was larger but otherwise no finer. When John was in the Azores or in Europe, his first consideration was buying specimens for his collection. A considerable part of his inheritance was spent on those purchases. At any rate, the mineral cabinet was part of the collateral that secured the loan. The first payment, $600, was due in April and be it said to John Webster's credit that he paid it.

Mr. Shaw interrupted to tell of a morning in April when John had come to him desperate about a $600 payment due on a loan, doubtless the loan George spoke of. Webster was in a frenzy. He insisted he stood in danger of losing his furniture to the sheriff's men. Well, as George had said, John was an old friend and many a fine evening the Shaws had spent in Webster's home, listening to his daughters sing — charming young women, those Webster girls — or discussing their mutual interest in spiritualism. Consequently, he offered to make John a gift of $1200 but John insisted that the money be a loan. He wrote out some kind of a mortgage which Mr. Shaw put away without reading, his eyes troubling him as they did. As a matter of fact, Mr. Shaw had never read the mortgage from that day to this although he probably had it someplace in his desk. All he knew about it for sure was that the loan was secured by his mineral chest.

George was suddenly furious. That cabinet was not Webster's to use in any way whatsoever, he thundered. This was an act of fraud, the betrayal of loyal, patient friends by a dishonest, deceitful man! George roared as only George could roar when he was convinced that a debtor had tried to cheat him. It was far from the first time he had heard George carry on like that. Mr. Shaw shook his head sorrowfully. In all likelihood George had met with foul play at the hands of a person, probably a tenant, whom he had subjected to just such a tirade as he had given vent to that November afternoon in State Street.

*

But Dr. Parkman's tenants did not agree. Even as they helped
search the property he owned, they told each other and the
police that Dr. Parkman would never be found either dead or
alive in any of his houses in the West End.

Sunday afternoon Mr. Calhoun from the foundry and Mr.
Trenholm of the police department had a long conversation
with Mr. Littlefield and seven or eight people who lived in the
West End. As they stood in Fruit Street they were within sight
of ꞏthe Medical College, a fine brick structure now three years
old. Everybody knew Dr. Parkman had given the Medical
College the land on which the building stood. All of them
remembered the dedication ceremonies when Dr. Holmes spoke
so warmly of Dr. Parkman.* Pleased, the Doctor had smiled and
showed his new teeth. He had ordered them for the occasion
because he thought he might be asked to speak (he wasn't).
They were uncomfortable and an hour before the ceremony
Dr. Keep was grinding at them, trying to give Dr. Parkman
more room for his tongue.

Despite Dr. Holmes' fine speech, the truth was that behind
his back Dr. Parkman's Beacon Hill friends laughed over stories
about how stingy he was, how he haggled at the markets, how
he walked all over Boston to save the cost of keeping a horse.
But the people in the West End knew from firsthand experience that Dr. Parkman was a landlord who never evicted a sick
tenant or one who lost his job through no fault of his own.
Rich Bostonians enjoyed a good laugh when the *Post* printed
such stories as the one about the Irishman who defended himself against a charge of theft by explaining that he had stopped
in at a lumber yard to get a few shavings to boil his tea kettle
— and picked up a ten-foot mahogany plank by mistake. But
West End people knew that the poverty of the Irish was no

---

* Dr. Oliver Wendell Holmes (1809-1894), author and physician, dean of the
Harvard Medical College, 1874-53, father of the Supreme Court Justice, Oliver
Wendell Holmes, Jr.

joke, and so did Dr. Parkman. So did Dr. Shattuck. Together they took care of the sick in the West End and, like as not, Dr. Parkman paid for any medicines their patients needed.

Somebody was telling how Dr. Parkman volunteered to loan several of his houses to the city to use as hospitals during the cholera epidemic when Dr. Webster appeared in the direction of Bridge Street, walking fast. Nodding a greeting to the others, he asked Littlefield when he had last seen Dr. Parkman. His manner was brisk.

"Mr. Littlefield, did you see Dr. Parkman the latter part of last week?"

Littlefield nodded.

"When?"

"Last Friday about half-past one."

"Where was he?"

"Right about this spot, sir."

"Which way was he going?"

"He was coming right toward the College, Dr. Webster."

"Where were you when you saw him?"

"I was standing in the front entry."

Dr. Webster struck the ground with the cane he carried. "Then you saw him just about the time I did." He looked at Littlefield sharply. "Now, can you tell me anything more? Did you see him go into my lecture room?"

Littlefield shook his head. "I didn't see him go into your lecture room and I didn't see him come out of it. I went into Dr. Ware's room and lay down on the settee. I was waiting for Dr. Holmes' class to let out so I could go up there and clean up."

Then Dr. Webster told about his meeting with Dr. Parkman, naming the exact amount of money that changed hands, reporting Dr. Parkman's hasty departure and his statement that he meant to go immediately to Cambridge. His story finished, Dr. Webster nodded and hurried off up Fruit Street going toward Blossom.

After Dr. Webster was gone, Littlefield had to listen to the question he heard every time he set foot outside his apartment. Why hadn't the police searched the Medical College? Several people had seen Dr. Parkman go *into* the Medical College but nobody had seen him come *out*. So what did that mean? It meant Dr. Parkman was still in the Medical College and that's where he would be found. And why hadn't *Littlefield* made a search? Could it be that he knew more about the Doctor's disappearance than he was telling? This last question, accompanied by nudges and sidelong glances, infuriated Littlefield. Late that night he told his wife he was sick and tired of having everybody tell him that Dr. Parkman would be found in the Medical College and nowhere else. Beginning in the morning he meant to search every inch of the College. Furthermore, he meant to keep an eye on Dr. Webster. Littlefield couldn't put his finger on the reason, but something in the Doctor's manner roused his suspicions. And now he remembered that on the Monday before Dr. Parkman's disappearance, Dr. Webster had asked all kinds of questions about the dissecting room vault. He wanted to know how it was built and how they got it fixed the time it leaked foul air, and whether you could get a light clear down into it. He had never asked questions like that before. Why now? And why was he so anxious to have blood from the hospital that Friday morning?

By ten o'clock Monday morning Littlefield hadn't unpacked the skeleton Dr. Holmes needed for his one o'clock lecture. In fact, he hadn't even started the sweeping. The truth was that nobody in the West End and few people in any part of Boston got much work done on Monday morning, November 26, 1849. The whole town was reading the handbill announcing a reward of $3000 for information leading to the discovery of Dr. Parkman if alive.

People looked at each other with dropped jaws. *$3000!*

"That'll do the trick," Tim Mallory said. "Now somebody

will find him if he's buried nine miles deep under the main wing of the State House."

"But you've got to find him *alive* to get the $3000," Joe Wheel told him.

Tim shook his head. "Too bad about you Unitarians, Joe. You people just don't know nothing about the Resurrection of the body, now, do you?"

So Monday morning the search began again. People living in Dr. Parkman's West End houses were plagued with requests and ruses all aimed at getting into their basements and poking around in their closets. The second growth down by the river out beyond the hospital was combed again. So were all the outbuildings in that area. Dr. Webster's story about Dr. Parkman's saying he was going to Cambridge sent crowds over there. The tollkeepers reported record business for a November Monday morning.

About noon Mr. Kingsley and Mr. Starkweather, a police officer, appeared at the Medical College. When they arrived, Littlefield was upstairs with Dr. Holmes setting up the anatomical exhibits for Dr. Holmes' one o'clock lecture.

"We can't trace Dr. Parkman to any place but here so we'd like to have a look around," Starkweather said when Littlefield answered the bell.

Dr. Holmes appeared on the stairs at that moment. He had his coat off and he did not look pleased at the prospect of an interruption.

Littlefield relayed Starkweather's request.

"I don't suppose you'll need to haul out all the anatomical specimens, will you?" Dr. Holmes asked.

Starkweather said no, they simply wanted to look over the building to make sure Dr. Parkman hadn't stowed himself away somewhere up in the attic or elsewhere.

Littlefield went with Kingsley and Starkweather to the top floor of the building, to the lecture room where Dr. Holmes met

with his students, his "large, uncombed youth," as he called
them. The room with the students' benches in steep tiers was
small and badly ventilated. Only Dr. Holmes could keep students awake in a room like that at the end of a long morning of
lectures. And he did keep them awake.

"Gentlemen," he began one lecture, "today we will discuss a
subject about which I assume you gentlemen have no knowledge. Female genitalia." Dr. Holmes' choice of language, as
well as his wit, flavored his lectures. The double-lobed brain
was like a walnut, the mesentery like old-fashioned shirt ruf-
fles, the end of the Fallopian tube like the fringe on a woman's
shawl.

After a glance into Dr. Holmes' office, a cubbyhole under the
stairs which he called his "crypt," Starkweather and Kingsley
went across the hall to the anatomical demonstration room.
Littlefield explained that this was the room where the dissec-
tions were done and where they kept the specimens Dr. Holmes
and Dr. Jackson used in their demonstrations. He opened the
chests and the closets in which various pieces of cadavers were
stored. When none of them yielded anything that might be a
clue to Dr. Parkman's disappearance, the three men went downstairs to the lecture room used by Dr. Ware, Dr. Walter Channing and Dr. Jacob Bigelow. After an inspection that included
a look into all closets and a glance around the doctors' private
rooms, they crossed the hall to Dr. Webster's quarters.

When there was no response to Starkweather's knock, Littlefield put his key in the lock, but the door was bolted on the inside. After they waited a few minutes longer, Littlefield
pounded the door hard. Dr. Webster opened the door without further delay. He was in his working clothes, a cap, blue
overalls, and an old coat. He stood in the doorway looking
questioningly at Starkweather and Kingsley, his manner pleasant but cold.

Mr. Starkweather said he knew that Dr. Webster was as concerned about Dr. Parkman's disappearance as the Doctor's

other friends and the police. He asked if Mr. Kingsley and he might see Dr. Webster's rooms as they had seen the quarters of the other Medical College professors.

Dr. Webster stepped back then and they entered his lecture hall, a large room with two tiers of raised benches. There were steps down to the area where Dr. Webster did chemical experiments for his students. His large, rectangular lecture table was solidly built. Separated from the lecture room by a partition was the small upper laboratory. Off the laboratory to the left was Dr. Webster's private room.

After a cursory glance into the upper laboratory, Starkweather and Kingsley, followed by Dr. Webster and Littlefield, went down the stairs that led to the lower laboratory. They looked over the equipment in the room, the two sinks, the furnace, the two stoves, and the hogsheads used for water storage. At Dr. Webster's suggestion they stepped out into the passageway so he could show them the room across the hall where the students practiced dissection. Directly outside the laboratory door was a vault with a soapstone lid held in place by two locks and a heavy chain. Dr. Webster explained that the vault was used to dispose of waste from the dissection room. The four men spent a moment or two in the dissection room and then walked back through Dr. Webster's laboratory to another passageway. This corridor, which was on the east side of the building, divided Littlefield's apartment so that his parlor and a bedroom were on one side of it and his kitchen and his second bedroom on the other. The corridor opened into a large carriage shed. A window in Littlefield's parlor looked out into the shed.

Starkweather and Kingsley left Dr. Webster in his lower laboratory. As Littlefield escorted them out of the building by way of the carriage shed door, Kingsley made no secret of his dissatisfaction with their visit.

"We weren't in that lower laboratory *three minutes!*" he told Starkweather.

Starkweather frowned. "Well, did you see anything that

made you think we ought to look closer? Did you see *anything* that gave you any *real* grounds for the suspicions I know you both have?" He included Littlefield in his question.

"Shouldn't we have looked — *and looked carefully* — into that vault where they dispose of stuff from the dissection room? Isn't that the logical place you'd try to get rid of something you were trying to hide?" Kingsley asked him.

Starkweather shook his head. "Too obvious. If you murdered somebody at the Medical College and were looking for some way to do away with the body, you wouldn't use the vault. You'd *expect* that place to be searched first."

"Even if you knew a lamp won't stay lit down there long enough for anybody to take a good look around?" Littlefield put in.

"We *have* to get a look into that vault. There's just no two ways about *that*," Kingsley insisted.

Starkweather looked at his watch. "I'm going over to see the Marshal now," he said. "I'll tell him about the vault. Maybe he'll authorize another search."

"Let me know, will you?" Kingsley was adjusting his muffler. "I'm going over to Cambridge to help search over there. I'm not very hopeful though. We didn't turn up anything yesterday and we spent pretty near the whole day looking."

When Starkweather walked into Marshal Tukey's office, he found the Marshal standing behind his desk studying the letter he held. He handed it to Starkweather. It read:

DEAR SIR,
    You will find Dr. Parkman murdered in a Brooklyn Hotel.

                                        Yours,

                                        M——
                                        Capt. of the Darts.

"Judging by the handwriting, this is the work of an educated person," the Marshal said.

"Is this the envelope?" Starkweather asked him, picking up a yellow envelope from the Marshal's desk.

The Marshal nodded. "Notice the postmark. It was mailed today right here in Boston."

Starkweather handed the letter back. "When did you get it?" he asked, as the Marshal seated himself at his fine oak desk.

"About ten minutes ago. I'll send a man down to New York tonight but I don't think we'll get very far by going in that direction. I'll be very much surprised if we don't find the culprit we're after right here in our midst." He looked up at Starkweather. "How did you make out with your investigation at the Medical College?"

Starkweather described the visit and relayed Kingsley's comments about the vault. "Littlefield agrees with him," he said in conclusion.

The Marshal studied his handsome brass inkwell in silence. Then he said, "I'll send Clapp over to take another look around the building tomorrow. Rice and Fuller can go with him and he might as well take Kingsley along. That's one way of stopping his complaints. On your way out, will you tell Clapp I want him?"

When Derastus Clapp, the Marshal's deputy, and the two police officers, Rice and Fuller, arrived at the Medical College about eleven o'clock the following morning, Littlefield was standing at the carriage shed entrance talking with Dr. Jacob Bigelow. He called Dr. Bigelow's attention to the three men as they came up North Grove Street.

"Looks like we're going to have the College searched again, sir," he said.

Dr. Bigelow was a kind, sensitive man and Littlefield could see that he was upset. Dr. Bigelow's concern about people was not limited to his close friends, like the Parkmans and the Websters. He cared about Boston and everybody in it. He had organized Mt. Auburn Cemetery because he worried about the impact of Boston's hazardous burial practices on the health of *all* the people. Unlike most of the successful physicians in town, Dr. Jacob Bigelow did not divide Bostonians into two groups, those who were his patients and those who were not.

Littlefield walked down the path a few steps to meet the police officers, all of whom knew Dr. Bigelow. At his suggestion, the Doctor and the men from the police department stepped into Littlefield's parlor to discuss the situation that concerned them all. Sitting there on the padded green furniture that was his wife's special pride, Littlefield was annoyed to see his carpet strewn with grape leaves. The previous morning the Cambridge and Boston Express had delivered a bag of tanbark, a large box, and a bundle of heavy faggots made from grape vines. Since the door to Dr. Webster's lower laboratory was locked, Mr. Sawin could not set them inside. Consequently, the children tracked them all over the apartment.

Mr. Clapp was speaking. He was a short, heavyset man with a slightly pompous manner. Addressing his comments to Dr. Bigelow, he said he refused to entertain the thought that Dr. Parkman had met with foul play at Dr. Webster's hands. Marshal Tukey had ordered another search of the College not because either the Marshal or he had any suspicion whatsoever of Dr. Webster, Littlefield's and Kingsley's hunches notwithstanding — and here he made a little mock bow to Littlefield — but as a justification for further investigation of some of the houses in the West End.

Dr. Bigelow spoke up. He said that as a friend of Dr. and Mrs. Webster's, he could not for one moment believe that Dr. Webster was capable of doing harm to anyone, let alone a lifelong friend to whom he was indebted for favors of an important nature. Yet, sorry as he was to say so, he believed Dr. Parkman was dead. Otherwise he would have found a way to get in touch with his family during these past four days. And the inescapable fact was that Dr. Parkman was last seen alive at the Medical College. What that meant, Dr. Bigelow could not imagine. He looked from one to the other of the men in the room. Who would want to harm Dr. Parkman? True, he was quick-tempered, but you don't murder a man for that reason, do you?

Mr. Clapp said briskly that it was the duty of the police to find the answers to the questions Dr. Bigelow raised. Furthermore, they had better be getting about that business. Incidentally, he said as he rose, had they all seen the new handbill out this morning? There was a $100 reward for information leading to the recovery of Dr. Parkman's watch. It was a turned-case Lepine and Dr. Parkman had bought it in London.

He turned to Littlefield. "Will you be good enough to take us to Dr. Webster's rooms? Mr. Kingsley was to join us if he could arrange his business so he could be here this morning."

Kingsley was waiting for them on the front steps. "There's a rumor over town that Dr. Parkman was smuggled on board a sloop at Long Wharf," he said to Mr. Clapp.

Mr. Clapp continued on up the front steps. "Yesterday it was Rowe's Wharf. But we'll check into it just the same. We are following all possible leads, no matter how flimsy."

They were at Dr. Webster's door now. When Mr. Clapp rapped, Dr. Webster, dressed in his working clothes, answered almost immediately. He waited for Mr. Clapp to speak.

Mr. Clapp's manner was deferential and his tone apologetic. "We don't believe for a moment, sir, that it is necessary to search your apartment," he said. "We are about to begin another search of the houses here in the West End and we thought we'd better start with the College or some people in the neighborhood might get their backs up."

Dr. Webster was polite but distant. He said his rooms had been searched yesterday. However, if these gentlemen wished to make another search, they were welcome to do so. Then he led the way from his lecture room to his upper laboratory.

From the laboratory he indicated the location of his private room. When Mr. Clapp took a step in the direction of that room, Dr. Webster added that the articles stored there were dangerous.

Mr. Clapp jumped. "I've no intention of going in there and getting my head blown off," he said. He looked into the room gingerly and held the door open only long enough for the men behind him to glimpse shelves of bottles of different sizes.

The party went down the stairs into the lower laboratory. While they were there, Mr. Clapp and Dr. Webster stood by the windows at the rear of the room discussing possible explanations for Dr. Parkman's disappearance. The others wandered about the laboratory. Mr. Rice and Mr. Fuller opened the tea chest and handled some of the minerals that formed a layer on top of the tanbark. Surreptitiously Mr. Kingsley stirred the ashes under the furnace but found nothing.

Mr. Clapp asked Dr. Webster about the fuel closet and Dr. Webster opened the door so he could see the coal, three kinds, cannel, Sydney, and charcoal. Under the stairs was a cubbyhole which had a door with a whitewashed glass panel. Mr. Clapp looked over at it. Was that Dr. Webster's private privy, he asked?

Dr. Webster nodded as he suggested that Mr. Clapp might want to see the room where the students practiced dissection. It was directly across from the laboratory. As they entered the passageway to go to the dissection room, Dr. Webster called attention to the vault outside the laboratory door, explaining that it was a repository for waste from the dissection room.

Mr. Clapp was interested. At his request Littlefield got his keys and lifted the lid from the vault. At Kingsley's suggestion he found a glass lantern and held it down inside the vault. The light went out almost immediately.

But Mr. Clapp seemed satisfied. "That's all right," he said to Littlefield. "We can see there's nothing down there but what belongs there." He studied the outside of the vault. "How big is that opening? About two feet square?"

"That's right, sir," Littlefield answered. "And it stands two and a half feet above ground and twelve feet below. If you were down under the building, you'd see how it runs right under Dr. Webster's coal pen."

"Is there any way to get down under the building?" Mr. Clapp asked him.

"There's a trap door at the far end of this passageway, a scuttle I call it. If you go down, you'll find a tunnel about four feet high that runs back sixty feet. That's the width of the building. It's not very comfortable walking but you can get to the back wall of the building if you have a mind to."

Mr. Clapp considered the situation. "Well, let's go down and have a quick look, anyway," he said.

All of them except Dr. Webster went down the trap door. However, Mr. Clapp and Rice went only a few feet along the tunnel. Mr. Clapp assigned Fuller to make the trip to the back wall with Littlefield. Later when they met again in the lower laboratory, Fuller described the damp, airless tunnel, and the difficulty of walking on the uneven earth. To add to their troubles the lantern went out every few minutes so most of the time they were in the dark. And Fuller wondered whether his back would ever be the same after walking hunched over for so long. They got all the way to the back wall, though. Speaking to Dr. Webster, Fuller said he sure was glad to see the brick vault that belonged to Dr. Webster's privy because Littlefield had told him that when they saw that vault, they would be within a foot or two of the rear wall and ready to turn around and start back. Later when he was alone with Kingsley, Fuller repeated what Littlefield had said about the vault. It was solid brick, probably five courses, and there was no access to it except by way of the privy hole twelve feet above.

As the visitors were leaving, Dr. Webster requested Littlefield to ring the bell for his twelve o'clock lecture. Littlefield
did not see him again until shortly after four when Dr. Webster's bell rang in Littlefield's kitchen. Littlefield went up
promptly and to his amazement, the Doctor presented him with
an order for a Thanksgiving turkey. The order was on Foster's in Scollay Square, next door to the Howard Atheneum.
Would Littlefield be good enough to go to Foster's this afternoon and tell Mr. Foster to send a bushel of sweet potatoes over
to Dr. Webster's home?

Littlefield went back downstairs and got his coat. All the
way out Cambridge Street he wondered why, after seven years
of no presents whatsoever, Dr. Webster had chosen this particular time to give him a turkey.

Wednesday morning Dr. Webster arrived at the Medical
College much earlier than usual. While the Littlefields were
still at breakfast, they could hear him moving around his lower
laboratory. Careful to make no sound, Littlefield went out
into the passageway by the laboratory door. He lay down full-
length in the passageway beside the wide crack under the door.
By pressing his left cheek against the floor, he could see Dr.
Webster's legs as far up as his knees. The Doctor was moving a
coal hod from the fuel closet to the furnace. Back and forth he
went; back and forth. He made eight trips while Littlefield
watched. There were drops of wet on the floor.

Littlefield heard his wife calling him. He scrambled to his
feet as she appeared in the passageway.

"Ephraim, we've still got most of our Thanksgiving marketing to do. Could you be ready to go uptown in a quarter of an
hour? You can do the chores when we get back, can't you?"

"Yes. Just give me time to sweep the front steps," Littlefield
told her.

He was on his way toward the front of the building, broom
in hand, when he heard the bell at the main entrance. He

went out of the building by the door under the front steps and
saw Mr. Trenholm up at the entrance, his finger on the bell.

"Aren't you the impatient one this morning," Littlefield
chided him. "You pushed that bell for the first time about
ten seconds ago."

Mr. Trenholm came down to him. He had a poster in his
hand. "I thought maybe you hadn't seen this yet. I just got
it half an hour ago. The Marshal has a crew out tacking them
up."

Littlefield read the handbill aloud. " '$1000 Reward. Where-
as no satisfactory information has been obtained respecting
Dr. George Parkman, since the afternoon of Friday last, fears
are entertained that he has been murdered. The above reward
will be paid for information which leads to the recovery of his
body. Robert G. Shaw. Boston, November 28th, 1849.' "

"The Marshal says they've printed twenty-eight thousand
handbills since the Doctor's disappearance. *Twenty-eight
thousand.* That's one for every five people in Boston, counting children, granted they sent a good many out of town, so you
can't count them all for Boston."

Littlefield handed the poster back to Trenholm. "I guess
that means they think he's dead all right." He sighed. "Well,
we're going uptown in a few minutes and I know what I'll
hear every step of the way. I'll hear that he's dead and he's
someplace in the Medical College. But where?" he asked Mr.
Trenholm. "Where can he be?"

At that moment Mrs. Littlefield appeared with her hat on.

"Ephraim, it's almost nine and time we got started." She
smiled at Mr. Trenholm. "Have a good Thanksgiving, Mr.
Trenholm, although it's hard to know how any of us can really
enjoy anything until this trouble about Dr. Parkman gets settled."

The Littlefields were away from the Medical College until
about one o'clock. As soon as they returned, Littlefield went

immediately to the dissecting room passageway to listen for
Dr. Webster. There were no audible sounds. To Littlefield's
annoyance the bundle of grape vine cuttings, the bag of tanbark, and the wooden box that Mr. Sawin had delivered Monday were still in the passageway.

Then inadvertently Littlefield made a discovery that alarmed
him. As he stood in the hall observing the grape vines, he became aware that he felt heat on his face. He knew that Dr.
Webster's furnace was on the other side of the wall at the
point where he stood. He reached over and found the wall so
hot he could barely stand to hold his hand against it. Littlefield felt a flash of panic. Would the building catch fire?

Quickly, he tried all the doors that opened into Dr. Webster's rooms and found them bolted on the inside. Then he
ran to his apartment, to the bedroom with a window in the
same relative position as the first window in the rear wall of
Dr. Webster's lower laboratory. He climbed out his window
and managed to inch his way along the rough bricks to the
laboratory window. It was unlocked and Littlefield let himself down inside the room and ran to the furnace. His hands
trembled as he cleared the furnace lid of the crucibles and
minerals that cluttered it. He could scarcely believe his eyes
when he saw only a small flame in the furnace. Puzzled, he
replaced the lid and carried the crucibles and minerals back to
it. Now he noticed a spout a dozen feet long lying on the floor
between one of the hogsheads and the movable sink. On impulse he checked both hogsheads. One was two-thirds empty
and the meter on the other showed it was dry. Littlefield
knew for certain that he had filled them both Friday morning.
He looked into the two kindling barrels and saw they were
both about half empty. He remembered clearly that they,
too, were full on Friday.

On his way up the stairs to the upper laboratory, Littlefield
noticed spots on the stair treads. They looked wet like the

spots he saw when he lay in the passageway looking into the lower laboratory from the crack under the door. He rubbed his finger across one of them and found it had an acid taste. He hurried on upstairs. The door to Dr. Webster's private room was unlocked. He saw the same wet spots on the floor. At that moment he thought he heard footsteps on the outside stairs leading to the main entrance. He ran back down the stairs to the lower laboratory and climbed out the window.

His wife was in the kitchen. At his urging she interrupted her baking to go into the parlor with him so they could talk without being overheard by the children. Littlefield told her about the water level in the hogsheads, about the quantity of pine kindling that had been used since Friday morning, about the wet spots on the floor. As he talked, he could see that his wife was growing increasingly upset. Her thin face was solemn with fear. He saw her glance around the room, at the marble-topped table she loved, at the green furniture that represented so much scrimping and saving.

Didn't Littlefield know he was getting into something that might endanger his position at the Medical College, she burst out? Did he want to lose the fine position he had had for seven years now? Who among their friends was as well off as they?

Patiently Littlefield told her he understood how she felt. He very well knew he was taking a risk, but he was going ahead with it just the same. She knew just as well as he that neither of them could go outside the building without being told that Dr. Parkman was still *in this very building where they lived*. Yes, there had been all kinds of rumors but there was no truth in any of them. Ask Rice or Trenholm or Fuller or anybody else from the police department. It all boiled down to this. The last time Dr. Parkman was seen alive was when Elias Fuller saw him walking up the steps of the Medical College. What was more, Littlefield said, as the days went by, *he* became

more and more convinced that Dr. Parkman *must* be in the
Medical College. So he had a plan. Speaking slowly he said
that the one place in the College that had not been searched
was Dr. Webster's private privy. The only way to find out
what was in that privy was to drill a hole in the vault, and
that was what he meant to do. Tomorrow after he got back
from the wharves with the lime Dr. Webster needed, he meant
to begin.

Mrs. Littlefield burst into tears. She tried to interrupt but
Littlefield continued. Since tomorrow was Thanksgiving, Dr.
Webster might not come over from Cambridge. They couldn't
be sure, though, so Mrs. Littlefield would have to stand guard.
If she saw Dr. Webster approaching the building, she would
give a signal. What signal Littlefield didn't know yet, but he
would work out something.

Thursday morning Littlefield went down to Mr. Hoppin's
wharf and got the lime. "Bring a piece about the size of your
head," Webster had told him. As soon as he got back, he did
the sweeping up. Shortly after two o'clock he went to a neighbor, Mrs. Harlow, and borrowed a hatchet. Then he stopped
in at the foundry and got a mortising chisel from Elias Fuller.
Elias guessed what he was up to. He shared Littlefield's suspicion of Dr. Webster. It was Elias who had urged Kingsley to
look into the ashes under the furnace the day Starkweather
and Mr. Clapp and he visited the Medical College.

Nervous as she was, Mrs. Littlefield agreed to stand guard.
Littlefield had figured out a warning system. If Mrs. Littlefield saw Dr. Webster approaching the college while Littlefield was down working on the vault, she was to run back to
their kitchen and rap on the floor four times with the hammer.
Since the kitchen was almost directly over the vault, Littlefield
was sure to hear. Before he went down under the building,

Littlefield locked all the outside doors to make certain Dr. Webster could not get into the building without Mrs. Littlefield's knowing he had come.

As Mrs. Littlefield took up her position by a window, she had one source of comfort. She knew her guard duty would not last long. Littlefield had promised they would not be late for the Sons of Temperance Thanksgiving dance and she believed him. Was there another man in all of Suffolk County who enjoyed dancing as much as Ephraim Littlefield?

Littlefield did not disappoint his wife. He worked on the privy vault for an hour and a half. In that time he got through two layers of brick. He figured he had at least three more to go. At four o'clock he knocked off work and came up to get dressed. The Littlefields were not late for the party and Littlefield danced eighteen of the twenty dances listed on the program.

CHAPTER IV

The Discovery

ABOUT ELEVEN O'CLOCK on Friday morning the Cambridge postmaster, Eli Kinsley, got off the Bowdoin Square omnibus and then hurried along Tremont to School Street, leaning against a sharp east wind for the whole distance. It was a relief to get to City Hall and he stood for a moment at the bottom of the stairs to catch his breath before he went up to Marshal Tukey's office. From the second floor hall he caught a glimpse of the Marshal and was pleased to find him in. But despite his insistence that his business was urgent and he had to get back to Cambridge as quickly as possible, the clerk in the outer office required him to wait there until the Marshal was advised of his arrival. In Eli's opinion this process took an unreasonably long time. By leaning forward in his seat he could see the Marshal at his big oak desk. As usual he was impeccably groomed. He wore a fawn-colored coat and a white stock. At the moment he was buffing his nails.

While he waited for the clerk to come back, Eli recalled with pleasure the rumors that the Marshal was out of favor with Mayor Quincy. According to those in a position to know, the Mayor had decided that Boston needed more protection and fewer parades. Mayor Quincy was following in his father's footsteps. The old man had made a practice of galloping around town in the hours after midnight to find out what went on

in Boston after respectable people were in bed and to see for
himself what the police did about it. On a winter morning at
2 A.M. a watchman new to the force arrested a man on a big
gray horse for riding in a manner that endangered public
safety. Everybody congratulated the watchman on his judgment if not his luck, for it was common knowledge that Mayor
Josiah Quincy (the elder) was a very bad horseman.

The clerk reappeared. Marshal Tukey would see Mr. Kinsley now.

The Marshal did not look up from his newspaper as Eli entered his office.

Eli reached into an inner pocket of his greatcoat. "Marshal,
this letter must have been dropped into the East Cambridge
Post Office about ten o'clock this morning or shortly after. Because of its peculiar looks, I stamped it myself and brought
it right over."

The Marshal's expression changed in the space of a second.
He stood up and reached for the letter. He turned it over several times, studying it.

"I'd say those letters were more likely made with a brush
than a pen," he said, scrutinizing the handwriting. "And how
long has it been since you've seen a letter in a red envelope?"

"Don't know as I ever saw one before," Eli said.

The Marshal opened the envelope carefully. It held a single
sheet of cheap white paper. The handwriting had the same
thick look as the address on the envelope. The lines were ir-
regular. The writing was barely legible.

Together the Marshal and Eli made out the words.

> Dr. Parkman was took on Bord the ship herculan and this is
> al I dare say or I shal be kiled. Est. Cambrge. One of them give
> me his watch but I was feard to keep it and thowd it in the water
> right-side the road to the long bridge to Boston.

There was no signature.

The Marshal looked at Eli. "I assume you know about the letter in the yellow envelope?"

Eli nodded.

"That one was written by an educated man," the Marshal went on. "You can't say the same of this one." He paused and then added, "Or so it would seem."

"Nothing come of the other one? Nobody in New York knew anything about the Darts?" Eli asked him.

"No, and Dr. Parkman was not registered at any New York hotel." The Marshal looked up at the wall clock. "I'll have a search made for the watch, but I can't say I have much faith in this letter. Something about it doesn't ring true." He laid the letter on his desk.

"What do you think of Dr. Webster as a suspect?" Eli asked.

The Marshal frowned. "There is absolutely no firm evidence that points to him. So Dr. Parkman was last seen alive going into the Medical College and Dr. Webster was the last man known to have talked to him. That doesn't mean Dr. Webster killed him, does it? And after this much time has elapsed since Dr. Parkman's disappearance, I'm afraid we must presume that he's dead, murdered in all probability. These whispered accusations against Dr. Webster are ridiculous. Those men were friends all their lives. They went to school together and, if I remember correctly, Dr. Parkman was instrumental in Dr. Webster's appointment to the Harvard faculty. I know what Kingsley and Littlefield think, but their notions are preposterous."

"I saw Dr. Webster just now," Eli said. "He was coming up Union Street carrying a small package. If he murdered Dr. Parkman and hid him in the Medical College, it sure doesn't show in his manner. Did you know he was at a party at Professor Treadwell's house Friday evening? Can you imagine a man murdering an old friend in the afternoon and then going to a party that night?"

*

Earlier that morning Dr. Webster had paid a visit to the
Medical College. He arrived at nine o'clock and Littlefield,
slow getting up because of the dance of the previous evening,
was still at breakfast.

Dr. Webster stepped into the kitchen. It was a cold morning and he wore a greatcoat and a muffler that half concealed
his face. He carried a folded newspaper. He said he hoped
the Littlefields had enjoyed a good Thanksgiving. Also, he
wanted to ask whether they had any news of Dr. Parkman.

After thanking Dr. Webster for the turkey, Littlefield said he
had heard no news for the past day or two, nothing since the
story about the Irishman who tried to pay a penny toll with a
$20 bill.

That wasn't a *story,* Dr. Webster told Littlefield firmly, that
was the *truth.* Furthermore, he, for one, was not satisfied with
the explanation the Irishman gave the tollkeeper. If Marshal
Tukey took his advice, he would have the matter looked into
more carefully. He himself had just come from Dr. Henchman's
apothecary shop and Dr. Henchman told about a customer, a
woman, who had seen a cab go by her with a large bundle
propped up by a window. Something about the bundle didn't
look right to her and she had presence of mind enough to
take the number of the cab. Later they found it abandoned
and the inside all bloody. Now what could be the meaning
of that?

"There are so many reports flying around it's hard to know
what to make of any of them," Littlefield said.

Dr. Webster was silent for a moment. Then he said, "Could
be Dr. Parkman will never be found. Maybe we'll never know
what happened to him." At that he nodded and excused himself. Looking after him, Littlefield thought he seemed more relaxed than he had at any time since Dr. Parkman's disappearance. Littlefield got up from the table. Just the same, that
privy would bear looking into and he meant to see for himself
what was in it before the day was out.

He finished his tea standing up and went upstairs to the demonstrator's room. He was hard at work unpacking the new batch of specimens from Dr. Warren's collection when Dr. Bigelow came in.

Littlefield took the opportunity to tell him about the privy vault. "I hope to get through it by teatime this afternoon," he said in conclusion.

"I feel terrible about this thing," Dr. Bigelow said sorrowfully. "But I think you had better get on with it and get it over with. I hope you get through that wall before you sleep tonight." He got a book from the desk and hurried out of the room, nodding to Littlefield as he left.

A few moments later Dr. Jackson came into the demonstrator's room, snow on the brim of his tall black hat.

"I met Dr. Bigelow as I came in," he said. "He told me about the vault."

Littlefield carefully set a human skull on the demonstrator's table. "I haven't got much more work before I'll be into it, sir. I'll get at it again as soon as I get these specimens unpacked for Dr. Holmes."

"What will you do if you find something?" Dr. Jackson asked him.

"I'll go right to Dr. Holmes," Littlefield answered.

Dr. Jackson shook his head. Dr. Holmes' colleagues all knew how he felt about cruelty. As a boy of seven he had watched a public hanging on Jones Hill in Cambridge and the experience had permanently colored his feeling about taking life, for any purpose, under any circumstances. He had been known to run out of the room while his assistant chloroformed a rabbit. And as Dr. Jackson was well aware, there were other reasons why the tragedy Littlefield might uncover would be hard on Dr. Holmes. Holmes had known both men all his life. Dr. Webster had taught him chemistry during his undergraduate days at Harvard. He himself occupied the

Parkman Professorship of Anatomy at the Medical College, a chair created to express appreciation to Dr. Parkman for his gift of the ground on which the Medical College stood. Moreover, within the year Dr. Holmes had given up both his private practice and his appointment as visiting physician for the Massachusetts General Hospital so that he could devote himself to his responsibilities as both the Dean of the Medical College and a member of its faculty. He planned to augment his income by appearances on the lecture platform. The debt on the College's new building had to be paid off by the Medical College faculty and Dr. Holmes was not a rich man. Dr. Jackson knew that a scandal at the College would have serious implications for Dr. Holmes personally, professionally, and financially.

He said to Littlefield, "You'd better not go to Dr. Holmes. Go to the elder Dr. Bigelow and then come to me. If I'm not at home, leave your name on my slate and I'll understand."

Shortly after two o'clock Littlefield went across the street and borrowed a crowbar from Leonard Fuller at the foundry. Next, he locked all the outside doors. Again, Mrs. Littlefield was posted as the lookout. Littlefield said they would use the same signal. If she saw Dr. Webster approaching the building, she was not to let him in until she had run back to their kitchen and rapped on the floor four times with the hammer. By watching from the front windows, she could see him far enough away so she could signal Littlefield and still get up to the entrance without making the Doctor wait a suspiciously long time. And remember, Littlefield told her, she was not to disturb him for anybody except Dr. Webster.

Littlefield got a lantern and went down the scuttle to the tunnel. Bent almost double, with a crowbar in one hand and the lantern in the other, he made his way over the rough earth to the privy vault at the rear of the building. After he had found a level place for the lantern, he picked up the drill and went to work. Cold as it was, perspiration ran down his face. He found it hard to breathe in the airless, dusty tunnel. By the time he had worked half an hour, his hands began to blister and he went up to his kitchen to find his heavy gloves. When he had gone back down and worked on the vault another twenty minutes, he found he needed a hammer and a cold chisel. He stopped work again and went over to the foundry. Elias Fuller gave him the hammer and the chisel he needed.

He was halfway through the fourth layer of bricks when he heard four taps on the floor above his head. He threw down the chisel, grabbed the lantern and, hunched over, ran the distance from the vault to the scuttle. He climbed through the trap door, ran down the passageway, out through the carriage shed and around the building to the front steps. There he found not Dr. Webster but Mr. Kingsley and Mr. Starkweather.

Mr. Kingsley looked him over as he wiped the sweat from his face with his shirt sleeve.

"Well, you look as though you'd been crawling around down under the building, Littlefield," he said. "What are you up to, anyway?"

Littlefield looked from Mr. Kingsley to Mr. Starkweather. "We sometimes have trouble with pipes in weather like this. It's up to me to keep an eye on them."

"We're sorry to disturb you, but we want to have another look around Dr. Webster's rooms," Starkweather said. "Kingsley here has an idea or two we'd like to investigate."

Littlefield shook his head. "Dr. Webster isn't here and I don't have keys to his rooms. Remember the last time you were here and we had to pound on the doors to rouse him?"

Mr. Kingsley persisted. "Isn't there some way we could get in? What would you do if the place caught fire? And don't you ever have to get things ready ahead of time when he's going to do an experiment for his class?"

Littlefield was shivering. "He used to leave the door to the lower laboratory open and that way I could get upstairs if need be, but lately he locks everything."

Mr. Starkweather considered the situation. "Well, if we can't get in, we can't, and we don't want to keep you standing out here in the cold," he said finally. "We'll stop around in the morning. Dr. Webster comes over on Saturday mornings, doesn't he?"

Littlefield shrugged. "Hard to tell. Lately he's been coming every day, but that doesn't mean he'll necessarily be here tomorrow morning."

To Littlefield's relief the two men turned to leave, Mr. Kingsley reluctantly. As they started off up North Grove Street, he saw Mr. Trenholm turning the corner from Fruit Street. Littlefield hurried to meet him. He shivered as he talked, but he told Trenholm his trouble wasn't just being cold. The closer he got to seeing into that vault, the more nervous he grew. It was a help to tell Trenholm how he felt. If Kingsley had been alone, he would have told him, too, but he didn't want Starkweather telling the Marshal what he was up to until he was sure his hunch was right. And the longer he worked on that privy vault, the surer he was that he *was* right. He could feel it in his bones.

At that moment Mrs. Littlefield appeared at the door of the dissecting room passageway. "Eph, there's Dr. Webster!" she cried. She gestured urgently toward Bridge Street.

Littlefield felt a moment's concern about the grime on his face and his overalls, but Dr. Webster gave no sign that he noticed.

"Remember about the Irishman and the twenty dollars?" he asked Littlefield. He turned to Mr. Trenholm. Had he heard that an Irishman had given the tollkeeper at Craigie's Bridge a $20 bill to pay a penny toll?

When Mr. Trenholm nodded, Dr. Webster told them both that this afternoon Marshal Tukey had sent over to Cambridge to ask him to come and have a look at the bill to see if he could identify it as one he had given Dr. Parkman. Dr. Webster went over to City Hall and studied the bill, but he couldn't be sure. The bills he gave Dr. Parkman were those he had received from students paying their fees, so they were of all denominations, big and little. The only bill he remembered with certainty was one on the New England Bank. His story about the $20 bill finished, Dr. Webster bowed abruptly and started off up North Grove Street.

Trenholm thought he seemed agitated.

Littlefield said he hadn't noticed. All he could think about was getting back to work on the vault. "Come over to the College in about an hour and I'll be able to tell you if there's anything in it that shouldn't be there," he said to Trenholm as they parted.

In twenty minutes Littlefield had finished the drilling on the fifth layer of bricks. Then he looked around for the crowbar he had borrowed from the foundry and in a matter of five minutes he knocked a hole in the vault. At first he could not get a light into it because of the draft. Finally he hit upon the idea of leaning into the vault so that his body served as a shield against the draft. In that way he was able to get his lantern into it without losing the light. Leaning forward, Littlefield focused the pale light on the part of the vault to his left. Slowly, very slowly, he rotated the lantern. Now that his eyes were accustomed to the darkness, he could see the streaks of wet made by the tides of the Charles River. In the dim light he could make out the great blocks of stone in the outer foundation walls on his left. Directly in front of him was a trench made by the high mounds of earth dug away from the walls as a protection against pressure.

Bracing his body as best he could, he got the lantern in both hands and tried to angle the light above him so he could figure the position of the privy hole in relation to the floor of the vault. Satisfied as to its location, he leaned forward again and lowered the lantern. He turned it to his right. There on the slope of the mound on the north side of the building, he saw a man's pelvis, a thigh from hip to knee, and the lower part of a leg. In the pale lantern light the pieces of the body looked ghostly white against the black earth.

At the sight below him Littlefield began to tremble so that he could barely hold the lantern. He managed to get it out of the vault, but the light went out. He did not try to re-light the lantern. Stumbling over bricks and tools, trembling so violently he could not stay on his feet, Littlefield crawled down the long black tunnel to the scuttle.

As he climbed out of the trap door, Littlefield screamed for his wife. He burst into tears when he saw her. She led him into the kitchen and as he sobbed out what he had seen, she wiped the earth and the blood from his hands. Littlefield insisted that he must go immediately to Dr. Bigelow. He would not wait for his wife to borrow a rig so he could drive; he would not even wait until she found his jacket. He ran along Cambridge to Belknap Street, then up Belknap, down through the Common into Winter Street and across Washington into Summer. Dr. Jacob Bigelow lived in a big wooden house four doors from the corner of Chauncy Place.

At the sight of Littlefield, coatless on a cold night, earth-stained and trembling, Dr. Bigelow's servant called Mrs. Bigelow. Littlefield asked urgently for the Doctor. Alarmed, Mrs. Bigelow said her husband was not at home but wouldn't Littlefield go around the corner to young Dr. Bigelow? Mrs. Bigelow was sure he would be glad to help. Would Littlefield leave a message for the senior Dr. Bigelow? He should be home within the hour.

Littlefield did not hear. He was already on his way to Chauncy Place, upset at the prospect of talking to Dr. Henry Bigelow at a time like this. He did not like young Bigelow with his high and mighty airs and his fancy French cabriolet. Littlefield didn't care if he did give free medical care to the poor in the basement of the First Church. He was an ill-tempered, haughty fellow.

Littlefield liked Dr. Henry Bigelow even less as he stammered out the story of what he had found in Dr. Webster's privy vault at the Medical College.

Dr. Bigelow grabbed him by the collar. "Damn you, Littlefield! What do you know about this business?" he thundered.

Littlefield cried that he had nothing whatsoever to do with putting those pieces of a human body in Dr. Webster's privy vault! He had known Dr. Parkman for twenty years. He *liked* the old man! He didn't *kill* him!

Dr. Bigelow seemed reluctant to let go of Littlefield's collar. Still glowering, he ordered Littlefield to go to Mr. Shaw's home and tell what he had found. Dr. Bigelow would get Marshal Tukey and meet him there.

Littlefield ran back down Summer Street. When he burst out that he brought news about Dr. Parkman, Mr. Shaw's servant took him directly into the study where Mr. Shaw was reading. Standing there on the fine carpet in his muddy shoes, the blood oozing from the cuts on his hands, he told what he had found in the vault. He was finishing his story when Dr. Bigelow came in with Marshal Tukey. The three men talked for a few minutes. Mr. Shaw thought Littlefield could be wrong about the remains; maybe they *were* specimens from the dissecting rooms. It would take a chemical analysis to tell for sure, he said. Dr. Bigelow disagreed. If he saw the parts of the body, he could tell whether they had had the chemical treatment used on specimens prepared for the dissecting room. He suggested they go over to the Medical College immediately.

Mr. Shaw wanted to send for Edward Blake before they went to the College. Also, there were two other matters he felt they should settle at this time. He hesitated, glancing from Marshal Tukey to Littlefield.

At that Marshal Tukey turned to Littlefield. He ordered Littlefield to go back to the Medical College. They would join him there very shortly.

But Littlefield did not go directly to the Medical College. He ran over to Dr. Jackson's office. The Doctor's door was open but he was not in. Quickly Littlefield wrote his name on the slate. Then he ran down Tremont to the Common. From the Common he went up Belknap Street, down the north side of Beacon Hill and along Cambridge to Bridge Street and the Medical College.

When he turned into Bridge Street, he saw Mr. Trenholm pacing the ground in front of the steps that led up to the main entrance. From a distance of a hundred yards he could sense how upset Trenholm was.

Now Trenholm looked in the direction of Bridge Street and saw Littlefield. Running toward him with the awkward gait of a tall, thin, middle-aged man, Trenholm burst out that he had seen the pieces of the body. He had come over to the Medical College just after Littlefield left to go to Dr. Bigelow. Mrs. Littlefield told him about the vault and he had gone down to see for himself. Trenholm shook his head sadly. He could not believe that one human being could do this to another, he said as Littlefield and he went into the building through the carriage shed entrance. And Dr. Webster? Was he capable of such a thing?

While Trenholm was speaking, Mr. Clapp came in followed by Dr. Bigelow, Marshal Tukey, Mr. Shaw, and Mr. Edward Blake. At Littlefield's suggestion they all stepped into his parlor and Mrs. Littlefield went for more candles. The men looked at each other in silence, their faces solemn. Then the Marshal told Littlefield they were ready to go down with him to view the pieces of the body. They waited while Littlefield got three lanterns. Marshal Tukey took one and Dr. Bigelow another. Littlefield carried the third.

Marshal Tukey motioned for Littlefield to show the way to the scuttle.

Was Littlefield *positive* there were no specimens missing

from the demonstrator's rooms, Marshal Tukey asked as the men walked along the passageway.

Littlefield said, yes, he was positive there were no specimens missing. They had reached the scuttle and Littlefield stooped down to lift up the trap door.

Despite Mr. Blake's urging Mr. Shaw did not stay behind. One by one the seven men descended the narrow wooden stairs. By the light of the three lanterns, they made their way along the airless, dusty tunnel toward the vault. Four times they had to stop to re-light the lanterns before they reached the pile of bricks Littlefield had taken out of the vault.

The hole Littlefield had made was about a foot and a half square. It was barely two feet above the ground so each man had to stoop to see into it. At Marshal Tukey's direction Littlefield held a lantern down into the vault and one by one the men looked into it in turn, the Marshal first.

"Are we *sure* those aren't dissecting room specimens?" Mr. Blake asked in horror while they waited for Littlefield to re-light his lantern.

"We are almost certain they are not," the Marshal said. "I have sent for Coroner Pratt. He will decide whether we need additional investigation of this matter." He looked over at Derastus Clapp. "How do you propose to get the remains out of the vault so Pratt can make a decision?"

Mr. Clapp addressed Trenholm. "You're the tallest of all of us so you probably have the longest arms. You step into the vault and hand the pieces out to Littlefield."

As he spoke, Mr. Blake picked up a lantern and Mr. Shaw and he started back toward the scuttle. In the shadowy darkness the other men saw Mr. Shaw pause momentarily and brace himself against the side of the tunnel. Marshal Tukey and Dr. Bigelow exchanged a glance.

"Mr. Shaw, would you want to sit down for a few minutes' rest if we can find something —" Marshal Tukey began.

Mr. Shaw interrupted in a faint voice. "I do not want to sit down," he said. "I want to go up." He continued on down the tunnel, feeling his way along the wall.

Dr. Bigelow spoke up for the first time since they had seen the pieces of the body.

"We can put the remains on this," he said, indicating the piece of board he held. "I found it leaning against the wall on the outer side of the vault."

Trenholm climbed through the hole. The pieces of the body were lying toward the outer wall, on the sloping mound of earth on the north side of the building. One by one he handed them to Littlefield, the pelvis, the right thigh, the piece of a left leg, the part from the knee to the ankle. Littlefield placed them on the board.

The Marshal said the remains must stay where they were until the Coroner gave his permission for them to be removed from the place where they were found. Littlefield and Trenholm had better find a level spot near the vault and put the board there.

When Dr. Bigelow, Mr. Clapp, and Marshal Tukey were back upstairs with Mr. Shaw and Mr. Blake, they went to Littlefield's parlor to consider what step they should take next. The unanimous decision was to arrange for Dr. Webster's arrest. All things considered, there was no alternative; this action must be taken.

Dr. Bigelow spoke up. He said that if the circumstances were different, he would be willing to help resolve the problem that confronted them all. He hoped no one in the room had a shadow of a doubt as to his sincerity on this point. However as things were, he must ask to be excused. If the suggestion was agreeable to Marshal Tukey, he would ask Dr. Martin Gay to serve in his place. Dr. Gay was a chemist as well as a physician and eminently well qualified to assume any responsibility that he might be asked to bear in this situation. Furthermore, he was a close friend of the Webster family and would be more than willing, Dr. Bigelow knew, to do all he could to comfort Dr. Webster in the days that might lie ahead.

Marshal Tukey nodded. There was no need for further explanation, he said. He appreciated Dr. Bigelow's offer to ask Dr. Gay to serve in his place. Would he do so immediately?

Every man in the room could understand Dr. Bigelow's wish to withdraw. They all knew that Dr. Bigelow's wife was Dr. Parkman's niece and that in the spring his sister, Catherine, would marry the Doctor's nephew, Francis Parkman.

Then Marshal Tukey said he had another request to make of Dr. Bigelow. Would Dr. Bigelow accompany the rest of them to Mt. Vernon Street to discuss the situation with Mr. Parker? They would need a warrant for Dr. Webster's arrest. Somebody would have to go before a magistrate and make a complaint against him.

When Dr. Bigelow nodded, the Marshal turned to Trenholm. He ordered Trenholm to stay with Littlefield at the Medical College. Littlefield was to lock all the outside doors and to admit no one except Jabez Pratt, the Coroner, Mr. Parker, the District Attorney, other members of the police force, or any of the men now in the room. Then he ordered Mr. Clapp to take Starkweather and Spurr with him and go to Cambridge to bring Dr. Webster to the Leverett Street jail. They were to hire a coach rather than to use one of the police vehicles. Dr. Webster was to be told simply that he was wanted at the Medical College.

It was close to eight o'clock when Officers Clapp, Starkweather, and Spurr arrived at Garden Street in Cambridge. They stopped the coach a few yards from Dr. Webster's home.

The Doctor was standing in his doorway saying good-bye to a guest, his plump figure outlined by the house lights behind him. As he turned to go into his house, Mr. Clapp approached him. The police were about to search the Medical College again, Mr. Clapp said, and Dr. Webster's presence was wanted.

Dr. Webster nodded. He said he would be glad to go over to the Medical College if Officer Clapp would excuse him while he stepped into his library for a moment. He reappeared wearing a greatcoat and his boots. On the threshold he felt for his keys and was on the point of going back for them when Mr. Clapp said that wouldn't be necessary. He was sure they already had all the keys they needed.

As he got into the carriage, Dr. Webster spoke to Spurr who was outside with the driver. His manner toward Mr. Clapp and Starkweather was friendly and easy. As they rounded the corner by Judge Fay's house, he asked if they knew that "Fair Harvard" was written in a second floor bedroom of the Judge's house. He thought the occasion was Commencement in 1826. He wasn't sure of the year but in any event it was a long time ago. They were in Harvard Square now and as he looked toward the Yard, Dr. Webster commented that it didn't seem so very long ago that he was one of those students over there. Dr. Parkman and he were friends when they were both at Harvard. Many a time he had heard Dr. Parkman say that the only reprimand he got during his four years at Harvard was a lecture from a faculty committee for unnecessary walking on the Sabbath. Dr. Webster turned to Mr. Clapp. Was there any news about Dr. Parkman?

When Mr. Clapp shook his head, Starkweather spoke up to say they had found a hat at the Navy Yard and the consensus was that it belonged to Dr. Parkman, although they hadn't found any other piece of clothing or anything else that might be a clue.

Then Dr. Webster said he understood Mrs. Bent had seen

Dr. Parkman late Friday afternoon. They weren't very far from where she lived. What about stopping by her house so they could hear her story first hand?

But Mr. Clapp said he thought they'd better get on over to the Medical College since they were expected. Dr. Webster took the refusal with no sign of resentment.

Ahead the lights of Craigie's Bridge dotted the darkness. As the carriage rattled over the old pine planks, Starkweather told how Marshal Tukey had ordered soundings made above and below the bridge on both sides. He did not add that the Marshal had issued the order after Eli Kinsley brought over the letter in the red envelope and that so far they had not found Dr. Parkman's turned-case Lepine.

Dr. Webster spoke up. "We've missed the turn. That was Second Street we just passed."

"I guess we have a green driver, but I'm sure we'll eventually get to our destination." Mr. Clapp's tone was light and pleasant, but Starkweather could sense his tension.

"Didn't I see another officer up with the driver?" Dr. Webster asked. "It's a wonder he didn't give the man directions."

"'I don't envy Spurr his seat. That's a bitter wind blowing northeast off the harbor," Starkweather said. As he spoke the carriage pulled up to the front of the Leverett Street jail. In the darkness the old gray stone building looked black.

Excusing himself Mr. Clapp got out on the far side and went into the jail. He was back in a moment; there were no spectators to clear from the office. He opened the door on Dr. Webster's side of the carriage. "Gentlemen, I ask you to come into the jail office for a few moments," he said to Dr. Webster and Starkweather.

Dr. Webster and Starkweather followed him into the cavernous building, Spurr behind them. Mr. Clapp picked up a lamp and started across the stone floor toward the inner office. "Suppose we go this way, gentlemen," he said.

Dr. Webster did not move. "Mr. Clapp, what does this mean?" he demanded.

Mr. Clapp turned to face Dr. Webster. He set the lamp on the desk to his right. When he spoke, his tone was no longer conversational. "Dr. Webster," he said, "you recall that Starkweather mentioned the soundings that have been made above and below Craigie's Bridge. Well, we are done with looking for the body of Dr. Parkman, and you, Dr. Webster, are now in custody on the charge of his murder!"

Dr. Webster gasped. He seemed to steady himself against the battered table he stood beside. "What! Me!" he cried.

Mr. Clapp's tone was cold. "Yes, you, Dr. Webster. You are in custody for the murder of Dr. George Parkman."

"I want you to send word to my family immediately!" Dr. Webster cried at him.

But Mr. Clapp said that would not be possible tonight. He added that in his opinion, it was a good thing. He said Dr. Webster's family would be spared a sad night, a very sad night indeed.

Then he wanted his friends, Dr. Webster persisted. Would Mr. Clapp kindly get a message to Mr. Prescott and Mr. Dexter as quickly as possible?

Mr. Clapp shook his head. That would have to wait until morning, too, he said. Dr. Webster could not see them tonight even if they did come. And Mr. Dexter lived clear out in Beverly. It would be totally impossible to get a message to him at this time of night.

But Mr. Dexter wasn't in Beverly. He was at the Revere House. Couldn't somebody take a message to him there, Dr. Webster pleaded.

But Mr. Clapp only shook his head. Dr. Webster's face showed panic. He looked beseechingly from Starkweather to Spurr.

Mr. Clapp was speaking to him. "Dr. Webster, it is my

duty to make sure that a prisoner does not take anything im-
proper into the jail. Will you be kind enough to give me your
personal possessions?"

Dr. Webster's hands trembled as he handed Mr. Clapp his
watch, his wallet, $2.40 in cash, an omnibus ticket-case, and
five keys, one of them a rusty iron key four or five inches long
with a pasteboard label marked *Privy* attached to it. In addition he gave Mr. Clapp three slips of paper. The first one,
wider than the others, had jottings of sums of money and several names written on it. On the second was written, *$483.64.*
The third slip of paper was a list:

> ax
> keys
> tin box
> solder

Mr. Clapp tied up Dr. Webster's possessions in a handkerchief
he took from his own pocket. Next, he gestured to Starkweather and Spurr to bring Dr. Webster and follow him into the
inner office.

There was a rush of cold air as the outer door opened and
Cummings, the turnkey, came in.

"I expected to find you here when we arrived," Mr. Clapp
said sharply. "Aren't you on duty?"

"Yes, sir, but I've been busy at the jail. Andrews isn't here,
so I'm alone and it's a lot for one man, sir."

"Where is Andrews?"

"It's his night off, sir."

"Can you get word to him to come over?"

"I can, sir, and I will," Cummings said. He started toward
the door. "I won't be gone but a moment this time."

As soon as he reached the inner office, Mr. Clapp locked
Dr. Webster's possessions in a desk drawer. Then he sat
down at the desk and wrote out a mittimus. That done, he

told Starkweather that Spurr and he would go in search of the Marshal. Starkweather and Cummings would stay at the jail with Dr. Webster. They were not to put the Doctor into a cell until Mr. Clapp returned.

As soon as Mr. Clapp and Spurr left, Dr. Webster asked for water. Starkweather brought an earthenware pitcher and a glass. He set the pitcher on the scarred deal table beside the couch where Dr. Webster sat. Dr. Webster emptied the glass three times.

"Tell me. Have they found Dr. Parkman?" he asked.

Starkweather looked at the Doctor kindly. "I wish you wouldn't ask me questions, Doctor. It's not proper for me to answer. You know that."

Dr. Webster persisted. "You might tell me something!" he cried. "Where did they find him? Did they find the whole body?"

Starkweather did not answer immediately. Then he asked, "Dr. Webster, did anybody else have access to your private room?"

Abruptly Dr. Webster stood up. He shook his fist as he cried, "Nobody but that porter, the villain!"

Starkweather leaned to adjust the lamp wick. As he straightened, he was sure he saw the Doctor take something from his vest pocket and put it into his mouth.

"Dr. Webster, didn't you take something? Didn't I see you put something into your mouth just then?"

But Dr. Webster shook his head. He sank heavily on the old black settee. He sat with his head bowed, his hands clasped between his knees, his shoulders hunched. He seemed sodden with despair. During the hour that elapsed before Mr. Clapp's return, he said nothing.

Starkweather, sitting in the shadows, watching by the light
of a single lamp, saw the Doctor trembling. He made no response when Starkweather spoke to him. He neither answered
nor turned his head nor in any way indicated that he had heard
Starkweather. Cold as the room was, the Doctor's face glistened
with sweat.

Starkweather heard Mr. Clapp and Spurr in the outer office
and a few minutes later Mr. Clapp came to say he had not been
able to locate Marshal Tukey or Mr. Parker. He had decided
to commit Dr. Webster on his own authority. Starkweather
could take him down to his cell. "If you need help, get Cummings," he said.

Even two men had difficulty getting Dr. Webster down the
narrow, dark stairs. He did not have the use of his legs so they
had to carry him. They had to hoist him onto his bunk. He
lay face down in the straw. Starkweather and Cummings stood
watching him for a few minutes and Starkweather thought the
Doctor's trembling was growing more pronounced. As they
left the cell, he cried out to them, begging them to get word
of his whereabouts to his family.

Upstairs Starkweather told Mr. Clapp he thought the Doctor
was having convulsions. He said he was positive Doctor Webster had taken something from his vest pocket and slipped it
into his mouth. After that he began to tremble. Hadn't they
better send for a physician?

Mr. Clapp did not think that was necessary. Just watch him,
he said. Keep an eye on him until Mr. Parker and the Marshal
get here.

"Can you believe Dr. Webster could be guilty of a terrible
thing like this?" Cummings asked Mr. Clapp.

Mr. Clapp pulled a chair opposite him to get his feet off the
cold stone floor. No, he couldn't believe the Doctor was guilty
of murder, particularly *this* murder. At the same time, there
was some evidence that would take a lot of explaining on the

Doctor's part. He told about a fragment of bone Littlefield had found in the furnace in the lower laboratory. "If I was to guess, I'd say it was a piece of skull. And who had access to the Doctor's lower laboratory twenty-four hours a day except the Doctor himself?" he concluded.

"Littlefield," Starkweather said. "I asked Dr. Webster about that tonight."

"Could be. Could be," Mr. Clapp said.

Cummings wanted to know if Dr. Webster could have burned the rest of the body. Wouldn't there have been a terrible odor? True, classes weren't in session but Littlefield and his family were there.

Mr. Clapp was sure there would have been an odor, all right. He remembered a summer night years ago when Dr. Strong was a young fellow with an office on Cornhill Street. About the middle of the evening the watchman began getting complaints about the terrible odor in Cornhill. It seems that Dr. Strong had got hold of the body of a pirate, got hold of it legitimately of course, and was trying to boil the flesh off the bones. Mr. Clapp grimaced at the memory. He'd remember that smell if he lived to be a hundred.

"You'd think it would take a mountain of fuel to do something like that," Cummings said.

"Well, if the rest of the body wasn't burned, and that doesn't seem very likely, what do you suppose happened to it?" Starkweather asked.

"Wherever it is, it's our job to find it, providing we don't freeze to death before the rest of them get here," Mr. Clapp said.

As he spoke, Mr. Parker came in with Jabez Pratt, the coroner, and Dr. Martin Gay. Marshal Tukey was with them and so were Mr. Shaw, Mr. Blake, and Mr. Kingsley. As usual Mr. Parker's manner was crisp. He directed Cummings to go downstairs and bring up Dr. Webster immediately.

Cummings was back in a moment or two to say he could not

manage the Doctor without help. He had never seen a man
tremble the way Dr. Webster was trembling at this moment.
The Doctor must have the trembling madness or convulsions
or something very serious. Starkweather told about seeing
the Doctor swallow something he had taken from his pocket.

Dr. Gay spoke up. "I'll be glad to go down and see John.
I'll look him over in the light of Officer Starkweather's comments and see if I can't get him calmed down a bit."

Mr. Parker nodded. "That would be a service, Dr. Gay. Cummings, you go down with him." He looked over the crowd of
men in the room. "Where is Jones? Is he here?"

Jones stepped forward. "Here, sir."

"You go downstairs with Dr. Gay and Cummings. It may
take two of you to get Dr. Webster up here if he is in as bad
shape as Cummings and Starkweather say."

Afterwards Dr. Gay said that in his entire professional career, he had never before seen a man in the condition in which
he found Dr. Webster. The Doctor's body was arched, so that
he rested on his head and his heels. His face was wet with perspiration. He gave no sign of recognition when Dr. Gay entered his cell.

Dr. Gay said Dr. Webster was having the spasms Starkweather and Cummings had reported. After he had watched
Dr. Webster for a few moments, Dr. Gay got a chair from a
corner of the cell. He asked Jones and Cummings to lift Dr.
Webster out of his bunk and set him on the chair. As the two
men got hold of him, Dr. Webster's face showed a flash of panic.
He gave a sudden spring and grabbed Jones around the neck
as though he were terror-stricken.

When Dr. Webster was seated on the chair, Dr. Gay began
to talk to him. He spoke of his long friendship with the Webster family, of his earnest desire to help him in every possible
way. Could Dr. Webster doubt the sincerity of a friend of forty
years' standing?

Dr. Webster spoke then. He asked for water but when Cummings brought it, he could not hold the tumbler. He spilled the water all over himself. Dr. Gay held the tumbler for him but even then he could not drink. He seemed unable to get the rim of the tumbler into his mouth. He snapped at it, like an animal. Finally he motioned for the water to be taken away.

"It's terribly cold down here," Dr. Gay said, glancing around the cell.

Dr. Webster stirred. "My legs are freezing," he said.

Dr. Gay began to talk to him again. Speaking gently he said that there were men upstairs who must talk with Dr. Webster about discoveries that had been made at the Medical College. He asked whether Dr. Webster was able to walk upstairs to see them.

When Dr. Webster said he could not walk, Cummings and Jones carried him up the stairs and put him in a chair facing the men who waited for him. He seemed scarcely able to sit upright.

Mr. Parker observed Dr. Webster in silence. Samuel Parker had distinguished himself as the District Attorney of Suffolk County. The son of an Episcopalian minister, the only Episcopalian clergyman in New England who did not desert his parishioners during the Revolution, his courage and his convictions were in the family pattern. Perhaps as he stood watching Dr. Gay and Cummings minister to Dr. Webster, Mr. Parker pondered the fact that he had already sustained one major blow involving the Parkman family. His wife's aunt, Mary Mason, was the woman who rocked Beacon Hill by divorcing Samuel Parkman.

Mr. Parker's manner with Dr. Webster was firm but not unkind. A short, thick-set man whose taste in dress was conservative and expensive, his appearance embodied his reputation as a strong, successful, and powerful public official. He stood in the pale lamplight, looking down at Dr. Webster. A whistle sounded from the harbor. Horses' hoofs thudded in the jail yard. The semicircle of men behind Mr. Parker were silent, their faces barely distinguishable among the shadows.

Mr. Parker's voice was low-pitched. He began by reminding Dr. Webster that he was a lifelong friend of the Webster family. He had known Dr. Webster's father well. Certainly Dr. Webster knew Mr. Parker meant him no harm in having him brought to the jail.

Dr. Webster burst into sobs. He cried out that he wanted his family. Why wouldn't they send for his family? He leaned uncertainly toward Mr. Parker. Cummings stepped forward quickly and put his hand on the Doctor's shoulder.

Mr. Parker ignored the interruption. He repeated that his intention in having Dr. Webster brought to the jail was to help him, certainly not to do him any harm. As it happened certain disclosures had been made at the Medical College. "We have come here to see if you wish to go there with us to make any explanations you feel are indicated," he concluded.

Again Dr. Webster burst out that he wanted his family. Cummings stood close to him, ready to catch him if he fell. "Why can't my family be told where I am?" he demanded of Mr. Parker. "Why can't . . ."

Mr. Parker interrupted. "There is another family that has been in great distress for a week, Dr. Webster. Perhaps if you can explain certain things that have happened at the Medical College, that family will be relieved." He added in a different tone, "We are on our way to the Medical College now. You are free to go with us or not, as you please."

Dr. Webster was weeping, but he managed to say, brokenly, that he would go to the Medical College. He had nothing to explain, he said.

Mr. Clapp spoke up. He addressed the men who stood in

the darkness behind Mr. Parker. "Is Mr. Andrews here?" he asked.

"Not yet, sir, but I'm here. Could I do whatever you have in mind, sir?" It was Leighton, the jail clerk.

"You and Cummings get Dr. Webster over to the Medical College," Mr. Clapp told him. "The rest of us will follow in the other carriages."

Dr. Webster was still unable to walk. Leighton and Cummings carried him to the coach and carried him up the steps to the main entrance of the Medical College. Gus Andrews, the jailer, joined them shortly after they reached the College. The night was bitter cold. The men on the steps were at the mercy of the sharp northeast wind. Dr. Webster was quiet but his face was wet. He was still racked with convulsions. He trembled so that he could not have stayed upright without the support Leighton and Cummings gave him.

Andrews could not understand why they had to wait so long on the steps. Finally he pounded the door with his fist. "Hurry up in there!" he roared in his stentorian voice. "We've got a sick man out here in the cold!"

Littlefield was very apologetic as he opened the door. With all that was going on downstairs, he simply had not heard the bell. He was sorry. He hoped Mr. Parker and the others would understand.

When Dr. Webster saw Littlefield, he burst into tears. "They took me away from my family, Littlefield! They didn't even give me a chance to say good-bye!" he cried. However, he gained composure as the party walked through his lecture room. He watched in silence while the others looked around the upper laboratory. During the inspection of his private room, somebody picked up a coat and began examining it.

"That's a coat I wear when I'm doing experiments during a lecture," Dr. Webster said. "There's nothing important about it. In fact, you won't find anything of importance in this room."

Mr. Clapp pulled open the drawers of a small chest. In the third drawer he found a bunch of keys. Many of them were rusted. He held them up and looked questioningly at Dr. Webster.

Dr. Webster faltered. "I — I don't remember just when it was, but I found those keys in the street one morning last spring. I think it was on Fruit Street up near Blossom. I threw them into the drawer there, thinking they might be of use sometime, and haven't looked at them since."

No one in the group commented. While the others watched, Mr. Clapp pushed the chest drawers closed. He had the keys in his hand as he left the room.

As Leighton and Cummings started down the stairs to the lower laboratory with him, Dr. Webster began to tremble again. The room was crowded and this seemed to upset him. In addition to Mr. Parker, Dr. Gay, Marshal Tukey, Mr. Clapp, Mr. Shaw, and Mr. Blake, young Parkman Blake was there. So were Coroner Pratt, and Trenholm, Andrews, Rice, Spurr, Starkweather, Adams, Littlefield, and Mr. Kingsley came in after Dr. Webster and the others were in the lower laboratory.

Mr. Parker gave orders to open the door of Dr. Webster's privy. When Mr. Clapp remembered that the Doctor's key to the privy was locked in his desk at the jail, Littlefield and Mr. Kingsley broke down the door.

Dr. Webster remained fairly calm while the men took turns examining the privy. Mr. Clapp had one of his men take the seat away. He and half a dozen of the others discussed the size of the privy hole in relation to the width of the shoulders of a man of Dr. Parkman's size. Would they go through or wouldn't they? As Coroner Pratt walked out of the privy, Littlefield approached him.

"I broke this off the side of the furnace," he said. He held up a piece of slag into which was fused a splinter of burned bone.

For a few seconds Mr. Clapp stared at the bone in shocked silence. Then he said to Littlefield, "Put it back. Put it back where you found it. Everything must stay as it is until the coroner's jury has acted."

It was when they started for the passageway that Dr. Webster began to tremble violently again. Sweat and tears poured down his face. He asked for water but he again could not drink. When Cummings held the tumbler for him, he seemed to choke on the water. He motioned it away. When he heard Marshal Tukey direct Littlefield and Trenholm to bring up the pieces of the body, he shook violently and he began to sob. Dr. Gay was unable to quiet him. He stood eight or nine feet from the trap door that led down to the tunnel. As Trenholm handed up the first piece of the body, the thigh, and it was placed in the shallow pan filled with sand that had been prepared for the purpose, Dr. Webster tried to spread his feet as though he sought to brace himself against the floor.

"Dr. Gay, are these the remains of a human body?" Coroner Pratt asked as the piece of leg and the pelvis were placed in the pan.

"Yes, they are," Dr. Gay answered.

Coroner Pratt made a note. "There is no doubt whatsoever?"

"None whatsoever," Dr. Gay said.

For a moment or two the group stood looking at the remains in silence. Dr. Webster turned his head away after a few seconds. Tears streamed down his face.

Andrews stepped up to Mr. Clapp. "Is Dr. Webster wanted here any longer? If not, I'll take him back to the jail."

Mr. Clapp looked over to Mr. Parker. He repeated Andrews' question and Mr. Parker nodded.

As Andrews and Cummings carried Dr. Webster up the laboratory stairs, they heard Marshal Tukey giving directions about the remains. They were to be put in a box in the privy for the rest of the night and the privy door was to be nailed shut.

Trenholm, Rice, and Adams were to spend the night at the
Medical College in the capacity of guards.

When Andrews and Cummings got Dr. Webster out to the
carriage to take him to the jail, he still seemed unable
either to hear or to understand what they said to him.
Also, his body had stiffened. In order to get him into the carriage, Andrews got in first and then drew the Doctor up as
though his body were a board. Later Cummings said that Dr.
Webster had perspired so much that he could feel the wetness
of Dr. Webster's pantaloons against his own leg.

Dr. Webster spoke once on the trip to the jail. "Why don't
they ask Littlefield? Why don't they ask Littlefield?" he
cried.

Leighton, the jail clerk, had ridden over to the jail on the
outside of the carriage. It was he who helped Cummings get
Dr. Webster down to his cell. They got him onto his bunk
and turned him over so he was on his back. When they took
off his outer coat, they found his clothes soaked with perspiration. It was still freezing cold in his cell. Cummings got him
another blanket. He seemed uncomfortable lying flat so
they found a bolster to put under his head.

Cummings went down to check on the Doctor twice during
the night. At two-thirty he set a lantern in the cell. As he went
back up the stairs, through the darkness he could hear Dr.
Webster sobbing.

CHAPTER V

Saturday Morning
at the Medical College

BEFORE EIGHT O'CLOCK Saturday morning two police carriages turned into North Grove Street and pulled up in front
of the Medical College. It was bitter cold. The crowd of forty
or fifty in front of the College were bundled in scarves and
greatcoats. Steam rose from the horses' flanks.

Marshal Tukey stepped down from the first carriage. His
stock showed milk-white above the fur collar of his coat. He
turned to address the crowd, his manner imperious.

"Will you people stand back so my men can get through?"
he demanded.

Respectfully the crowd moved a foot or two. Every one of
them had heard frightening rumors about the Marshal, how
he got a confession out of a prisoner when he wanted one and
he didn't care *how* he got it.

A man in a knitted cap spoke up. "Where's the rest of Old
Chin, Marshal? Any news yet?"

For answer the Marshal turned his back and started toward the
College.

The other men jumped down from the second carriage.
Adams, Butman, Heath, Eaton. The crowd knew them all.

"Hey, Adams! Where's Fuller and Trenholm? Here on
guard all night? There was *somebody* here."

Adams only shook his head.

A woman with a red wool muff called to Heath. "They've got Dr. Webster over at the Leverett Street jail, don't they?"

"Could be," Heath answered.

"Do you think he did it?"

"Did what?" Heath parried.

"Why, chopped up poor Dr. Parkman, what else?" the woman told him. "Have they found his head and his hands yet?"

Heath moved off toward the College but a tall man behind the woman answered her. "I can tell you where his hands are easy enough. They're in somebody else's pockets. That's the place to look for *them.*"

A murmur went through the crowd. The woman turned to see who had spoken.

"Who said that?" she demanded. "Was it *you,* Jim Tully? Was it *you?* And you knowin' perfectly well that Dr. Parkman never had his hand in *anybody's* pocket unless he had good and fair reason to have it there!"

Another woman shook her fist at Jim. "You just ask your Letty who it was that got Dr. Shattuck to come to see Amos last summer when you thought he had the cholera. And while you're at it, ask her who paid for the very medicine that kept Amos from *dying.* You ask her those questions, Jim Tully, and *then* let's hear what you have to say about Dr. Parkman!"

Jim sighed. "Are you telling *me* about Dr. Parkman? Me, that's been renting a house from him for thirteen years? Yes, he got the doctor for Amos and, yes, he paid for the medicine, but I *still* say he was a mighty close reckoner when there was money due him." Then he went on in a different tone, "I didn't mean no harm to the old man's memory. Can't a man try to warm up a cold morning with a little joke without getting all his neighbors at his back?"

"Not if your little joke is disrespectful to a good man that's helped the West End folks for years and years!" a third woman told him.

A man at the edge of the crowd stepped forward. His hat was tied on with a scarf and his hands plunged deep in the pockets of his ragged coat. He spoke to Jim. "If you're looking for a man that's made *trouble* for the people around here, you don't need to look no farther than Dr. Webster. Remember the ruckus he kicked up last summer when Littlefield wanted to rent his back room to a student? He said Eph had no right to make money for himself by rentin' out College property. Well, it was Eph's apartment, wasn't it? And his living quarters is part of the pay he gets from the College, so —"

Marshal Tukey shouted down from the entrance at the top of the steps.

"Get a move on, men. We've got work to do this morning."

Littlefield opened the door. In the shadows behind him Fuller and Starkweather stood in the doorway of Dr. Webster's lecture room.

"It's dark in the building this morning, sir," Littlefield said deferentially to Marshal Tukey. "I've been getting extra lamps ready."

The Marshal made no comment. While the others watched, he drew off his fawn-colored leather gloves, smoothed them, and put them into his coat pockets. Then he took off his coat, folded it wrong side out, and handed it and his hat to Adams who happened to be standing at his elbow.

Adams looked uncertain and uncomfortable.

Littlefield spoke up. "You could put the Marshal's wraps on the settee in Dr. Ware's room," he said to Adams, indicating the room directly across the hall from Dr. Webster's lecture room. "And the rest could put their coats on the students' benches."

The Marshal was speaking to Fuller. "Where are Trenholm and Rice?"

"Downstairs on guard at the privy where the pieces of the body are. If you remember, sir, we were supposed to stand guard all night, two of us at a time —"

The Marshal interrupted. "You can rest assured that when I give an order, I remember that I gave it, Fuller. Now, have you anything to report?"

"There was a crowd outside until long past midnight, sir. Three times some of them came up the steps and hammered on the door. Nothing more than that, sir, but I will say we were a little nervous with just the four of us here. If there'd been —"

The Marshal interrupted again. "Could you see who came up? Did you know any of them?"

Fuller shook his head. "We held lamps up to the sidelights every time there was anybody at the door, but we couldn't see much. Only figures moving around."

"And that's the extent of your report, I take it."

"That's all, except we made a test. I guess you could call it that."

The Marshal looked interested. "A test? What kind of a test?"

"Well, sir, Littlefield told us Dr. Holmes was upstairs lecturing at the time the men over at the foundry saw Dr. Parkman on his way up the front steps of this building. Dr. Holmes' lecture room is directly above Dr. Webster's so we took turns going up to his lecture room to find out if you could hear noise up there from down below. We tussled and knocked over a couple of seats and generally made a racket, but the fellows upstairs couldn't hear a thing, even with no classes going on."

"Good work, Fuller. For once you used your head," the Marshal said. He looked at his watch. "As soon as Coroner Pratt gets here, we'll go down and have a look into that assay furnace where Littlefield found the slag with the bone fused to it." He paused. "On second thought, I think we'll start now and work until the Coroner gets here. We're going to make a final search of this building this morning and we might as well get started."

"You want us to divide up into groups, sir?" Fuller asked him.

"Yes, but first, the four of you who were here all night go uptown and get breakfast. Be quick about it. We have a lot to get done before the coroner's jury gets here this afternoon."

"That won't be necessary, sir," Fuller told him. "Mrs. Littlefield already gave us a fine —"

"That being the case, we'll start work immediately. Rice, you stay here at the door. Don't let anybody in unless he's one of our men or he has a message from the Mayor's office. Coroner Pratt excepted, of course. And don't send anybody to see me unless I know ahead of time that he's coming. Keep Tarleton up here with you. Send him down to me if anybody comes or if anything happens that makes you think trouble is brewing outside." He gestured toward the crowd.

On the Marshal's orders, Starkweather, Fuller, and Adams went down to the lower laboratory. Heath, Eaton, and Butman stayed upstairs.

The Marshal walked into Dr. Webster's shadowy lecture room. He glanced down the rows of benches that faced the lecture table. Then he turned to his left and walked along the rear wall, observing the row of pegs that served the students as a coatrack. Now he turned to his right and stood at the first of the three tall, arched windows that looked out on North Grove Street. The sky was leaden and there was a spit of snow in the air. The crowd, noticeably larger, stood around a fire, the one bright spot on a dull gray scene.

Butman was at the Marshal's elbow. "Excuse me, sir, but we've found something over here we'd like you to look at." He indicated Dr. Webster's lecture table and Marshal Tukey crossed the room toward it.

Heath said to the Marshal, "I ran my fingers along the under-

side of the table top and found a metal handle. I pulled it
and found this pocket-shaped bin."

"Bring another lamp, Eaton," the Marshal ordered.

Butman said, "It's lined with metal, sir. I think it's zinc, and
there's another pocket just like this one in the other end of the
table."

"It's damp," the Marshal said, feeling the inside of the bin.
"Where's Littlefield? Littlefield!"

"Over here, sir," Littlefield answered, as he emerged from
the stairway that led to the downstairs laboratory.

"When did you wash these bins last, Littlefield?"

Littlefield couldn't remember. Dr. Webster rarely used
them so there was no need to scrub them routinely. He hadn't
any idea when he'd last cleaned them. He couldn't imagine
why they were damp.

The Marshal got out a black pocket notebook. "Well, this
is something we'll want to ask Dr. Webster."

As the Marshal put away his notebook, Heath got down on
his knees to have a closer look at the underside of the table.
In so doing he saw on the floor a pine stick about six inches
long and the thickness of a quill. A wad of cotton was tied to
one end of it with a thread. The cotton had black stains on it.

Heath handed the stick up to the Marshal. "What do you
suppose this is, sir?"

The Marshal studied the stick and the wad of stained cotton.
"Looks as though somebody has been doing some painting," he
said.

Butman called over from the center window. "Coroner
Pratt is here, sir. He's getting out of his rig now."

"We'll leave the stick here on the table until the coroner's
jury has seen it," the Marshal said. He took a step closer to the
lamp to see his watch and bumped into Eaton.

"Confound you, Eaton! Don't you have brains enough to
keep out of my way!"

Eaton held out a small china plate smeared with what looked like black dye.

"Where did you get that? Speak up, man!" the Marshal roared at him.

"Over on the bench under the far window," Eaton answered in a small voice.

The Marshal put the plate on the table without comment, and at that moment Jabez Pratt entered the room. His step was light and quick, as always, and his manner brisk.

"Good morning, Marshal, and all," he said pleasantly, glancing around the room as he unbuttoned his heavy overcoat.

Butman stepped forward, but the Coroner waved him away. "I can do for myself, thank you, and what's more, I prefer to do for myself, although I appreciate your offer of help."

"May I ask if you have arranged for a coroner's jury to view the human remains that were discovered in this building last evening?" the Marshal asked.

"You may and I have," Coroner Pratt told him.

"And who is on the jury?"

The Coroner laid his folded overcoat on one of the benches and deposited his hat on top of it. "Let's see. There are six of them." He counted off names on his fingers. "There's Osmyn Brewster, the printer, there's a John Anderson, a clerk, and a Lewis Jones who sells stoves. There's a fellow by the name of Martin who sells carpets, and Tom Restleary, the chemist. That's five of them. Now who's the other one?" The Coroner was in the act of reaching into his pocket when he remembered. "Ah, Merrill, the undertaker. How could I forget *him?*"

"Sounds like the usual run," the Marshal commented.

The Coroner nodded. "And I sent young Blake around with a message for Doctors Winslow Lewis, Martin Gay, and Charles Jackson. They can call in any others they need. They'll be here after dinner, before the jury arrives. That will give us

time enough to make a search of this building and tend to the
furnace. Is Deputy Clapp here?"

The Marshal shook his head. "I sent him and Spurr over
to Cambridge to search Dr. Webster's place for evidence
bearing on the payment of money he says he made to Dr. Parkman."

He gestured toward the stick with the cotton tip and the
china plate. "This may be evidence and also these drawers."
He felt for the handle that released the metal-lined bin.
"There's another one at the other end of the table. Feel the
inside. It's damp."

Coroner Pratt felt the bin. He picked up the stick and
looked at it briefly.

"Well, with Rice and Tarleton on guard at the door, these
things are safe here. Let's get down to that furnace. I'll be glad
when that job's done. The Lord himself knows what we may
find before we get to the bottom of the thing. I'm assuming
the pieces of the body are still nailed up in the privy."

"We haven't moved them. The men stood guard all night,
but with all of us in the building, that precaution is now unnecessary." The Marshal turned to Littlefield. "Are there
plenty of lamps? It's still like night in this place even though
it's past nine."

"I'll get some from my place, sir. Dr. Webster doesn't like
lamps so there's only candles down there," Littlefield said.

Coroner Pratt led the way down the stairs to the lower laboratory.

It was Littlefield who pointed out the spots on the walls
and the stair treads. He held his lamp close to the wall. The
spots there were pale green and they were raised like water
blisters. Those on the stairs looked black.

Coroner Pratt studied the wall and the stairs. "Looks to me
as though some kind of liquid was splashed against the wall
and dripped on the stairs as it was being carried down to the

lower laboratory. Would you have any idea what it might be?" He addressed his question to Littlefield.

"No idea at all, sir," Littlefield answered.

The Coroner touched one of the spots. "They're still damp. Maybe Dr. Jackson can get some of the stuff off with his filtering paper and give us an analysis." He wiped his fingers on his pocket handkerchief. "Now let's get on downstairs."

The lower laboratory was dark. The windows overlooking the Charles River were patches of gray in a gray wall. Starkweather and Adams, each carrying a candle, emerged from the fuel closet. Trenholm, a candle holder beside him, was intent on examining the dry sink in the middle of the room.

"Find something of interest?" Coroner Pratt asked him.

Trenholm continued to rub his fingers along the inside of the sink. "I'm just wondering how long this sink has been gouged and chipped like this," he said. "Dr. Webster doesn't strike me as the kind of man who would put up with battered equipment."

Littlefield stepped over to inspect the sink. "This sink hasn't been this way for more than ten days," he said to Coroner Pratt. "Since Dr. Parkman's disappearance, Dr. Webster has taken to keeping his rooms locked so I haven't had the chance to clean the way I usually do. All I can say is that the last time I cleaned this sink, there wasn't a mar on it. I'm positive of that, sir."

Coroner Pratt turned to the Marshal. "There's something else for you and your men to investigate, Marshal."

The Marshal got out his notebook. He had trouble finding the page where his notes ended. "Littlefield!" he roared. "Where are those extra lamps? A man can't see his hand before his face down here. And stoke up your furnaces, will you? This place is cold."

Littlefield held a lamp so that the light fell on Marshal Tukey's notebook. "There are four extra lamps over on the table under the windows, sir. I didn't get them handed around yet because I've been busy spreading newspapers on the floor around the furnace. I thought that might be a good idea. And I think the heat will be all right in a few minutes, sir. I stirred up the furnaces good when I was out getting the newspapers from the furnace room."

Adams and Starkweather lifted the soapstone lid from the assay furnace.

"That was a good idea about spreading newspapers on the floor," said Coroner Pratt to Littlefield. "Now could you find us a couple of boxes?" He pushed back his coat sleeves and reached into the furnace. "This must be the piece you found, Littlefield. That's bone all right." The piece of slag was the size of a tea cup. The Coroner handed it to the Marshal. The Marshal accepted it gingerly.

"There's plenty more of it here," the Coroner said as he felt along the sides of the furnace. "I'll need something to pry it off with."

Littlefield found him a bent poker.

"This will work fine, Littlefield." The Coroner pried off half a dozen small chunks and handed them around to the men. "There's going to be a lot of this stuff. You men start separating the pieces of bone from the cinders. I know I don't have to tell you to do it carefully. Put the bone on the newspaper and throw the slag into the boxes. We'll want it for chemical analysis and the same goes for the ashes."

"I'll get some files," Littlefield said. "Maybe they'll be a help in digging the bone out of the cinders."

Starkweather stepped over to Coroner Pratt. "I've finished separating the bone from the cinder in the chunk you gave me, sir, and I think I've got the bone from a finger. What do you say?"

The Coroner stopped digging with the poker and studied

the bone Starkweather held. "I'd say you're right. I'd say that's the terminal phalanx of a human finger."

Eaton shuddered visibly. He looked at the furnace with horror. "Somebody actually burned up parts of a human body in there?"

"Here's a big one." The Coroner used both hands to lift a chunk of slag over to Butman.

Butman laid the slag on the paper by the furnace. He dug at it for a few moments and then stared in silence at what lay in front of him.

The other men gathered around him.

"What have you got there, Butman?" the Marshal asked him.

"A long, slender bone, sir. I don't know what it is."

Coroner Pratt picked up the bone. "I'd guess that's a right tibia, the right shin bone in common parlance. We'll get Professor Wyman over here. He's the man you need when you have to identify bones."

The men watched in silence while Coroner Pratt laid the long bone beside the others.

"How could you tell it was the *right* tibia?" Starkweather asked him.

"By the way it curves. Think of a man standing. Think how his shin curves a little to the right or the left, depending on whether it's his right leg or his left."

Eaton shivered again. "All those little pieces look like chicken bones, but that big one — " He turned away from the bones.

The Coroner handed him a piece of slag. "Here, Eaton. Keep busy and it won't bother you so much."

Eaton took the slag, turned it over, and reached for a file.

The Marshal was looking over Eaton's shoulder. "Wait, Eaton! Don't break into that one!" He took the slag from Eaton and held it out to the Coroner. "What's that pink color?"

The other men had a look at the splashes of pink on the slag the Marshal held.

"I don't know what it is," the Coroner said finally. "That'll be another job for the chemists. Could you find me a box for this piece, Littlefield?"

As he spoke, there was the sound of footsteps on the stairs. Deputy Clapp and Oliver Spurr entered the room. Kingsley was behind them.

At the sight of the bones spread on the paper, Kingsley stood stock-still. "Are — are those *human* bones?" he asked.

"Yes," Adams told him. "We must have fifty pieces over here and we're not through yet, not by a long shot."

Marshal Tukey drew Deputy Clapp aside. "Find anything over in Cambridge?" he asked.

Clapp shook his head. "Not much. Just a bankbook on the Charles River Bank that shows a deposit of ninety dollars made the day after Dr. Parkman disappeared. I left it at your office. I didn't like to press Mrs. Webster. She was very upset. She'd only found out about the Doctor's arrest about an hour before we got there." Maybe we should go back there later.

"Hear anything uptown?"

"Well, Mr. Parker went over to the Revere House to see Mr. Dexter early this morning, as he had promised Dr. Webster. Mr. Dexter went over to Cambridge and then to the jail. I hear Mr. Prescott has been there, too. By the way, I got Mr. Cunningham to go with us to Dr. Webster's. I thought that would make it easier all the way around since he is such a close friend of the Webster family. He's going over to the jail this afternoon."

"Anything else?"

"There's all kinds of rumors around town. Some say there'll be trouble here tonight. There's talk about the people taking the law into their own hands to find what they're sure is hidden someplace in this building."

"Look!" Coroner Pratt cried out. He held up a piece of a dental plate with two teeth attached to it.

Eaton turned away after the briefest look at the teeth. He pulled at Marshal Tukey's coat sleeve. "I think I'm going to be sick, sir," he said as he wiped his forehead.

"Go ahead and *be* sick but get out of here!" the Marshal yelled at him.

Eaton made for the passageway that divided the lower laboratory from the dissecting room.

The Coroner said to Littlefield, "Dr. Keep lives next door to Dr. Lewis. Dr. Lewis could ask him to make an examination for us." He paused. "Come to think about it, I'm pretty sure Dr. Keep was Dr. Parkman's dentist." He put the teeth and the dental plate into the box Littlefield handed him and went back to work on the furnace.

"Here, Spurr, you haven't had a turn at this." He handed Spurr three small pieces of cinder. "And I think that's about the end of the slag," he added as he worked the poker through the ashes in the furnace. "No, I'm wrong. There's another batch down here on this side right in front of me." He dug out big chunks and distributed them among the men.

"Can you tell me what this is?" Adams asked, showing the Coroner two small pieces of bone that seemed hinged together.

"I'd say that's probably the terminal phalanx of a little toe with the middle phalanx still attached."

"And this one?" Butman held up a slender bone fragment four or five inches long.

The Coroner studied the bone a few seconds. "Couldn't even make a guess about that one." He looked over at Starkweather. "How about you?"

Starkweather shook his head. "Neither can I."

The Coroner sifted the ashes with his fingers. "I thought I saw something white in here a minute ago. It was round and flat — ah, here it is. It's a shirt button, a pearl shirt button. Let's put it over here in the box with the teeth."

"Are you down to the bottom yet?" the Marshal asked.

"I think so." The Coroner dipped his hands into the ashes again. "Here are more teeth. Three of them. And this one looks as though a dentist had filled it, see? Here, Heath, put these in the box with the other teeth, will you?"

The Coroner scooped down into the ashes on the bottom of the furnace again. "I thought I felt something else down here." He brought up a handful of little round pieces of metal with holes punched in them. "They're copper, wouldn't you say?"

Heath spoke up. "There's a lot more of them in the chest up in Dr. Webster's private room, the chest where the keys were."

Eaton observed the pieces of copper in the Coroner's hand. "Maybe Dr. Webster got them from the foundry to use in his chemical experiments," he suggested. "They look like pieces they might have left over around a foundry."

The Marshal turned to Eaton. "Eaton," he said, "it could be that you aren't as stupid as I think you are, but I doubt it."

"What would they be doing in the furnace? He wasn't doing any chemical experiments in there, was he?" Clapp directed his question to Littlefield.

"I never knew Dr. Webster to do any experiments that required putting pieces of copper in this furnace, but he could have been working on something I didn't know about," Littlefield answered.

The Coroner wiped the back of his hand across his forehead. "We'll add a question about the pieces of copper to our list for Dr. Jackson. I think we've finally got this thing empty now. I'm going to shake the grate so we can be sure there's nothing still lying on the bottom."

As Coroner Pratt shook the grate, Trenholm stooped down to the hearth and picked up another piece of dental plate with five teeth attached to it.

"Well, we have a good sample of teeth for Dr. Keep, whoever they belonged to," the Coroner said. "Put them over in the box with the others and then give Littlefield a hand with getting

the rest of the ashes into the boxes." He took the towels Littlefield offered. "After I wash my hands I'll join the rest of you
in searching the building. It must be after eleven now — "

"Ten minutes before eleven," the Marshal said.

"And we have only until three o'clock to go over this building," the Coroner continued. "Since the place has been searched
a number of times, I can't believe we'll find anything of major
significance. Nevertheless, it is our responsibility to give the
building one more going over to make certain, once and for
all, that we have found everything, *everything,* that could be
classified as evidence." As he finished, he looked over at Littlefield. "Since we've got the privy nailed up, where will I
wash?"

"You're welcome to use my apartment, sir," Littlefield said.
"If you go out into the dissecting room passageway and turn
right, the room you want will be the second on your left after
you pass the furnace room."

As the Coroner disappeared into the corridor, the Marshal
gave orders for the search. "Fuller, you and Starkweather and
Trenholm cover this laboratory and the dissecting room across
the hall. Adams, you take Heath and go up to Dr. Webster's
lecture room. Kingsley can go along with you. You can do
Dr. Ware's room, too. Butman, take Spurr and Eaton and go
over Dr. Holmes' lecture room and the demonstrator's room.
You can do the library. Don't do the specimen closet. Dr.
Ainsworth can tell us whether there's anything in there that
shouldn't be. Littlefield, go down to the vault to make sure
nothing escaped our notice last night." Then he addressed the
whole group. "Coroner Pratt, Deputy Clapp, and I will be
circulating through the building. If you come across anything
out of the ordinary, get hold of one of us immediately. It's
five minutes after eleven now. At one o'clock we'll begin
taking turns going to dinner."

*

The men separated and Fuller began to search the area of
the lower laboratory between the fuel closet and the door
leading to the passageway by the dissecting room. He decided
to start with the recess in the wall just beyond the furnace.
On the table against the wall he found a paper-wrapped bundle that proved to be two cheap cotton comforters the size of
bed sheets. They looked new. Above the table were two
shelves crowded with glass bottles, the kind chemists use.
Most of them were empty. Fuller uncorked several in an unsuccessful attempt to identify their contents by odor.

When he was finished with the shelves, Fuller turned his
attention to the small wooden chest pushed against the wall
below them. The chest gave off an unpleasant odor not sur-
prising because, as Fuller knew, Dr. Webster stored minerals
there. Opening the chest, Fuller saw paper-wrapped packages,
the contents of each package noted in ink on its wrapping. The
writing on some of the packages looked fresh. On others it was
faded. Fuller moved several of the packages and found they
formed a layer on top of tanbark. He reached down into the
tanbark and came up with a jackknife. He opened it, looked at
it, saw nothing remarkable about it, snapped it shut, and put it
in his pocket.

He reached down into the chest again and felt a cold, damp
object. Something in the texture of the thing his fingers
touched made him cry out at the top of his voice. "Here!" he
shouted. "There's something in this chest!"

Coroner Pratt and the other men in the lower laboratory
were with him in a second. Marshal Tukey came pounding
down the stairs with Kingsley and Rice close behind.

Fuller and Starkweather were dragging the chest into the
center of the room.

"Turn it out!" Coroner Pratt ordered.

They dumped the contents of the chest onto the floor.

Coroner Pratt was on his knees, Starkweather and Fuller
beside him. "Good God! It's a human torso!" he cried.

The torso lay on its stomach. It was headless and without arms. Tanbark clung to the hair on the back.

"It's half burnt!" Starkweather said, his voice almost a whisper.

The men stood motionless in shocked silence. Eaton crossed himself.

Then Kingsley turned away. He brushed the back of his hand across his eyes.

Adams patted Kingsley's arm. "We don't know who it is yet," he said comfortingly. "Maybe it's not who you think it is." Then he added, "Don't think the rest of us don't have any feelings, Kingsley. It's just that we're all constables and every one of us has seen his fill of dead human bodies." He looked back at the torso. "Maybe not many of them as bad as this, but bad enough."

"What's that cord tied around it?" the Marshal asked the Coroner.

Coroner Pratt bent down to the torso. He turned it over. There was an incision from the neck to the pubis.

"I think the cord's holding something inside it." He took hold of the torso, reached down into the cavity, and pulled out a thigh. He looked up at the Marshal. "That's why the cord was there."

"Somebody sawed his head off just below his Adam's apple," Starkweather said.

Rice stepped forward. He was holding a butcher's saw twelve or fifteen inches long. "I'd just found this behind the door in Dr. Webster's private room when I heard Fuller yell."

"That's probably what did the job," the Coroner said. "Any blood on it?"

"None that I can see, sir."

"Put it up on the lecture table with the other stuff. We'll ask Professor Wyman to do a microscopic examination of it. Maybe Dr. Jackson can run some tests on it, too."

The men began to move about the room. Eaton went over to the bench under the windows and sat down. Kingsley went back upstairs. Adams and Butman asked for water and Little-field directed them to the sink by the windows. There were two tin cups hanging on nails beside it.

Starkweather was still on the floor beside the torso. He had started to brush the tanbark away but the Coroner stopped him. "Better leave it just as it is until after the jury sees it this afternoon," he said.

"He's had his breastbone removed," Starkweather observed.

The Coroner studied the torso. "You're right. I'm surprised I didn't notice that."

"Does it look like a professional job to you? Would you say it was done by somebody who knew something about surgery?" the Marshal asked the Coroner.

The Coroner squatted beside the torso again. He examined the incision. "I'd say so, but the doctors can give you a better opinion than I can," he answered the Marshal.

Fuller was behind the Coroner. "Is there anything at all left inside him?" he asked.

Starkweather peered inside the torso. "Well, he's still got his left kidney and his lungs. They're collapsed, but they're there. And he's got that, whatever it is." He pointed.

Coroner Pratt took a look. "That's his spleen."

Starkweather continued, "He's missing his heart, his kidneys, his bowels, and his liver."

"Why is he green under his left armpit?" Adams asked.

"That means he's starting to decompose," Starkweather told him.

"Turn him over, will you?" the Coroner said to Stark-weather.

"Hairy cuss, whoever he was," the Marshal commented as Starkweather laid the torso on its stomach.

"Now that you mention it, I don't think I ever saw a human body with this much hair on it," the Coroner said. "It's an inch long from his shoulder blades to his hips, and thick, too. I'll bet you wouldn't see another one with this much hair in twenty years of looking."

Butman spoke up. "Why is the hair sandy-colored up at the shoulders and black lower down — " He broke off in mid-sentence. "Is that because of fire, sir?"

The Coroner nodded.

The Marshal pointed to a diagonal dark red stripe across the back of the torso, beginning at the left shoulder. "What caused that, do you think?"

The Coroner ran his fingers along the stripe. "It's hard to say, but it's my guess that's the reaction of some chemical agent. That's only a guess, though." He picked up the thigh he had taken from the torso. "I think that's why this thigh looks so different from the one we found in the privy vault last night. The one in the vault is dead white because it's water-soaked. In my opinion this one looks so much smaller and darker because it has been exposed to chemicals that have shrunken it and changed its color. It's been exposed to fire, too." He pointed to a blackened area at the head of the thigh bone. "I'm sure that's because of fire."

"His thighs have been hacked off," Starkweather said. "Notice the ragged edge along his hip sockets. That's no expert dissection job."

"Maybe not," the Coroner said, rising from his squatting position. He brushed sand from his hands. "We'll leave these pieces of the body here on the floor until after the jury has seen them this afternoon. Where's Littlefield? Maybe he could find some paper to slip under them."

"Littlefield!" the Marshal bellowed.

Littlefield was standing behind him. He was holding three or four pieces of wet, stained cloth.

"What have you got there?" the Marshal asked, his eyes on the cloth.

"They're towels, sir."

"Where'd they come from?"

"I found them downstairs in the vault, sir."

The Marshal reached for one of the pieces of cloth. It was badly stained and full of holes.

"This one is practically new," Littlefield said, holding up another towel. "I remember putting it out for Doctor Webster a day or two before classes were out for Thanksgiving. It's a roller towel."

"Do they all have this?" the Marshal asked.

The other men crowded around to see the small *w* stamped in the corner of the towel in his hands.

"Yes, sir," Littlefield answered.

Deputy Clapp spoke up. "That doesn't mean much, Marshal. Anybody could have got in here and got hold of Dr. Webster's towels."

"Don't you think I realize that, Clapp?" the Marshal snapped.

While the men were still gathered around the Marshal and Littlefield, Tarleton came down the stairs. As he stepped into the laboratory, he had an unobstructed view of the torso. He stood stock-still.

"Well, Tarleton," the Marshal said. His tone was testy.

Tarleton didn't move a muscle.

"Tarleton!" the Marshal yelled at him.

Tarleton started. "Yes, sir?"

"Did you have a reason for coming down here, Tarleton, or are you just sauntering around the building?"

"Sir, Officer Rice sent me down to tell you the crowd is a good bit bigger than it was an hour ago and he wonders —"

The Marshal turned to Spurr. "Get over to Mayor Bigelow's office. Tell him I think we'd better alert the military, including the two companies at Roxbury. Go out the door at the end of the dissecting room passageway and go up around behind the building so you'll attract as little attention as possible. Where's Trenholm? *Trenholm!*"

Trenholm answered from across the room.

"Go up and tell Butman and Heath to stand guard by the carriage shed entrance. Then you and Adams get out to the door at the end of the dissecting room corridor."

Deputy Clapp looked worried. "We just might have some serious trouble around here by nightfall," he said.

The Marshal nodded. "And if we do, some Boston people are going to learn a lesson they won't forget for a while. You can take my word for that. Before we came over here this morning, I made sure every man had his revolver and six rounds of ammunition." He started for the stairs. "Come on. Before that crowd starts trouble, I want to find out whether there is anything else hidden in this building that we should know about."

CHAPTER VI

Dr. Webster in Jail

ON MONDAY EVENING Dr. Webster sat at the narrow table in his cell writing to his daughter, Marianne.

I had a good sleep last night and dreamt of you all. [he told her] I got my clothes off for the first time last night and awoke in the morning quite hungry. It was a long time before my breakfast came from Parker's and it was relished, I can assure you. At one o'clock I was notified that I must appear at Court. All was arranged with great regard for my comfort and avoidance of publicity, and this first ceremony went off better than I anticipated. On my return, I had a bit of turkey and rice from Parker's. They send much more than I can eat, and I have directed the steward to distribute the surplus to the poor ones here.

It was a ten minute carriage ride from the Leverett Street jail over to Court Street, to the gloomy old stone courthouse with its Greek pediment and pillars. There were few people in the building this dark winter afternoon and in Judge Cushing's courtroom attendance was limited to those whose presence was essential to the matter at hand. The Judge sat with his back to the tall windows. In the half-light his long, bony face was barely distinguishable. Samuel Parker, District Attorney for Suffolk, was there, his manner characteristically crisp and businesslike. Coroner Pratt waited quietly at his elbow. Charles Kingsley stood a little apart from them. He looked upset and ill at ease. He folded and refolded the paper on which Mr. Parker had helped him write the formal statement of the charge he had agreed to make against Dr. Webster the night of his arrest.

Dr. Webster, relaxed and poised, stood with Franklin Dexter, who was acting as his attorney. But this was the last time, Dexter promised himself. He meant to get clear of this dismal business the moment he could find somebody else to undertake John Webster's defense. Nine years ago when he successfully defended Mrs. Kenney against the charge that she had murdered her husband, he had vowed he was through with murder cases and he meant to keep his word. Furthermore, he was through with the law. He had served Massachusetts as District Attorney and as a state senator. Now, at fifty-six, he felt he had earned the right to retire to Beverly and spend the rest of his life painting. He knew people said the Dexters were a queer lot. Periodically somebody reminded him about old Timothy Dexter, who wrote a book with all the punctuation in the back so the reader could salt and pepper to suit himself. Well, Bostonians were free to say whatever they liked about him. *He* would be in Beverly.

Now Judge Cushing was speaking.

At a signal from Mr. Parker, Kingsley began to read from his paper. He read awkwardly. "I, Charles Kingsley —"

When Kingsley finished, the Judge turned to Franklin Dexter.

Dexter took a step forward. He said his client would waive examination.

The Judge looked inquiringly at Dr. Webster, who nodded his assent to his counsel's statement. He said he had nothing to add to Mr. Dexter's remarks.

Judge Cushing paused briefly. Then he said, "In the light of his counsel's statement, the prisoner will be remanded to the Leverett Street jail to await the action of the grand jury."

Sheriff Joseph Eveleth, a stout old man with pleasant, old-fashioned manners, walked toward Dr. Webster. Unobtrusively he slipped the wrist irons on his prisoner and led him down the courthouse stairs to the waiting carriage.

It was all over in less than fifteen minutes.

Everybody who visited Dr. Webster in the days immediately after his arrest spoke of his composure. True, Mr. Prescott confided to the family and to close friends that the Doctor was very much upset on the Saturday morning when Mr. Prescott visited him in jail for the first time. He cried a good deal on that occasion, alarmed for his family — not for himself. But since that interview he had handled himself with dignity and composure. He protested his innocence, certainly, but he did so calmly and confidently. During those first days after his arrest the Doctor's colleagues lost no time in calling at Leverett Street. Dr. Daniel Treadwell came and so did Dr. Benjamin Pierce and Dr. Charles Jackson, the chemist, Emerson's brother-in-law. Another old friend who came was Dr. Eben Horsford from the Lawrence Scientific School. And among the first to call was Dr. Cornelius Felton, the hearty, good-natured Irishman who was Harvard's professor of Greek Literature. It was heart-warming to hear Dr. Felton's unequivocal condemnation of anybody and everybody who would so much as dare to *imply* that Dr. Webster had any connection whatsoever with the ghastly crime committed at the Medical College.

The Reverend Charles Lowell came, old and frail and a little garrulous.* He stayed a long time and talked about the West Church and how he had preached his first sermon there forty-three years ago last Thanksgiving morning. The Leverett Street almshouse was built a few years before he came to Bos-

---

* Father of James Russell Lowell (1819-1891), the famous American author, teacher, and diplomat.

ton but not the jail. He had watched the jail going up from the back windows of his church. Bulfinch designed them both and he designed George Ticknor's mansion shortly after the almshouse was built. Only Ticknor didn't own it then. It was Thomas Amory's house. The Board of Selectmen gave Amory special permission to build his wine cellars far out under Beacon Street. The cost of those wine cellars alone was enough to ruin any man in Boston and Amory was no exception. He got word of his bankruptcy a few hours before his guests arrived for his sumptuous housewarming. And about the time Amory built his house Christopher Gore lived around the corner on Beacon Street, near where the Athenaeum stands. A colorful character he was, rolling around the countryside in his orange coach with his footmen in matching orange livery. Too colorful for the thrifty Massachusetts farmers. They turned him out after one term as governor. Did Dr. Webster know that as a young man Daniel Webster read law with Christopher Gore?

The Reverend Mr. Lowell paused. There was deep sorrow in his face as he said he knew why he talked so much about the past these days. It was because for him the present was heartbreaking. His wife's mind was clouded now and nobody could help her. She sat in her room, month after month, worrying and crying. She never came down anymore, not even when their oldest friends called. Then the old man made a visible effort at cheerfulness. But he had his blessings despite his terrible unhappiness. James and Maria and the babies were at Elmwood. He was grateful for that. Had the Doctor read *The Biglow Papers?* He would ask James to bring a copy when he came over to Leverett Street. His faded eyes twinkled. He doubted whether Dr. Webster would endorse James' political philosophy, but he might find the book amusing. And James could write about nature. Those lines about the fox grape vines among the scrub oak, for example. They had charm.

Another friend who came often, almost every day, was
Charles Cunningham. It was he who supplied the fresh fruit
Dr. Webster enjoyed so much. Apples, bananas, oranges, all
up from the Azores. The Cunninghams boasted that the finest
fruit in Boston was to be had on Rowe's Wharf the days their
Harbinger put in from Fayal. And here's proof of the Cunninghams' claims, Dr. Webster would say as he urged a visitor
to make a selection from the bowl of fruit he offered.

Dr. Webster was grateful to the Cunninghams for their generous gifts of fruit. He was equally grateful to William Prescott for arranging to have his meals sent down from Parker's.
How could a man who was something of a gourmet have survived on an unvaried diet of beef, bread, and something they
called "skilly," a dish made by mixing Indian meal with the
broth from the beef? Moreover, Dr. Webster had memories
of an incident that heightened his feelings about jail food.
Seventeen years earlier, at the request of Governor Levi Lincoln, he had called at the Leverett Street jail to examine prisoners thought to be ill from food poisoning. The prison
authorities suspected the grain used in the jail kitchens, particularly the rye. In the end Dr. Webster decided that the inmates' illness was not caused by food. Dr. Jacob Bigelow, who
did the analysis of the rye, said the jail grain was of higher
quality than the samples he procured elsewhere in Boston.
But the memory of those wretchedly sick men and women,
more than two hundred of them, had stayed with Dr. Webster,
and try as he would, he could not disassociate their illness
from the prison fare.

Dr. Webster enjoyed the meals that came down from Parker's, breakfast about ten and dinner around three. He enjoyed the Cunninghams' fruit and the cigars his other friends
provided for him. Also, when his family came, as they did on
Monday and Thursday afternoons, the girls always brought
him some little delicacy as a treat. So as far as food was

concerned, he certainly had no complaints. Furthermore, he found his cell tolerably comfortable. It was very small, barely large enough to accommodate his cot, a narrow table, and a bench. But the whitewashed walls looked clean and the heat was adequate. At first the stone floor was very hard on his feet, but he was able to get permission to have a carpet so that problem was solved. The light was not good and this was hard on a man who spent most of his time reading, but he managed. His only serious complaint was about the noise. His cell was a narrow rectangle with two openings in the long wall across from his cot. He realized that the openings were there so Andrews, the jailer, and Jones, the turnkey, could look in on him and pass in food and parcels without the trouble of unlocking the cell door. It so happened that the cells on the lower floor were occupied by prisoners awaiting trial. They were a noisy lot and Dr. Webster found their endless questions and comments most unpleasant, to say nothing of their raucous laughter and their ribald jokes. But by and large, he was very well treated, Dr. Webster told his visitors. As long as he could see his family and his friends, he was happy. They were what mattered to him. Not the bad light and the disturbing noise.

Dr. Webster's friends, particularly his Cambridge friends, were convinced that his calmness and the good nature with which he bore his appalling situation constituted evidence of his innocence. Could a man of John Webster's volatile temperament behave in such a way if he were guilty of *murder?* Furthermore, after he had committed murder, could he have appeared totally unchanged in his social and professional relationships? Certainly not! And there were plenty of people in Cambridge who had known John Webster for twenty years ready to testify that he was characteristically warm and genial *on the very evening of the day on which he was alleged to have murdered his old friend, Dr. Parkman!*

Dr. Treadwell told about the gathering at his home the eve-

ning of Dr. Parkman's disappearance. Dr. and Mrs. Webster
were frequent guests in the Treadwells' home. On this
Friday evening they came in about half-past eight. It was a
pleasant, crisp night and they had escorted their daughters to
a party at the Batchelders' and then walked on out North Avenue to the Treadwells'. Dr. and Mrs. Morrill Wyman were
there when the Websters arrived. Old Judge Fay stopped in
later. Most of the evening they played whist. At one point during their conversation Mrs. Wyman asked about methods for
preserving wedding cake.

"Not difficult at all," Dr. Webster told her and described
the process.

When she still seemed uncertain, Dr. Webster, obliging as
always, offered to do the little job for her. He'd stop at Wymans' to pick up the cake on his way into Boston one morning
the first part of the week.

Was that the behavior of a man, an excitable man at that,
who had just come from murdering a friend he had known
since his school days?

And what about the Thanksgiving party at Cunninghams'?
By that time Dr. Parkman's disappearance was the main topic
of conversation in Boston. Everybody at the party asked Dr.
Webster how Dr. Parkman had seemed during their interview.

"You may have been the last person to see Dr. Parkman
alive," the ladies said to Dr. Webster. "Tell us about him. Describe how he acted."

Dr. Webster obliged. He said Dr. Parkman didn't seem different from usual. They all knew him. He walked fast and
talked fast and was generally in a hurry as he was when he
rushed out the door of Dr. Webster's lecture room, calling
back over his shoulder to say he was going to satisfy the mortgage Dr. Webster had just paid off.

John Sibley, the librarian of Harvard College, heard about
the Thanksgiving party when he stopped in at Dr. Felton's

home early Saturday afternoon, the day after Dr. Webster's arrest. Louis Agassiz was there when Sibley arrived. This afternoon it was the explosive Agassiz who was trying to soothe Cornelius Felton, for Felton was in a rage.

Striding up and down his drawing room, Dr. Felton stormed that the *very idea* that a man who was a scholar, a generous host, and the father of four lovely daughters could be a *murderer* was simply preposterous! The accusation against Dr. Webster was not only preposterous, it was an insult to Harvard College and the citizens of Cambridge! What firm evidence was there that Dr. Webster had any connection whatsoever with this terrible thing that had taken place on North Grove Street? Hadn't those spots on the stairs leading to his lower laboratory proved to be tobacco juice, not blood? And hadn't his friends — the Treadwells and the Cunninghams and plenty of others — been able to account for his whereabouts every evening since Dr. Parkman's murder, if it *was* Dr. Parkman? So what was all this talk about Dr. Webster spending all his time, day and night, at the Medical College since Dr. Parkman's disappearance?

Sibley looked doubtful. It was certainly true that nobody in Cambridge had the least doubt of Dr. Webster's innocence, but you couldn't say the same for Boston. There the current ran the other way.

Boston people, Dr. Felton burst out. *Boston* people! His anger made him look taller than his six feet and heavier than his two hundred pounds. Do *Boston* people know John Webster as well as *we* do, he demanded. Who in Boston has played whist with him two or three times a week for years? And is it the *Boston* Musical Association he belongs to?

Sibley persisted. The people of Boston —

The people of Boston enjoy thinking the worst of anybody who doesn't live in Boston, Dr. Felton told him. When somebody pointed out the site of the new Charitable Eye and Ear Hospital to Julia Ward Howe, she said she was surprised to learn there were any charitable eyes and ears in Boston, and she had a point.

But that doesn't change the fact that in Boston feeling is running high against Dr. Webster, Sibley continued. For instance, all the ardent churchgoers, and that's a mighty big crowd, are convinced that Dr. Webster's incessant smoking is the mark of a man deficient in moral principles.

Did this mean that Dr. Webster would be more acceptable to the sanctimonious if he gave up smoking and chewed peanuts all the time like the almighty Henry Ward Beecher, Dr. Felton snapped.

Sibley said he knew he was playing the devil's advocate, but he thought Dr. Webster's Cambridge friends ought to know about the talk in Boston. Right now there was a great deal of discussion about his father's will. The prevailing opinion was that Redford Webster entailed his will because he had doubts about his son's integrity. Otherwise he would have left the estate to him outright and —

Dr. Felton interrupted impatiently. "Nonsense! A generation ago many men left their estates entailed. It hasn't been more than a year or two since Mr. Prescott told me that his mother had finally decided to relinquish control of the fortune old Judge Prescott left. She wrote Prescott a letter telling him she felt it was now time for his wife to be the mistress of a home of her own. Prescott said he'd been married twenty-seven years by the time his mother made that decision."

"And there's something else about the will," Sibley went on. "There's a story that Redford Webster left a bequest of a dollar a week for the support of an indigent niece in Amesbury, a girl by the name of Mary Bagley. They say Dr. Webster never paid the money and that the girl died in the Amesbury almshouse."

Dr. Felton frowned. "We'd better look into that tale, although I don't believe it, not for a moment. We'll get John Whittier to work on it. He knows everybody in Amesbury.

Moreover, I know he's interested in John Webster's plight, or will be when he hears about it, granted he hasn't heard already. You know how he feels about capital punishment."

Louis Agassiz spoke up then. He said Lizzie had ridden into Boston with Dr. Webster on the Cambridge omnibus the Saturday after Dr. Parkman disappeared. They talked about Dr. Parkman a little but mostly their conversation was about the Musical Association's concerts. Then, glad of an opportunity to change the subject, Dr. Agassiz told Sibley that Lizzie Cary and he were engaged.

Sibley extended congratulations. That meant Dr. Felton and Dr. Agassiz would be brothers-in-law, both married to Cary girls. And that was reason for congratulations, too. When would the engagement be announced?

"Tomorrow at a party at the old Perkins mansion," Dr. Agassiz answered.

Dr. Felton smiled for the first time that afternoon. "It will take every inch of that old house to hold the Cary-Perkins-Agassiz-Felton connection. It's a fine old house," he added. Did Sibley know that the huge front door was made from wood taken from the hull of the *Constitution* when Joel Barker rebuilt her in '34?

Yes, Sibley knew.

And had Sibley seen the armchair Napoleon used at St. Helena? Lafayette gave it to Colonel Perkins as a gift of gratitude when the Colonel got Lafayette's son out of France so he could escape conscription during the Revolution. After all, the boy was only fourteen.

Yes, Sibley knew about the armchair.

Dr. Felton commented that of all the relics in that house, none was as interesting as the Colonel himself, tall, white-haired, majestic, as handsome in age as he was in youth. He had read some of the old man's letters from his seafaring days. He was in Paris during the Reign of Terror and he described it all for his family, how the prisoners arrived in carts and were kept in a

room directly under the scaffold until they were taken up the
ladder, one by one, to the platform where the guillotine was.
He was a good letter-writer and he knew it. "Save my letters,"
he wrote home to his wife. "Don't let the girls use them for
curl papers."

Doubtless the old Colonel would enjoy the wedding, Sibley
said. Family functions meant so much to him these days.
When would it take place?

In the spring, Dr. Agassiz answered. In April at King's
Chapel.

And speaking of King's Chapel, Sibley said, rising, he understood Ephraim Peabody was to officiate at Dr. Parkman's funeral service.

How could anybody be sure the remains they'd found *were*
Dr. Parkman, Dr. Felton asked?

The rumor is that there were some markings on the torso they
found Saturday that made a positive identification possible,
Sibley told him.

"That's the first I've heard of anything like that," Dr. Felton
said, and he looked upset again.

Sibley looked at his watch. "By the way, did you two see the
Transcript? Epes Sargent quoting Hamlet in his article about
the murder. Shakespeare on the front page of the *Transcript*.
That's a measure of how upset Boston is."

"Oh, I don't know," Dr. Felton told him. "You would hardly
expect less from the man who wrote in his newspaper that the
hearts of Bostonians were 'as cold to President Polk as the
marble that lies unused beneath Pentelicus.' "

"And what did he mean by that?" Sibley asked.

"I think he meant to show off," Dr. Felton answered.

John Sibley hurried along Harvard Street as far as Concord,
glancing down Concord to see the fine house John Webster had
built with most of the money he inherited from his father. As

all his friends knew, it was with deep regret that Dr. Webster had sold it to Harvard College. Even then, almost fifteen years ago, the poor man was harassed by financial troubles from which his friends — the Bigelows, the Wymans, the Parkmans, the Prescotts — were constantly trying to rescue him.

Sibley turned to his right on his way to the new library, Gore Hall, down by the river. It occurred to him then that the last conversation he had had with Dr. Parkman was on the steps of Gore Hall. Dr. Parkman was returning a book on Brahms. He had enjoyed the book, he said, though his taste leaned toward Bach and Beethoven, Bach especially. There were few pleasures that he enjoyed more than listening to a good organist playing Bach. His nephew, Samuel Tuckerman, was a fine organist. Folks were kind enough to tell him that they'd never had a finer organist at St. Paul's than Samuel.

Sibley crossed Massachusetts Avenue and saw Dr. Jacob Bigelow coming toward him, his shoulders hunched against the sharp wind. He had to get up close before Dr. Bigelow recognized him. The old man wasn't wearing his glasses. Bad as his eyes were, it was a wonder he could get around Cambridge, Sibley thought.

Was it true that the Medical College would suspend classes beginning next Monday, Sibley asked him? That was the rumor around Boston.

Dr. Bigelow nodded. In all likelihood that's what would happen. Later in the afternoon the Medical College faculty was to meet at his house and decide the question. He himself felt they had no choice but to suspend classes. How could you teach with a crowd milling around your building, looking for a chance to get inside? In his opinion the wisest course was to open the building and let the public satisfy its curiosity.

"I'm sure it's too soon for the Medical College faculty to have had any word from Dr. Webster," Sibley said.

"As a matter of fact we have had word," Dr. Bigelow said.

"Mr. Curtis brought me a message about an hour ago. Dr. Webster requests that we find a substitute to give his lectures while he has to be away. That's another piece of business we'll have to attend to this afternoon."

"You don't think for a moment that Dr. Webster had any connection with this grisly affair, do you, sir?" Sibley asked.

Dr. Bigelow started off across Massachusetts Avenue. "I don't know," he said. "I just don't know what to think."

The Medical College faculty met at Dr. Bigelow's house on Bedford Street that afternoon. A hickory fire blazed in the Doctor's big, comfortable library, a welcome sight on a windy December day. Everybody was present except Dr. Webster. Dr. Oliver Wendell Holmes, the Dean, Dr. Jacob Bigelow, Dr. Henry Bigelow, Dr. John Ware, Dr. Walter Channing, Dr. J. B. S. Jackson — they were all there. And they all asked each other just what exactly had happened at the Medical College. It was impossible to believe that John Webster had any part whatsoever in this unspeakable crime. But as Edward Everett had said — he had known Dr. Webster from earliest childhood — it was impossible to believe Dr. Webster was guilty of this terrible murder but at the same time it was just as difficult to believe that so much incriminating circumstantial evidence could attach itself to an innocent man.

It was a relief to get down to the business of the meeting. First, Dr. Bigelow told of the message Dr. Webster had sent by way of Benjamin Curtis. Dr. Holmes and Dr. Ware were appointed a committee to discuss the situation further with President Jared Sparks. Dr. Holmes stressed the temporary nature of the arrangement they would make; they needed only a *temporary* substitute for Dr. Webster. Somebody expressed compassion for President Sparks. All Jared Sparks' close friends knew he never wanted to be president of Harvard. He had succumbed to Edward Everett's urging only to please his wife. Left to himself he would have stayed in his house on Kirkland Street with its beautiful gardens and its serpentine walk and devoted his life to the writing of history. That was what he loved to do, write history.

Dr. Bigelow steered the discussion back to the business at hand. Should they open the building on North Grove Street to the public? Wasn't this the only way to satisfy the curiosity of the crowds that made it impossible to hold classes in the building now? The decision was to close the building. Dr. Bigelow and Dr. Holmes were appointed a committee to determine when the lectures at the Medical College would be resumed.

On Monday mornings the College schedule called for a lecture on *materia medica* and clinical medicine, a lecture Dr. Jacob Bigelow delivered at the Massachusetts General Hospital which stood five hundred yards or so to the rear of the Medical College building on North Grove Street. But on Monday, December 3, there was no lecture delivered to the students who appeared at the hospital. Instead, Dr. Bigelow spoke to them on behalf of the Medical College faculty. He said that in consequence of the solemn and appalling events of the past week, the lectures at the College would be suspended for three days. The faculty had made this decision as a gesture to the memory of Dr. George Parkman, a patron of medical science and the generous benefactor of the Medical College, as well as the friend of many of the faculty and the students at the College. Classes would be resumed on Thursday, December 6.

Dr. Bigelow bowed and walked rapidly toward the door. He wished to avoid the questions he was sure the students were eager to ask. In the hall he purposefully avoided a young man waiting to talk with him, a large-boned country boy, one of the College's "uncombed youths," in Holmes' phrase. What was the

boy's name? Preston? Dr. Bigelow wasn't sure. Come to think
about it, wasn't it Preston who said he saw Dr. Parkman entering the College the Friday afternoon he disappeared?

Now Dr. Bigelow himself was going up the steps to the entrance to the Medical College. From the hall he stepped into
Dr. Webster's lecture room to find Dr. Jeffries Wyman at work
at the lecture table. He was cutting swatches from spotted overalls.

"What have you got here?" Dr. Bigelow asked after he and
Dr. Wyman had exchanged greetings.

Dr. Wyman went on cutting up the overalls. "About an
hour ago Heath and Adams found these in the clothes closet at
the top of the stairs leading down to the lower laboratory."

Dr. Bigelow examined several of the spots. "Well, that's
blood, all right. You hardly need a laboratory test to tell that,
except for legal purposes. Any identification on them?"

For answer Dr. Wyman put down his scissors and folded back
the waistband of the trousers. Inside was stamped in ink *Dr.
Webster*.

"And I suppose these are his, too," Dr. Bigelow said, as he
picked up one of the carpet slippers that lay on the lecture
table. There was blood on the toe of the left slipper. "Of
course this is only circumstantial evidence. He could have got
blood on himself doing an experiment."

"True," Dr. Wyman said. "But if so, it was an experiment
done sometime prior to Dr. Parkman's disappearance. Littlefield says Dr. Webster hasn't used blood in any of his experiments since the week before Thanksgiving."

"Littlefield could be wrong." Dr. Bigelow felt some of the
spots. "This seems like fairly recent blood. Notice the shape of
the spots. They aren't elongated as they would be if the blood
had been dropped from height. Webster — or whoever it was
— must have been carrying whatever it was the blood came
from."

"Did you know the right kidney was found in the ash bin yesterday?"

"No. Who found it?"

"Sanderson, I think." Dr. Wyman studied Dr. Bigelow's face. "You thinking of Littlefield?"

Dr. Bigelow nodded. "He did have access to the Medical College at all hours, as they keep saying in Cambridge." Then he shook his head. "But somehow I don't think he's guilty."

"Did you hear about the markings near the penis and on the lower back? Maybe you already know that Mrs. Parkman has identified them so there's no longer any doubt about who was murdered."

"I didn't know where the markings were but I heard something about them from Longfellow yesterday afternoon. He told me he went to a lecture on Dante in Boston Saturday night. He said the lecture was dull but the conversation afterward wasn't. Mrs. Farrar was there and reported that some peculiar markings had been discovered on the torso found at the College. She said that of course nobody could identify them except Parkman's wife and Longfellow found that remark amusing."

"They found something else today," Dr. Wyman said. He removed the newspaper wrapping from a knife in a silver sheath.

Dr. Bigelow picked up the knife. "I remember this from the old building on Mason Street. It's Turkish and I think you call it a yataghan. If I recall correctly, it has figures carved on the blade." He took the knife out of the sheath and held it to the light. "See, there they are. Hunters and animals of some kind." He leaned down to examine the blade closely. "It's been cleaned recently, hasn't it? And what's this on the handle, blood? Here, hold it while I take some scrapings." He tore a piece from the newspaper.

"I hear the Medical College faculty has voted to open the building to the public beginning at noon today. That right?"

Dr. Wyman asked as Dr. Bigelow folded the newspaper with the scrapings and put it into his pocket.

"Assuming your committee is through by then," Dr. Bigelow said. "Who's downstairs, anyway?"

"A crowd. Lewis, Gay, Jackson, Stone, Jabez Pratt, Deputy Clapp, and a half-dozen constables. Tukey left a little while ago."

"I'm going down and have a look," Dr. Bigelow said. "The Medical faculty meets at my place again this afternoon and I have some things to get done before then, but I think I'll take the time to go down anyway."

"I'm through up here so I'll come along. When I was down earlier, they were cutting out sections of arteries to test them for the preparation Dr. Ainsworth uses to preserve specimens. I'm taking the bones over to my office. I can do a better job of cataloguing them over there."

"Did Jackson work on the stains on the wall and the steps?" Dr. Bigelow asked as they started down the stairs.

"They are copper nitrate," Dr. Wyman told him.

Dr. Bigelow shook his head. "Well, if there's anything better for removing blood stains than copper nitrate, I haven't heard about it."

When they reached the lower laboratory, Dr. Jackson stepped over to the windows that looked out on the Charles River. "It just occurred to me that these windows can't be more than two feet above the river at high tide, two feet at the most. For some reason I never noticed that before."

A knot of men was standing around Dr. Webster's privy, which was directly under the stairs. The two doctors saw that the privy seat was raised and Littlefield was holding the torso down into it.

"Well, I guess we have the answer as to why the torso was put in the chest and not down the privy vault," Deputy Clapp said to Dr. Bigelow. "It's too big to go through."

Eaton spoke up. "Why didn't whoever killed him use the dissecting room vault? Wouldn't that be the place you'd expect somebody to use to get rid of remains?"

"And risk having some student come in while he was doing it? Littlefield says there are likely to be students working in the dissection room at just about any hour of the day or night."

"How would he have got the keys to the dissection room vault? There's a double lock and nobody has the keys but me," Littlefield told him. "Nobody can use the vault without me knowing about it."

Dr. Wyman and Dr. Bigelow joined the doctors gathered around a board on the floor at the center of the room. Dr. Lewis and Dr. Stone were squatted beside the board, examining the leg found in the vault.

"Leg muscles well developed, probably from walking a good deal," Dr. Lewis observed. He looked up at Dr. Bigelow. "Whom does that remind you of?"

Dr. Bigelow nodded. He looked at the box on the floor beside Dr. Stone. "What's in here?"

Dr. Jackson answered. "Specimens from the thorax muscles. I'm going to test them for alkali."

Dr. Gay called over to the men standing around the privy. "Could somebody bring the trunk and the other thigh over here? You can have them back in about fifteen minutes if you aren't through with them."

Dr. Bigelow consulted his watch. "When do you think you'll be through?" he said to Dr. Lewis.

"Another hour," Dr. Lewis said. "We're just about through except for the description of the fleshy parts of the body. We did most of our work yesterday afternoon. Dr. Wyman has to catalogue the bones, but he's taking them over to his office so that won't delay us. Coroner Pratt says the Medical College faculty wants the building opened to the public at noon. Is that the case?"

"If you've finished by then," Dr. Bigelow told him.

"We will be. Pratt says the undertaker will be here around eleven."

As Dr. Lewis spoke, Littlefield placed the torso on the board, laying it on its back. Fuller brought the thigh found in the privy vault and put it in the natural position in relation to the torso. Dr. Gay laid the thigh from the mineral chest on the board and Dr. Stone placed the left leg below the left thigh.

"Look at the difference in the size of the thighs," Dr. Stone said. "The one found in the vault must be a third bigger than the other one."

Dr. Bigelow stepped closer to the board and leaned down to look at the torso. "What's that hole under his left nipple? I don't remember seeing that before."

Dr. Jackson studied the torso. "Do you suppose that's the stab that killed him?"

Dr. Stone touched the wound carefully. "Doesn't look like a stab wound to me. The edges are too ragged. Looks as though it might have been made recently. The flesh over his ribs is soft and spongy and the skin breaks easily. Maybe somebody inadvertently made this hole in the process of examining the torso."

"Come to think about it, when I was here Saturday, I saw one of the constables using his cane to brush off some of the tanbark," Dr. Gay said.

"I hope you don't remember who it was," Dr. Wyman said. "Tukey will have him strung up by his thumbs for a month of Sundays."

"*I* won't remember who he was, but there were others in the room. As a matter of fact, somebody warned him to stop using his cane for fear of doing just such damage as this."

Dr. Lewis was measuring the length of each piece of the remains with great care. He made a notation of each measurement in the notebook on the floor beside him. Then he rose and studied his figures for a moment or two. He said to Dr. Stone, "According to my calculations, the height of this man was five feet, ten inches."

Dr. Stone reached into his pocket for a slip of paper. "According to his passport, Dr. Parkman was five feet, ten and a half inches tall."

CHAPTER VII

Wanted: Counsel for Dr. Webster

THE THERMOMETER at Faneuil Hall stood at four below zero on Thursday afternoon, December 6. Despite the cold, crowds lined the streets of Boston as Dr. Parkman's funeral cortege moved toward Trinity Church. Slowly the carriages came down Walnut Street, black bands on the coachmen's tall hats, black crepe on the horses' harnesses. The carriage windows were shrouded, but everybody knew that only the immediate family was present at the brief service Dr. Ephraim Peabody had conducted at Dr. Parkman's home. Everybody knew, also, that the remains had been embalmed in spirits, sealed in a lead box, and then placed in a casket. Interment was to be in one of the crypts under the square gray towers of Trinity Church in Summer Street. The rumor was that in the spring, the remains would be removed to the family's plot at Mt. Auburn Cemetery.

The procession passed the Ticknor mansion at the corner of Beacon and Park as George Ticknor watched from the windows of his second-floor library. To Ticknor, a man who held himself personally responsible for Boston's moral standards, the sight was truly appalling. Hundreds of Boston people waiting in the bitter cold to witness the funeral procession of the victim of the worst crime in the country's history! This was more of the ghoulish curiosity that had led 5000 people to visit the Medical School the first two days it was open to the public.

Abruptly George Ticknor turned from the window back to his library with its elegant hanging lamps, its fine carpets, and the portrait of Sir Walter Scott, painted at Abbotsford, above the mantel. His glance fell on the priceless collection of books that were the cornerstone of his *History of Spanish Literature*, to be published within the month.

George Ticknor was well aware that Boston's leaders were sharply divided over the question of the extension of slavery into the territory acquired from Mexico after the war and he saw this situation as a terrible threat to all New England. But it was impossible for him to believe — *impossible* — that Boston's moral fiber was weakened to the extent that two Harvard men, both physicians, both with graduate training in European universities, both allied to Boston's first families, could under any circumstances become involved in a vulgar quarrel over money, a quarrel that culminated in murder.

Looking up at Sir Walter in his green hunting jacket and his buff waistcoat, Ticknor thought about the great Reverend William Ellery Channing. "Don't make Iago too attractive," the Reverend Mr. Channing had warned when Ticknor began his teaching career at Harvard. Across all the intervening years he had remembered that warning. He had devoted all his adult life to stamping out those forces that jeopardized the finest and the best in Boston culture and Boston tradition.

He knew there were people among his peers who said he was as cold as the marble stairs that led up to his library. He knew that a recent dinner guest had said she was chilly for days after an evening with Tête Noir and La Mère Glacé. Such comments did not disturb him in the least. What *did* disturb him was the defection of men of his own class. How could they be so blind as to refuse to support the values that had sustained Massachusetts throughout its long and dis-

tinguished history? Could they see no parallel between themselves and Louis XVI sitting in his gardens writing "nothing"
in his diary the day the Bastille fell? It was Ticknor's deep
conviction that the higher a man's status by virtue of family,
education, and wealth, the greater his obligation to provide
leadership for those less fortunate, the kind of leadership that
buttressed proven values and age-old tradition. Despite his own
undistinguished looks — he was a thick-set man with a heavy
face — Ticknor believed that quality was manifest in a man's
appearance as well as his behavior. He had said as much
to Thackeray and was not amused when Thackeray smiled
and questioned whether Ticknor's comment was appropriate
for one broken-nosed man to make to another.

Because he felt as he did, Ticknor could not accept socially
— or in any other way — those peers who departed from his
own Federalist philosophy. Charles Francis Adams, the son
and the grandson of United States Presidents; Charles Francis
Adams, a member of the Free Soil Party, a party that threatened
the very foundations of the Union in the opinion of Daniel
Webster himself. Wendell Phillips, the son of Boston's first
mayor, associated with that rabble-rousing abolitionist fa-
natic, William Lloyd Garrison. James Russell Lowell, the rosy-
cheeked young man with the taffy-colored hair who wrote the
scandalously disrespectful *Biglow Papers,* was the grandson of
Judge John Amory Lowell, for thirty years a judge on the
Supreme Court of Massachusetts. And Ephraim Peabody, the
rector of King's Chapel, openly harboring Frederick Douglass,
a runaway slave, another man's property!

In addition to defection, there was deterioration among the
class of men whom Boston rightfully looked to for leadership.
Ellery Channing was the nephew of the saintly and brilliant
Reverend William Ellery Channing. And what was Ellery
Channing? A morose, unproductive poet who dressed like a
peddler and half the time never bothered to tie his shoe-

strings. It was only by chopping wood for Emerson that he staved off starvation. Emerson was his closest friend and that was probably the seat of his trouble. That Concord crowd was a disgrace to Massachusetts. Henry Thoreau who stood neck-deep in Walden Pond for hours on end watching birds, *he* had the audacity to say that Harvard taught all the branches of learning and none of the roots. And Hawthorne, the queerest of them all. Hawthorne was so preoccupied with his own thoughts he couldn't be trusted to do his job at Brook Farm, which was feeding the pigs.

In Ticknor's philosophy there were responsibilities that transcended the claims of friendship. How many times had Charles Sumner been among the Ticknors' guests when they entertained the finest men in New England? Daniel Webster, Rufus Choate, Edward Everett, Robert Winthrop, the Honorable Abbott Lawrence, Benjamin Curtis. But after Sumner abandoned the old values, after he challenged Timothy Dwight on the prison reform issue, he was no longer received at the Ticknor mansion. Sumner had gone from bad to worse. He had allied himself with the Free Soil crowd and what was he doing right now? Stirring up trouble for the Boston School Committee by bringing suit in the name of a nine-year-old Negro girl, charging that she was wrongfully denied her constitutional rights when she was "forced" to go to the African school!

George Ticknor knew that John Webster had friends whose philosophy of friendship was different. They were men who looked upon Webster as a troubled human being in need of help. They could not — or would not — see him as a man who had brought about a new and terrible assault on all that Boston's leaders had worked to uphold generation after generation. The whole country was talking of what had happened at the Medical College in Boston. Charles Francis Adams wrote home from Washington that when he met Henry Clay at an evening affair, Clay's questions were about the murder. In Ticknor's philosophy, a man who brought this shame on his class, on Harvard University, and on the city of Boston deserved to be shunned. Yet he knew that this was not to be. In the weeks and months ahead people of education and breeding would meet at the Leverett Street jail. And that was not the worst of it. Who among Boston's foremost attorneys would have to soil his hands by defending John White Webster? Daniel Webster? Rufus Choate? Franklin Dexter? Benjamin Curtis?

Who indeed?

That question worried Franklin Dexter, for despite all his efforts, he could not find counsel for Dr. Webster. How would it look to a jury, he asked William Prescott, if no New England attorney was willing to undertake John Webster's defense?

The first man Franklin Dexter had approached was Daniel Webster, and he was not unprepared for Webster's refusal. Everybody knew Daniel Webster was staggering under a terrible load of work in an effort to pay off some of his mountainous debts. These days he was trying to wring a little money out of his beloved Marshfield. "Mr. Stevens at the Revere House will take all the potatoes we can supply," he wrote his Marshfield manager. Moreover, Webster was far from well. His eyes still had the fire of black diamonds and he was always carefully dressed in his double-breasted coat with the brass buttons, but his walk was slow and he no longer stood as erect as an Indian. His close friends knew his trouble went deeper than his worry over his debts and his bouts with his old enemy, rheumatism. For Daniel Webster was a bitter man, bitter over the Whigs' failure to nominate him for the Presidency, bitter because President Taylor had not offered him a Cabinet post. He said if he had his life to live over again, he would have no part of politics. *Poor Richard* was right; the first mistake in public business was going into it at all.

Also, Daniel Webster had never recovered from the blows he had sustained a year and a half earlier, in July, 1848, when his only daughter, Julia Appleton, the gentle, lovely Julia had died of tuberculosis at twenty-six. The very day of her funeral the body of Major Webster, Daniel Webster's first-born, reached Boston, a victim of Mr. Polk's war with Mexico. Webster did what he always did in time of trouble; he went home to Marshfield. There he planted two weeping elms and named them Sister and Brother. Webster loved trees and he could think of no finer memorial to his children. He stayed on in the country until autumn, tending his fields and his foals, but this time even Marshfield could not help him. He was a broken man.

Daniel Webster said he was sorry he was too overburdened with work to undertake John Webster's defense. He was certainly very much interested in the case, he said, and very much amused when an English newspaper carried an account of the murder with Daniel Webster in the role of the accused and Judge Isaac Parker as his victim. During the trial Webster was heard to complain that John Webster got better newspaper coverage than he did. The trial began twelve days after Webster's March 7 speech and by that time he was well aware that there were many people in Massachusetts who felt that his crime in supporting the proposed compromise on slavery was even worse than the charges against John Webster.

But now in December, the trial was still in the future and Franklin Dexter had not yet been able to find counsel for Dr. Webster. At one point he turned to Rufus Choate, a man who had many times served as Daniel Webster's junior counsel and who himself had a brilliant record of success with juries. Rufus Choate and Franklin Dexter were well acquainted so-

cially and professionally. They were both close friends of the
Ticknors'. Choate had assisted Daniel Webster when the latter
successfully prosecuted the Knapp brothers for the murder of
Captain Joseph White in Salem. Franklin Dexter was the attorney for the defendants and although the Knapps were eventually hung, Dexter's handling of the defense was masterful.
The two men met again professionally when Choate made his
first appearance before the United States Supreme Court and
lost his case because Franklin Dexter was able to defend his
client against the charge that he had infringed on the plain-
tiff's patent for improvements in the construction of a plow.

There was never any question as to Choate's brilliance as
an attorney and there was no question, either, that his
personal mannerisms were a major factor in his success with
juries. Rufus Choate was a tall, angular man with big, bony
hands and, in middle life, a face seamed with a network of
wrinkles. He took no interest whatsoever in his appearance.
He rarely combed his thick, curly black hair and he regularly
wore jackets with missing buttons and trousers that stopped far
short of his shoe tops. Choate was always cold during the long
Boston winters and often he wore as many as five overcoats
topped with a kind of lamb's wool stole. His hat was an ancient
beaver and in cold weather his big feet were always encased
in large rubber overshoes. When he was trying a case in the
wintertime, it was Choate's practice to sit in court bundled
in all his overcoats until the attorney for the opposition was
about to reach the climax of his presentation to the jury. At
this point Choate would quietly rise and begin to divest himself of his various coats, a process that never failed to fasci-
nate a jury.

After he had laid aside his coats, Choate usually felt the need
to refresh himself. He achieved this objective by giving his
whole body several bone-jarring jerks and then suddenly bow-
ing from the waist until his fingers touched the floor. After a

moment or two in this position, he would stand bolt upright and breathe deeply in a way that could be heard in every corner of the courtroom. Wendell Phillips once remarked that Rufus Choate's courtroom behavior reminded him of a monkey with convulsions, and those who had seen Choate in action said the description was apt. Like Daniel Webster, Choate was a graduate of Dartmouth College. It was in September of his senior year that Choate heard Webster argue the Dartmouth College case at Exeter, an experience that resulted in his decision to become a lawyer himself.

Along with their genius for the law and their close friendship, Webster and Choate shared a monumental inability to manage their personal finances. Bostonians told of a winter morning when Choate lived in Chauncy Place and Webster had a house in High Street.

The two men met on Summer street, Choate in a battered beaver, as usual, and Webster wearing his immaculate stovepipe hat.

"I was on my way over to see you," Webster told Choate. "I want you to come up to the Exchange Bank and endorse my note for five hundred dollars."

Choate considered the request for a moment or two. Then he said, "Make it for one thousand dollars. No man in Suffolk County needs five hundred dollars worse than I do."

In January, 1850, Rufus Choate moved his office to 7½ Tremont Street, to the old house where the Parkmans had lived before Samuel Parkman built his Bowdoin Square mansion. In December, however, he was still on Court Street and Franklin Dexter found him in his littered office with his old horsehair sofa and the stand-up yellow pine desk that had once belonged to Judge Prescott. Red was Choate's favorite color, and among his treasures was the red rug on his office floor, an item purchased second-hand by his cleaning woman for an outlay of $2. For almost three hours Choate listened to Dexter urge him to serve as defense counsel for John Webster. Years later Choate said that he had never heard a more eloquent plea than Franklin Dexter made that December afternoon in his old office at 4 Court Street.

Choate had anticipated an approach from Dexter. Consequently, to prepare himself for the decision he knew Dexter would ask of him, he discussed the murder with Daniel Webster and he had a long talk with Ephraim Littlefield. After Franklin Dexter had concluded his argument, Choate began to talk. He reviewed the facts in the case as Dexter and he knew them. He recounted Littlefield's description of Dr. Webster's unusual behavior after Dr. Parkman's disappearance. When before, in all his years at Harvard, had Dr. Webster been known to spend any holidays working at the Medical College? And Choate felt they should not overlook the fact that by his own admission, Dr. Webster had himself set the date for that last interview with Dr. Parkman and he had chosen the day preceding the beginning of the Thanksgiving holidays, a period during which no classes would meet at the Medical College. Could he have planned it that way to give himself time to dispose of a body? Choate raised other questions. Knowing Dr. Parkman as they both did, Choate asked Franklin Dexter whether he thought it likely that Dr. Parkman would make a mistake in computing the interest due him — which he had done if John Webster spoke the truth — or that he was a man to rush off to settle a mortgage with no consideration of the fact that there were other names on that mortgage in addition to his own.

Then Choate said that he appreciated the generosity of Dr. Webster's friends. The $2000 fee they offered was twice what he would have asked for. However, he would consider serving as Dr. Webster's counsel only on the condition that Dr. Webster would state that Dr. Parkman had died in his presence. On the basis of that admission by Dr. Webster, Choate would ask the Prosecution to show *how* Dr. Parkman died. He continued,

"The Prosecution would be asked to show whether Dr. Parkman died by visitation of God, as the result of an attack made
on the prisoner by the deceased — so that Dr. Webster acted in
self-defense — or as the result of a violent altercation. Possibly the idea of murder might be suggested, but with no more
reason than apoplexy or any other form of sudden death. Since
under the law the prisoner himself could not speak, the question would narrow down to the alternative of justifiable
homicide or manslaughter." In any event, Choate said, if a
defense were presented in this way, he was certain Dr. Webster
would escape the gallows.

"Moreover," Choate added, "if Dr. Webster would say that
Dr. Parkman died in his lecture room or his laboratory, his
subsequent behavior, otherwise so hard to explain, could be
presented as the action of a man who out of fear made the mistake of failing to immediately disclose what had happened.
Having made this mistake, he was faced with the problem of
disposing of the remains." In summation he said again that
he could not consider undertaking Dr. Webster's defense unless Dr. Webster was prepared to meet the condition Choate
had specified.

Franklin Dexter rose. He said that as an attorney, he could
appreciate Choate's interpretation of the evidence and his rec-
ommendations for Dr. Webster's defense. At the same time,
he was sure that neither Dr. Webster nor his friends would
consider for even a moment a defense based on Dr. Webster's
statement that Dr. Parkman had died in his presence.

And Dexter was right. An innocent man plead guilty to
murder! Dr. Webster and his friends were incensed that Rufus
Choate would dare to make such a suggestion.

By the latter part of December Dr. Webster, hitherto calm
and confident, began to worry about Franklin Dexter's failure
to find counsel for him. By that time both Charles Loring and

Benjamin Curtis had declined to serve, both on the basis that
they were members of the Harvard Corporation and therefore
it would be inappropriate for them to have a part in litigation
involving a man on the Harvard faculty. Dr. Webster decided
to take a more active role in this matter of securing an attorney
for his defense. Accordingly, he wrote to Charles Sumner, asking him to call at the Leverett Street jail. On Friday afternoon,
December 21, Sumner went up to Mt. Vernon Street to talk
over the situation with Charles Francis Adams.* Sumner said
he knew Webster wanted to sound him out about serving as
his defense counsel. What did Adams think he ought to say?

Adams looked into the fire thoughtfully. He said he wondered how many times he had come into this very room on a
winter afternoon and found his father and Dr. Parkman sitting
before this fire. More often than not, they were both asleep.
He remembered his father's hands on the arm of that chair
over there. The fingers of his right hand were invariably ink-
stained, for he was always writing something, journals, his-
tories, memoirs of his days as John Quincy Adams, President of
the United States. Dr. Parkman and his father saw a good deal
of each other socially. It was at a dinner party at the Parkmans'
that the old man had astounded Fanny Kemble with his pon-
tifical appraisal of Shakespeare. He informed her unequivocally
that *Othello* was disgusting, *King Lear* was ludicrous, and
Romeo and Juliet, childish nonsense. Afterward Fanny said
she was so at a loss as to how to respond to such remarks from a
former President of the United States that she filled the moment by seizing the water tumbler in front of her and drink-
ing it dry.

Adams paused. He recalled Dr. Parkman as a high-strung
but kindly man. It was significant, he thought, that John Web-

---

* Charles Francis Adams (1807-1887), son of President John Quincy Adams and
in 1848 the candidate for Vice President on the Free Soil ticket. During the Civil
War he served as United States Minister to England.

ster had chosen Dr. Parkman as the creditor to keep waiting. According to rumor, he had recently made payments to some of the others, Dr. Bigelow, for example, and Mrs. Prescott.

Charles Sumner said that he had given careful consideration to the whole situation, to Dr. Webster's statements, Littlefield's description of what went on at the Medical College, particularly after Dr. Parkman's disappearance, to John Webster's long-standing financial difficulties and Dr. Parkman's personality. Regretful as he was to have to say it, he had arrived at the conclusion that John Webster was guilty of murder. Nevertheless, guilty or innocent, the man had a right to be defended. The question was, who would undertake that responsibility? Should he offer his services?

Adams shook his head. He, too, was convinced of Webster's guilt. Certainly somebody had to defend him, but if Sumner took his advice, he would steer clear of the whole affair. Sitting there in his library, looking at Sumner, Adams may have thought about Sumner's talent for getting carried away by his feelings, frequently landing in very hot water. Wendell Phillips said that Sumner was like a cat without smellers; he could not assess what was going on around him. He could not judge the impact of his own words. On the other hand, Holmes said Sumner's trouble was his lack of a sense of humor. "If I told Sumner the moon was made of green cheese, he would immediately say, 'No, it isn't, Holmes,' and proceed to line up a long list of weighty arguments." But then no wonder Sumner had no sense of humor, a man who had a hangman for a father.

Whatever his reasons, Adams hoped Sumner would not get involved in Webster's problems. But Sumner could not make up his mind. Finally he decided that the one man in the country who could save John Webster from the gallows was Rufus Choate. Three years earlier Choate had won an acquittal for his client Albert Tirrell by convincing the jury that Tirrell had been asleep when he murdered his paramour. A man who could convince a jury with *that* story could convince a jury of anything. The day would come when Sumner and Choate would be bitter enemies, but they were still friends in December, 1849, when Sumner called at Choate's office. Choate and Sumner went over the case against Dr. Webster. As he had told Franklin Dexter, Choate said he would consider defending Dr. Webster only if Dr. Webster was ready to state that Dr. Parkman had died in his lecture room or in his laboratory or in some other room of the Medical College where they were together. In Choate's opinion there was no other tenable defense for Dr. Webster. As for any other line of argument, well, you might as easily try to persuade a jury that Dr. Parkman shook himself to pieces in a fit of ague. Choate went on to say that although he certainly recognized the right of the accused to counsel — regardless of the question of his guilt or innocence — still he did not feel obligated to go into court and present a defense that he could not believe to be the truth.

Sumner could not persuade Rufus Choate to defend John Webster and in the end he decided not to take on that responsibility himself. Franklin Dexter felt a growing conviction that John Webster would be defended by counsel appointed by the court. There was just no other way to secure help for this unfortunate man.

Late in December Dr. Webster began to write a brief for his own defense. Word leaked out that his two main points were that the remains of the body found at the Medical College were not those of Dr. Parkman and that he, John Webster, was the victim of a conspiracy planned with the objective of collecting the reward for information leading to the discovery of Dr. Parkman's body. Also, by the end of December Dr. Webster had a spiritual advisor, the Reverend George Putnam, a Unitarian minister from Roxbury. He told his family and his friends that his discussions with Dr. Putnam were a great source of comfort to him.

Rufus Choate knew the Reverend Mr. Putnam. One morning when they met on Tremont Street he inquired about Dr. Webster.

"How is your charge at the Leverett Street prison?" he asked.

"Well," replied Dr. Putnam, smiling, "I always find him in."

Choate's eyes twinkled. "And I wager it will be quite some time before you find him out," he said.

CHAPTER VIII

The Indictment

DID THE Prosecution have a witness who had seen Dr. Webster dismembering Dr. Parkman's body?

On a snowy afternoon during the second week in December, William Hickling Prescott called at Franklin Dexter's rooms at the Revere House to discuss that rumor. His mother had heard it and, understandably, she was very upset. After all, Mrs. Webster and she were half-sisters. They had grown up in the same household on Fayal in the Azores and they had always been very close. Mr. Prescott had come to see Mr. Dexter in the hope of taking a word of comfort back to Beacon Street.

Mr. Dexter got up to stir the fire. Yes, he, too, had heard the rumor and he did not believe there was any truth in it. Neither did he think it would be possible to make a positive identification of the remains with both the head and the hands missing. Consequently, it was his opinion that under no circumstances could Dr. Webster be convicted of murder in the first degree.

But when Mr. Prescott sighed with relief, Mr. Dexter held up a restraining hand. He did not want Mr. Prescott to go away with a false sense of security where Dr. Webster's situation was concerned. It was very likely that the coroner's jury had some strong evidence not known to the public at large. Where there was so much smoke, there must be some fire. At any rate they would know in a day or two when the jury completed its work.

In answer to Mr. Prescott's question, Mr. Dexter said the jury's findings would not be made public, as Mr. Prescott had been informed. But as Dr. Webster's acting counsel, he would see the documents to be submitted to the grand jury, granted the jury of inquest found against Dr. Webster. He had settled that when Samuel Parker called to discuss the possibility of barring the public from the jury's sessions.

"What did you say to him?" Mr. Prescott asked.

Mr. Dexter said that as far as he was concerned, speaking as Dr. Webster's counsel, the District Attorney was free to make whatever decision he thought best. In his opinion Mr. Parker was right in raising the issue. If the Coroner's investigation was open to the public, what man could keep from forming an opinion as to the part Dr. Webster had played in the tragedy? Even as things stood now, it would probably be next to impossible to get a jury of impartial men for the trial.

As he rose to leave, Mr. Prescott asked about counsel for Dr. Webster. He referred to the announcement in the *Transcript* that Dr. Webster would be defended by Mr. Dexter, Benjamin Curtis, and Edward Sohier.

Franklin Dexter shook his head. Certainly he had made no secret of his sentiments on this subject. He was not prepared to offer his services as Dr. Webster's counsel. Furthermore, he was eager to get the matter settled so he could leave for Beverly. Mr. Curtis also had declined to defend Dr. Webster, and his refusal came as no surprise. All Boston knew how Mr. Ticknor felt about the murder. To have his nephew involved in such a sordid affair was doubtless more than he could tolerate. As for Mr. Sohier, he had expressed his willingness to serve if he could share the responsibility with a colleague experienced in criminal law. At the moment Mr. Dexter awaited the names of the men the court stood ready to appoint as Dr. Webster's counsel.

He expected to receive them a day or two after the jury of inquest returned its verdict, assuming the verdict went against Dr. Webster. When and if he received the names, he would go over to the jail and consult with Dr. Webster, for he had the privilege of choosing among the men the court made available to him. Dr. Webster's attorneys, whoever they proved to be, would have the privilege of reviewing the evidence on which the jury had based its verdict, again assuming the coroner's jury found against Dr. Webster.

The jury of inquest was hard at work during the first two weeks of December. When the jurors emerged from the Medical College or the ward room at the courthouse, their feelings about the gravity of their responsibility showed in their faces. The first of their sessions, all of them held in secret, was at the Medical College on Saturday afternoon, December 1. They arrived at the College as the Medical Committee was finishing the work of writing a description of the pieces of the body. The jurors took careful view of the remains, noting the diagonal stripe of hard, purplish skin across the back of the torso, the perforation in the left side of the chest, the difference in size between the thigh found in the privy vault and the one from the tea chest. They subjected Dr. Lewis' Medical Committee to a barrage of questions. Was the body dismembered in a way that showed training in dissection? Was it possible that the remains were anatomical specimens used by the medical students? Could the committee tell for sure whether the remains were all from the same body? How did a physician decide about the age of the victim in a situation like this? After the jury had viewed the pieces of the body to their satisfaction, Coroner Pratt released the remains to the undertaker waiting upstairs in the hall. After another hour during which the jurors questioned Professor Wyman about the bones found in the furnace — he said he needed further study before he could supply the answers

requested — Coroner Pratt dismissed the jury with an unnecessary reminder as to the seriousness of their responsibility and
orders to be back at the College no later than nine o'clock the
following Monday morning.

The jury of inquest spent Monday and Tuesday at the
Medical College. Monday morning they began their inspection of the College building. Beginning with Dr. Holmes'
lecture room on the top floor, they examined everything in the
entire building, every table, every cabinet, every cubbyhole,
every box. They interrogated Dr. Ainsworth about the specimens in the demonstrator's closet, his special responsibility at
the College. They checked his record book to satisfy themselves
that all specimens were accounted for and none were missing.
When he was questioned on the subject, Dr. Ainsworth said he
was positive that Dr. Jackson's chemical analysis of the blood
vessels dissected out of the remains found in the privy vault
and the tea chest would show none of the solution that was
always injected into specimens prepared for the medical
students.

When the jury reached Dr. Webster's quarters, they went
through his rooms almost inch by inch. In his private room
off his upper laboratory, they examined the contents of every
drawer in his storage chest, noting the bunch of keys, the balls
of cord, the grapples. When they got to the lower laboratory,
they studied it with the same meticulous care, examining the
sink, the furnace, the fuel closet, the privy. Finally, they
climbed down under the building and made their way back
to the privy vault. Littlefield was requested to accompany
them to point out where the pieces of the body lay when
he first saw them.

After their investigation of the College building was complete, the jury began their questioning of Littlefield.
Patiently and carefully Littlefield told his part in the tragedy
beginning with Monday, November 19, when Dr. Parkman

came to the Medical College late in the afternoon while Little-field was helping Dr. Webster prepare materials for his lecture the following day. The jury asked Littlefield to show them how it was possible for him to lie with his face pressed against the floor in the lower passageway and see Dr. Webster moving about his lower laboratory. And at the jury's request he demonstrated how he edged his way along the outside of the building and climbed into Dr. Webster's lower laboratory the afternoon he thought Dr. Webster's furnace might set the College afire. The word spread through town that Littlefield had answered all questions patiently and thoughtfully and that the jury, finding no contradictions in his story, credited him with telling the truth.

Then beginning on Wednesday, December 5, the jurors held their sessions in the ward room of the courthouse. On Thursday, the day of Dr. Parkman's funeral, they did not meet. They resumed their sessions on Friday and met the following Saturday, Monday, and Tuesday. Their meetings lasted from nine o'clock in the morning until seven in the evening. In the course of their investigation they interrogated sixty people. On Thursday, December 13, at six o'clock their work was complete. Their foreman, Osmyn Brewster, presented for the grand jury's consideration a locked portfolio that held eighty-four large pages of foolscap.

While the coroner's jury was in session, the feeling against Dr. Webster seemed to grow hourly in Boston. The town was inundated with stories that purported to show him as an unstable, insensitive man. Somebody looked into the Faculty Records for the years Dr. Webster was an undergraduate and reported that he had been disciplined for misdemeanors many times. He was disciplined for absences from prayers and recitations, and for being away from the College without permission. And on at least one occasion he was guilty of an offense more

serious than a misdemeanor. In April, 1810, he was suspended
for eight months for behavior that included expressing his displeasure with his tutor by violently and repeatedly slamming
the door of his room. At the very least this was very childish
behavior, and the general opinion was that Dr. Webster continued to exhibit childish behavior when he was a grown man.
Consider, for example, his insistence that the committee charged
with planning Dr. Sparks' installation as President of Harvard
include a display of fireworks in the ceremony. Even the students knew of his determination to influence the committee in
this respect. "Sky-rocket Jack," they dubbed him. Was this
proper and dignified behavior in a member of the Harvard
College faculty?

And the story of Dr. Webster's strange and certainly undignified behavior at one of the Websters' dinner parties
was told and retold in Boston. Longfellow was among the
Websters' guests on that occasion. He said that after the wine
all the candles in the room were extinguished. After a moment
or two a servant brought in a large bowl of phosphorus and
placed it on the table in front of Dr. Webster. While the room
was in darkness, Dr. Webster had put a piece of heavy rope
around his neck. With the red glow from the phosphorus on his
face, his head cocked and his tongue lolling out, he looked for all
the world like a man in the act of being hanged. Longfellow
said the effect of the scene was blood-chilling.

Also, Dr. Webster's management — or lack of it, rather —
of the fortune he inherited was cited as additional evidence of
his irrational nature. Why was it that simple arithmetic did
not show him that the cost of his Cambridge mansion, his lavish
entertaining, and his extensive travels in Europe were leading
him down the road to financial ruin? The truth was that
throughout his life Dr. Webster had shown himself incapable
of charting his course in terms of unwelcome facts. When he
was up against a situation that was not to his liking, his behavior

was emotional, not rational. He lived his life in terms of his pleasures, not his responsibilities.

Bostonians told each other that on the afternoon of November 23 Dr. Webster was again faced with a set of facts not to his liking. On that occasion, as on so many others, had the erratic, irresponsible side of his nature got the upper hand — to the extent that he committed murder?

As for his brutal treatment of the body of an old friend, a man to whom he was indebted for many kindnesses, well, there was evidence that Dr. Webster was indeed capable of insensitivity where other human beings were concerned. The death of his cousin Mary Bagley in the Amesbury almshouse was a case in point. And people said Dr. Webster's callous disregard for the well-being of others was manifest when a student in his lecture room narrowly escaped serious injury as the result of an accident during a chemical experiment. According to the other students, Dr. Webster was very cool about the incident. He seemed totally unmoved by the fact that a student might have been seriously hurt because of a situation for which he alone was responsible.

Also, there was Joseph Willard's story about Dr. Webster's abuse of a dog. According to Willard, the dog in question was a nice pup, a stray the boys at the Medical College had adopted. The dog was usually to be found in the neighborhood of the College building and one day Dr. Webster dragged him into class for the purpose of using him in an experiment. Willard said that Dr. Webster repeatedly hit the dog on the head with a sledgehammer. When he could not beat the animal into unconsciousness, Dr. Webster allowed the dog to drag himself out of the building. Later the boys found him at the bottom of a well, slaughtered, to use Willard's word, and they held Dr. Webster responsible. Willard said that for a time the feeling against Dr. Webster ran very high among the medical students.

The attorneys in Boston said that Dr. Webster's counsel would be up against far more serious problems than community feeling over stories about their client's alleged cruelty to a dog. For example, why didn't Dr. Webster give Dr. Parkman the money in question when he called at Walnut Street the morning of the day Dr. Parkman and he met at the Medical College? Why was it necessary to make the appointment for the meeting at the College if all Dr. Webster intended was to hand over the money? Also, why were *both* notes in Dr. Webster's possession? It was proper that he should have had the smaller note, the one representing the debt he owed Dr. Parkman before a group of his friends, Dr. Parkman among them, made him the larger loan. But how did it come about that at the time of his arrest, Dr. Webster had in his possession not only the smaller note but the larger one as well? He had not satisfied *that* note. And what about the endorsement on the back of the smaller note; was the handwriting Dr. Parkman's — or Dr. Webster's? Furthermore, there was the question of the fires at the College during Thanksgiving recess. Dr. Webster had never needed fires during any other recess period throughout his long association with the College. Why this time? And where did he get the money he said he gave Dr. Parkman? The Attorney General was sure to ask about that.

Then on Friday, December 14, the newspapers carried the story of the jury's findings. In their verdict the jury stated unequivocally that the parts of the body the jury had viewed "have been identified and proved to be the remains of the dead body and limbs of Dr. George Parkman." Moreover, Dr. Parkman had died at the Medical College "by a blow or blows, wound or wounds, inflicted upon him with some instrument or weapon, to the jury unknown, and by means not yet known to said jurors, and that said blow or blows, wound or wounds were inflicted upon him and said means were used by the hands of said Dr. John W. Webster by whom he was killed."

Everybody in New England — indeed everybody in the country who read the newspapers — knew that the coroner's jury had found against Dr. Webster. But the evidence that led the jury to its verdict was kept secret; it was locked in the portfolio Osmyn Brewster delivered to the grand jury. In the absence of information as to the facts on which the jury based its conclusions, Boston again seethed with speculation. According to rumor, the jury had proof that Dr. Webster had tried to bribe Littlefield to help him dispose of the body. That a search of Dr. Webster's house in Cambridge had yielded evidence that established his guilt beyond any reasonable doubt. That a student had come in on Dr. Webster when he was in the act of severing Dr. Parkman's head. That Dr. Webster had had an accomplice. In addition, Mr. Waterman, the tinsmith, told everybody about the large metal box with "good, strong handles" that Dr. Webster had ordered. Mr. Waterman was positive this box was not to be used to ship plants from Fayal. He had made Dr. Webster plenty of boxes for that purpose and none of them was anywhere near the size of this one. Wasn't that proof enough that Dr. Webster meant to use this box to dispose of the pieces of Dr. Parkman's body?

But through it all Dr. Webster had his defenders. "The findings of a jury of inquest show nothing of a man's guilt or innocence," the Cambridge *Chronicle* reminded the public. "They are no more than a statement showing there are grounds for complaint." Dr. Webster's friends professed to be undismayed by the jury's verdict. They said that all the rumors, every piece of speculation making the rounds in Boston, were simply stories about what *might* be circumstantial evidence, nothing more. If the coroner's jury had mistaken circumstantial evidence for facts, well, that was a sad commentary on their capabilities as jurors, but their errors did not make Dr. Webster guilty of murder. True, Dr. Webster had in his possession at the time of his arrest an unsatisfied note showing his indebted-

Sketch of Dr. Parkman
Courtesy of the Harvard Medical Library in
The Francis A. Countway Library of Medicine

Sketch of Dr. Webster
*Courtesy of the Harvard Medical Library in
The Francis A. Countway Library of Medicine*

Bowdoin Square in 1822 showing the Parkman mansion, the Blake-Tuckerman house built by Samuel Parkman for two of his daughters, and Charles Bulfinch's birthplace

Massachusetts Medical College, Harvard University

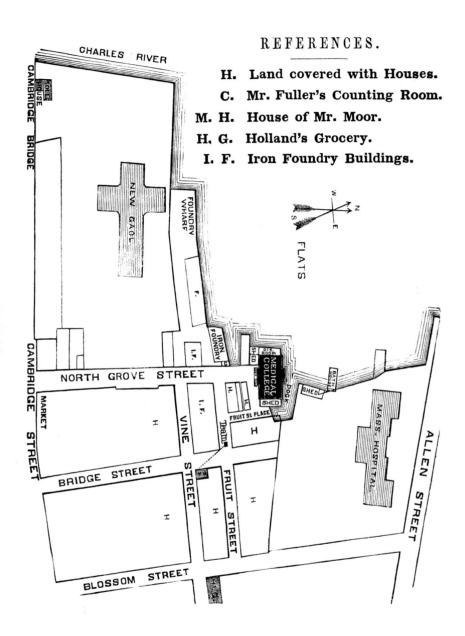

REFERENCES.

H. Land covered with Houses.
C. Mr. Fuller's Counting Room.
M. H. House of Mr. Moor.
H. G. Holland's Grocery.
I. F. Iron Foundry Buildings.

Map showing the location of the Medical College in the West End

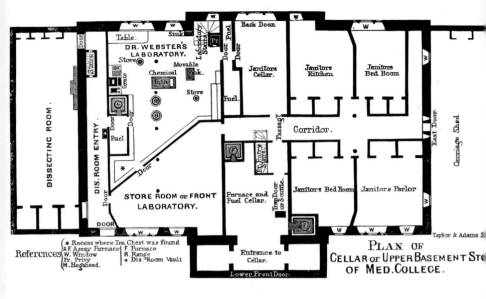

Table. DR. WEBSTER'S LABORATORY. Stove. Movable Table. Chemical Table. Stove. DISSECTING ROOM. DIS. ROOM ENTRY. Fuel. STORE ROOM or FRONT LABORATORY. DOOR. Laboratory Stairs. Door Fuel. Door. Back Door. Janitors Cellar. Janitors Kitchen. Janitors Bed Room. Fuel. Passage. Corridor. Furnace and Fuel Cellar. Trap Door or Scuttle. Janitors Bed Room. Janitors Parlor. Carriage Shed. East Door.

References { * Recess where Tea Chest was found / A. F. Assay Furnace / W. Window / Pr. Privy / H. Hogshead } { F. Furnace / R. Range / + Dis. Room Vault }

Taylor & Adams S[...]

PLAN OF CELLAR or UPPER BASEMENT STO[...] OF MED. COLLEGE.

Entrance to Cellar.

Lower Front Door.

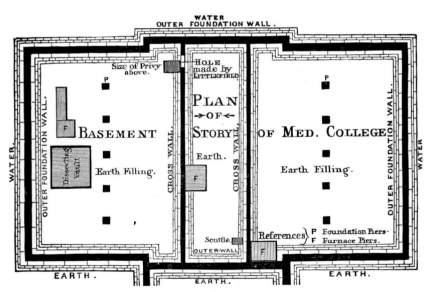

WATER
OUTER FOUNDATION WALL.

Size of Privy above. HOLE made by LITTLEFIELD. PLAN →OF← STORY OF MED. COLLEGE

WATER. OUTER FOUNDATION WALL. CROSS WALL. CROSS WALL. OUTER FOUNDATION WALL. WATER.

BASEMENT. Dissecting Vault. Earth Filling. Earth. Earth Filling.

References } P Foundation Piers. F Furnace Piers.

Scuttle. OUTER-WALL.

EARTH. EARTH. EARTH.

Floor plan of the basement of the Medical College where Dr. Webster's lower laboratory was located and a drawing of the foundation of the building

The Massachusetts General Hospital and the Medical College
across the street

Facsimiles of a note
Marshal Tukey received
after Dr. Webster's arrest

Mr. Tukey
Boston.

Dr Parkman was took on Bord the ship
herculan and this is al I dare to say or I
shal be kiled. Est Cambrge. one of the men

give me his Watch but I was feard to
keep it and thowd it in the water right-
side the road to the long brige to Boston.

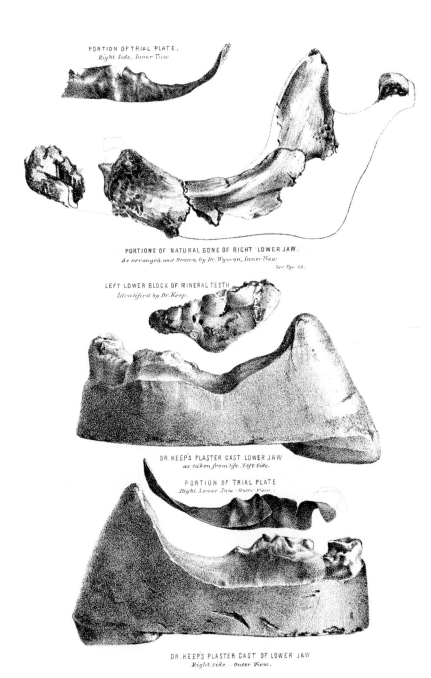

Dr. Keep's plaster casts of Dr. Parkman's jaws and the drawing Dr. Wyman made from pieces of bone found in the furnace in Dr. Webster's lower laboratory

Rufus Choate. From a contemporary engraving

Lemuel Shaw. From a painting by William Morris Hunt

ness to some of his friends. Yes, in the normal course of events, Dr. Parkman would have simply entered Dr. Webster's payment to him on the back of the larger of the two notes and retained it. But Dr. Parkman was an excitable man. Dr. Webster had explained that as soon as Dr. Parkman received the money, he ran out of Dr. Webster's lecture room in a rush to get to the bank. In his hurry he forgot to pick up the note. Was it so hard to believe that an excitable man like Dr. Parkman could have been guilty of such an oversight?

Also, was it not possible that Dr. Parkman was the victim of foul play at the hands of the thief he had prosecuted within the year? Wasn't that the thought that occurred to the Reverend Francis Parkman when he first learned of his brother's disappearance? And what evidence was there to establish the fact that the murder was committed at the Medical College? Students were in and out of the College by way of the dissecting room entry at all hours of the day and night. That was common knowledge in both Boston and Cambridge. The murderer could have watched for a chance to get into the building to deposit the remains there for the very purpose of throwing suspicion on Dr. Webster. What about the letter in the New Orleans *Times* in which a man *confessed* to the murder? What about *him?* In his letter he said he was on his way to California. Wasn't there some way to institute a search for him?

Over at Leverett Street Dr. Webster continued to have many visitors. All of them reported that he was relaxed and in good spirits, the very embodiment of a man with complete confidence that his innocence would be proved and his good name cleared. As a man who looked upon his acquittal as a foregone conclusion, Dr. Webster had no interest in discussing his trial. He disposed of that subject with the statement, repeated frequently, that he was innocent of all charges brought against him and that his trial would establish that fact. With Franklin Dexter's help he selected the names of Judge Pliny Merrick and Mr. Edward Sohier from the list of attorneys the court stood ready to appoint as his counsel. Dr. Webster told everybody how pleased he was with both men. Judge Merrick's father, also a prominent attorney, had served Massachusetts as a state senator. The Judge, a Harvard graduate and a classmate of Mr. Prescott's, had relinquished an appointment to the Court of Common Pleas to become president of the Worcester and Nashua Railroad. By happy chance this was the year Judge Merrick decided to leave the railroad and return to the practice of law. Now in his late fifties, Judge Merrick was a fine figure of a man, tall, well built, and always very well dressed. True, the Judge had a reputation for being hard on the opposition's witnesses, but he was always a gentleman whatever his professional objectives. Dr. Webster had assurances from Mr. Dexter on that score.

Dr. Webster was equally pleased with Edward Sohier, also a Harvard graduate, a member of Dr. Holmes' class. Mr. Sohier was a relative of the Ticknor family by marriage; his nephew had married George Ticknor's daughter. Anyone with a first-hand knowledge of Mr. Sohier's performance at the bar was not misled by his odd felt cap and the tweed coat with the mother-of-pearl buttons that he seemed to wear year round. Make no mistake about it, Dr. Webster said, Edward Sohier — or Ned as they called him around Boston — was a brilliant man as well as a man with a great deal of personal warmth. Also he was a man with a clever tongue. They were always repeating his bons mots over at the courthouse.

Recently somebody had commented to him that the motto of the Police Court, *Suim Cuique*, could be improved upon.

Mr. Sohier disagreed. "Not so," he said. "It couldn't be better. 'Sue 'em quick.' "

*

To the consternation of his attorneys, Dr. Webster felt no more interest in discussing his trial with them than he did with his other visitors. He made it clear that he had nothing to add to the story that was already public knowledge. Dr. Parkman had called on him at the Medical College about half-past one on Friday afternoon, November 23. During their brief interview Dr. Webster made a payment of $483.64 on the debt he owed Dr. Parkman. He had accumulated that amount over a period of time, mainly from students' fees; he could not be more specific than that. Dr. Webster said he had asked Dr. Parkman to come to the College to receive the money, rather than delivering it to his home on Walnut Street, because in Dr. Webster's opinion that was the proper way to manage the situation. He knew nothing whatsoever about the pieces of the body found at the College. He had the utmost confidence in his attorneys and in the power of the truth. Therefore, he felt no concern about his trial.

No matter how Judge Merrick and Mr. Sohier approached a discussion of the events that took place at the College on the day of Dr. Parkman's disappearance, no matter how hard they pressed him, Dr. Webster denied any knowledge of how Dr. Parkman met his death, granted, he said, that the remains found at the College *were* those of Dr. Parkman. It was Judge Merrick and Mr. Sohier who were anxious about Dr. Webster's fate; the defendant himself was consistently complacent and confident. Moreover, before Judge Merrick and Mr. Sohier had visited him very many times, Dr. Webster made it obvious that he saw no reason for further discussion of his defense. He made it apparent, also, that what he hoped for from his visitors, his attorneys included, was news of Boston. He was interested in everything that happened around town, even events of the most trivial nature.

Charles Curtis, whose two-wheeled chaise arrived in the jail yard at least once a week, was a good source of news both

major and minor. During one of his January visits Curtis told
about hearing Fanny Kemble read *Julius Caesar* and *Romeo
and Juliet*. The bad weather kept the audience small but
Curtis said Fanny did very well. Dr. Webster had seen the
notices of Fanny's engagement in the papers. He said that
in his opinion she was a woman of rare talent. He recalled
how he had requested the privilege of introducing her when
she read at Harvard in 1848 but Longfellow had won that
honor. (At the time of the trial Fanny spoke of Dr. Webster's
request and added that she was thankful she had not "put her
hand in the hand of a murderer.") Most of Fanny's admirers
knew how deeply she suffered in her unhappy marriage. Consequently Dr. Webster was glad to learn from Curtis that she
planned to spend the coming summer in the Berkshires with
her two little girls. The Berkshires, the loveliest spot in New
England. Dr. Holmes could never find enough time to spend
at his place near Pittsfield, the farm he had inherited from his
grandmother Wendell. James Russell Lowell said that Herman
Melville, Judge Shaw's son-in-law, was planning to buy a place
in the Berkshires and Hawthorne yearned to do likewise. Hawthorne hated Concord and small wonder, considering the bad
luck he had had there. Right now he was in a desperate financial
situation. Lowell was thinking about collecting a fund for him
from their friends.

And Lowell had other worries. He was beginning to be
seriously concerned about the slavery issue. Had Dr. Webster
heard that Mr. Calhoun boasted that one day southerners
would sell slaves at the foot of the Bunker Hill monu-
ment? Doubtless Dr. Webster had read in the papers that
President Fillmore had signed the bill admitting California
into the Union as a free state. But did he know that the night
after the bill was signed, Henry Clay, old and sick, plodded
through a snowstorm to have a talk with Daniel Webster? Could
it be possible that Webster would even *consider* supporting a
compromise bill that would entail planting the institution of

slavery in free territory? Was it conceivable that Daniel Webster might bring such shame on Massachusetts?

Dr. Webster knew that Lowell's concerns must include his father, for the old man was failing rapidly. He seemed more frail every time he came to Leverett Street and he had grown garrulous and forgetful. Around the time the Second Church decided to move from Hanover Street, he got to talking about Samuel Parkman. He rambled on and on apparently oblivious to how his discussion might affect Dr. Webster. He talked about what a fine man old Sam was and how the congregation of the Second Church had once given him a sterling silver pitcher, a handsome gift but none too fine for a man like Sam Parkman. You'd be hard put to find a man who had made a more generous contribution when they were collecting the money to build the hospital and he honored his pledge, too, even after all that trouble about young George not getting the appointment as the superintendent of the Asylum. Did Dr. Webster know it was Sam Parkman who commissioned Stuart to do the portrait of George Washington that hangs in Faneuil Hall?

After a visit from Dr. Lowell, it was reassuring to have a call from Dr. Bigelow, another old man, but one who was always in good health, in good spirits, and apparently in full possession of his faculties. It was Dr. Bigelow who reported how pleased everybody at the Medical College was to have Professor Horsford take over Dr. Webster's responsibilities during his absence. The entire faculty was of the opinion that Professor Horsford was eminently qualified to teach chemistry at the Medical College. Consequently they had agreed to the remuneration Professor Horsford requested, ten dollars a lecture plus seventy-five dollars for materials and the services of an assistant. Dr. Bigelow talked about the rise in the salaries of teachers during the past half-century. He remembered hearing Sam Appleton say that when he taught school as a young man, granted he taught in a writing school and not at Harvard, he earned room and board and sixty-seven cents a week in cash. Furthermore, nobody, including Sam Appleton, thought he was underpaid. But that was a long time ago, Dr. Bigelow said reflectively. That was a very long time ago.

At the end of one of his visits, Dr. Bigelow pulled from his pocket an old book on herbs, a book he had used thirty years earlier when he wrote his *American Medical Botany*. He said he knew Dr. Webster's interest in botany continued despite his indifferent success with the plants his daughter Sarah sent up from Fayal. He thought Dr. Webster might find this old book amusing. Dr. Webster had a fine time with that book. He read excerpts from it to everybody who called on him the following week. His visitors left the Leverett Street jail the wiser for knowing that fifteen peony seeds taken in wine helped rid a man of nightmares whereas lettuce taken with a little camphor would relieve him of immoderate lust. On the other hand, nettles had the power to stir lust — as well as to strengthen the limbs and stop whooping cough. It was good to know that a common herb like yarrow could cure falling hair and backaches. But Dr. Webster advised his friends that if they had to get along with only one herb, they had better settle for parsley. He read from Dr. Bigelow's book, "Parsley can provoke urine, relieve dropsy, draw down the menses, bring away afterbirth, ease a cough or a stomach ache, and take the venom out of a spider bite." So what were rubies and diamonds compared to parsley, Dr. Webster would inquire of his visitor as he closed the book.

Then on the last Friday in January, the twenty-sixth, Sheriff Eveleth called at the jail to deliver to Dr. Webster a certified copy of the indictment that the grand jury had returned against him three days earlier. The Sheriff, pleasant and courteous as always, handled his business with careful regard for Dr. Webster's feelings. All the same, the indictment was a jarring thing and Dr. Webster was glad Judge Merrick had forewarned him as to its content. That evening when he was alone, Dr. Webster re-read the indictment by the light of his single candle.

> John W. Webster, with a certain knife which he then and there in his right hand had held, the said George Parkman then and there feloniously, willfully, and of his malice aforethought, did strike, beat, and kick, in and upon the head, breast, back, belly, sides, and other parts of the body of him, the said George Parkman, and did, then and there, feloniously, willfully, and of his malice aforethought, cast and throw the said George Parkman down, unto, and upon the floor, with great force and violence there, giving unto the said George Parkman, then and there, as well as by the beating, striking, of him, the said George Parkman . . .

The description went on and on.

> . . . of which said mortal strokes, wounds and bruises, he, the said George Parkman, then and there instantly died. And so the Jurors aforesaid, upon their oath aforesaid, do say that the said John W. Webster, him, the said George Parkman, in manner and form aforesaid, did kill and murder . . .

Dr. Webster waited until the following morning to write the letter breaking the tie that was his one firm hold on the status, social and academic, that meant so much to him. It was a hard letter to write, even as a gesture. But he had no choice. The letter was addressed to President Sparks. It read:

> DEAR SIR:
> I request you to make known to the Hon'ble and Rev'd Overseers and the Corporation of the University my resignation of the Ewing Professorship with my wishes for the increasing prosperity and usefulness of the institution with which I have so long been connected.
> > I am
> > Most Respectfully yours,
> > JWWEBSTER

CHAPTER IX

The Weeks of Waiting

ON A WINTRY EVENING in February, 1850, the Reverend Francis
Parkman sat alone in the library of the old Parkman mansion
in Bowdoin Square. As he sat at his desk, the firelight outlined
his fine aquiline profile. At the moment he was immersed in
reflecting on the events of the day. He knew there were Bostonians who said his eagerness to have Dr. Webster brought to
justice was unbecoming in a minister of the Gospel. Well, he
forgave them. How could they know what it meant to a man
to have his only living brother murdered by a lifelong friend
beholden to him for many, many kindnesses? He dipped his
pen and under the day's date, February 9, he wrote in the
journal that lay open on his desk.

> This morning at ten o'clock Dr. Webster was arraigned before the
> Supreme Court of the Commonwealth having been indicted for
> the willfull murder of my brother. He pleaded not guilty.

Dr. Webster's arraignment was no surprise to anybody in
Boston. The grand jury returned its verdict on January 26
but a week earlier, on Saturday, the 19th, the *Courier* advised
its readers that "the Grand Jury has not yet announced the results of their investigation but a common report is that a true
bill has been found wherein Professor Webster is charged with
murder." Since everybody knew that both Dr. Webster's coun-

sel and the state preferred an early date, it was no surprise, either, when March 19 was set for the beginning of the trial.

During the five weeks that intervened between his arraignment and March 19, Dr. Webster had even more visitors than usual. Now that the crisis was at hand, all his old friends called at Leverett Street. Professors Felton, Treadwell, and Horsford came over from Cambridge. So did Professor Jeffries Wyman and his brother, Dr. Morrill Wyman. Dr. George Putnam, Charles Curtis, and Charles Cunningham continued to visit regularly. Many of Dr. Webster's visitors came with a gift, a book, perhaps, or a bottle of Madeira. All of them brought him the warmth of their concern and their loyalty. And as the days passed, Ned Sohier often stopped in at the jail for a few minutes' conversation. On those occasions there was rarely any discussion of matters pertaining to the trial. Dr. Webster looked forward to those visits, brief as they were. Ned Sohier's strange clothes and his awkward, slouching stance did not conceal his compassion and his kindness.

James Russell Lowell came frequently, even though his own troubles were heavy. Little Rose had died, little Rose with the beautiful gray eyes. First Blanche and now Rose. And Lowell's mother continued to be a source of heartache. She was always in tears now and nothing they could say or do comforted her. Lowell could not bear to watch his father trying so hard to comfort her. Why did a man like his father, a man who had spent his life in the service of the Lord, have to suffer so in his old age?

And Lowell was increasingly upset over the slavery issue. Daniel Webster had risen in the Senate to speak in support of Henry Clay's compromise bill. Two hours before the Senate convened, the chamber was jammed. Ladies sat on piles of documents in the aisles and even on the steps of the Vice President's rostrum. Dressed in his famous blue coat with the brass buttons, Webster spoke for three hours and eleven minutes. He began, "I speak today not as a Massachusetts man, nor as a northern man, but as an American." In Boston his speech caused a furor among the Free Soilers and the Abolitionists. Daniel Webster was right; he did *not* speak for Massachusetts. Compromise on the slavery issue? Never, Lowell said, and he flayed Webster in the *Standard,* the organ of the Anti-Slavery Society.

Unbeknownst to Dr. Webster another of Lowell's concerns was the Webster family. "Dr. Webster's family needs all our sympathy," he told their friends. The Webster family needed sympathy for many reasons. One reason was their financial situation; they were destitute. Moreover, they were determined to support themselves. Harriet taught music, Marianne gave drawing lessons, and they took in sewing. Despite all their efforts everybody knew that the Webster girls earned barely enough money to pay for the family's food.

When Fanny Longfellow called at Garden Street, she never saw Mrs. Webster; nobody had seen her since the night of Dr. Webster's arrest. But the girls were always home. Fanny said their devotion to their father was a moving thing to see. They spoke of his beautiful letters and of their joy in anticipating the day when he would be home again, working in his garden, reading to them in the evening as he so often did. Understandably the girls were terribly upset by the letters they received offering to reveal the name of Dr. Parkman's murderer —for a price. Gently their friends helped them to see that those letters were cruel ruses and nothing more, that a person with bona fide information about the murderer would approach Mr. Shaw, Dr. Parkman's brother-in-law. The reward he offered was a greater sum than any of the letter writers had asked of the Webster family.

Now and then Fanny prevailed upon Longfellow to visit Dr. Webster. After Clay's speech in February, Dr. Webster talked about the slavery issue. Most of his close friends, the Curtises, the Cunninghams, the Dexters, and the Prescotts, were conservative Whigs. Dr. Webster repeated their comments to Longfellow. Why all this uproar about slavery? Hadn't people in high places always had slaves? What about Madame Vassall over in Christ Church cemetery in Cambridge — Dr. Webster stopped short. Come to think about it, hadn't Madame Vassall once owned Longfellow's home? Hadn't she lived in Craigie House?

Longfellow nodded. Smiling, he said that Craigie House had a history of strange owners, including Thomas Russell who was supposed to be so rich he ate sandwiches made out of two slices of bread and a hundred-dollar bill.

"About Madame Vassall," Dr. Webster persisted. "Was it true she was buried with a slave at her head and another at her feet?"

That was the legend, Longfellow said. As far as he knew there was only one way to find out whether there was any truth in it. With a shovel.

From Longfellow Dr. Webster heard the literary news of Boston. Hawthorne's new novel was to be published in March. *The Scarlet Letter*, he had titled it. Everybody hoped the book would be a success, for Hawthorne was in terrible straits financially. Emerson tried to help him by buying his apples at a dollar a barrel, but a man can't support his family on that. Dana's novel, *Two Years Before the Mast*, was having a big sale ten years after publication. It was the only book in print that offered a description of California to a public very much interested in the gold rush. Dana was jubilant.

During the weeks immediately preceding the trial, Dr. Webster took special pleasure in Charles Cunningham's visits. The fruit Cunningham brought was very welcome, as always, but even more welcome was his news of Fayal. Dr. Webster's eagerness for news of the Dabneys and Fayal was Harriet's approaching marriage, for in April Harriet would go to Fayal to marry

her suitor, Samuel Dabney, her sister Sarah's brother-in-law.
The marriage was a good one; there was no doubt of that. Hard
as it was to have Harriet — a delightful, dependable girl and
lovely to look at — leave Cambridge it was a comfort to think
of her in Fayal with its hedges of beautiful camellia trees and
its fields of blue flax. What wonderful times Harriet and Sarah
would share, Harriet at the piano and Sarah, singing. Both
girls were accomplished musicians. How proud their parents
were when they gave concerts for the Musical Association in
Cambridge. Dr. Webster wondered whether there was a group
in Fayal similar to Cambridge's Musical Association. He must
remember to ask Cunningham about that. His wife had grown
up in Fayal, so she would know.

Then on Monday afternoon, March 18, Dr. Webster's attorneys made another trip to Leverett Street. On this occasion
they were both unusually solemn. Once more Judge Merrick
asked Dr. Webster whether he had anything further to say to
his counsel. Was he absolutely certain that he had omitted
nothing when he described what took place at the Medical
College when Dr. Parkman kept his appointment with Dr. Webster on Friday afternoon, November 23 last? When Dr. Webster, complacent as usual, said he had nothing to add to the
information he had already given, Judge Merrick said that Mr.
Sohier and he wished they could share Dr. Webster's optimism
about the outcome of his trial. They wished Dr. Webster to
know that they would do their very best, but in fairness to him
they must say that they felt his situation was most precarious,
most precarious indeed.

While Judge Merrick spoke, Dr. Webster nodded absently,
as though his attention were elsewhere. When the Judge finished, there was a pause. Then without any reference to his
counsel's comments, Dr. Webster asked about the arrangements
for the trial. He understood it might be held someplace outside the courthouse, someplace bigger. As Judge Merrick an-

swered, he looked incredulous and perplexed. He told Dr. Webster that there had been talk of holding the trial elsewhere but in the end Judge Shaw decided to use the courthouse.

"Judge Shaw." Dr. Webster repeated the Judge's name musingly. His father had known Lemuel Shaw in the days when the Judge was a poverty-stricken young attorney and the Websters lived on Garden Street in the North End. Governor Hutchinson himself lived in no finer house than the Webster mansion. Dr. Webster smiled over the memory of the handsome parquet floors and the beautiful carvings of the house in which he spent his youth. When Judge Merrick and Mr. Sohier rose to leave, his manner was hearty. He offered each of them his hand and urged them both to be of good cheer.

By 1850 Lemuel Shaw had been Chief Justice of the Supreme Judicial Court of Massachusetts for twenty years. While he held that office, his court achieved a reputation for excellence unsurpassed in the history of the American judiciary. When he heard *Commonwealth* v. *Webster,* Judge Shaw was sixty-eight years old, a stocky, powerfully built man with heavy features and a head of iron-gray curly hair. He took his responsibilities with utmost seriousness and he exacted the same standard of professional behavior from the attorneys who appeared in his court. Furthermore, those who out of apathy or ignorance did not measure up to the Judge's expectations were fated to feel the full impact of his wrath, and Judge Shaw's wrath was something to reckon with.

One spring morning when he was a practicing attorney in Boston, Benjamin Butler left his house accompanied by a young pup, a recent acquisition.

"Where are you taking your dog, Ben?" inquired a friend when they met on the Common.

"Over to the courthouse to listen to Judge Shaw so he can learn how to growl," Butler replied.

For all the years he was on the bench, Judge Shaw's growls were a source of sorrow to the attorneys in the Boston area. Judge Emory Washburn was heard to say that as a young man, he would have preferred to lay his head on a railroad track and let a train run over it rather than to argue a case before Judge Shaw. Rufus Choate, a close friend of the Judge's, was one of his warmest admirers. Choate said he felt toward the Judge as a Hindu must feel as he bows to his idol: I know you are ugly but I feel you are great. Yet even Choate felt the Judge's sharp tongue on occasion. Once after he had been severely rebuked by the Judge in open court, Choate whispered to his colleague, "I don't suppose anybody ever thought the Chief Justice was much of a lawyer but nobody can deny he is a man of pleasant manners."

Lemuel Shaw had accepted the appointment as Chief Justice reluctantly at the urging of Daniel Webster. In after years Webster said that if Massachusetts owed him nothing else, she owed him a debt of gratitude for persuading Judge Shaw to accept that appointment, for Shaw was "an honor to the ermine." When Webster first approached him about the appointment, Judge Shaw's answer was an unequivocal "no." The Judge said that after years of struggle, he was at last comfortable financially. Moreover, these were the years he needed money. He had a family to take care of, children to educate. He should give up an income of $20,000 a year for a stipend of $3000? Never. He simply could not afford such a change.

Daniel Webster talked for a very long time. By the end of the afternoon he could barely see Judge Shaw behind the smoke from his thick black cigars. Webster began by recalling Judge Shaw's interest in public service in years past. He reminded the Judge of his service on the School Committee, of his work as a member of the Massachusetts Constitutional Convention, of his terms in the state legislature. Massachusetts needed Judge Shaw as the Chief Justice of her Supreme Judicial Court. Was the Judge prepared to say that money was more important to him than service to his state and to his country?

As he talked, Daniel Webster must have thought of the day when as a young man, he, too, had to make a hard choice involving money. The sons of a farmer who could barely get a living from the rocky New Hampshire soil, Daniel Webster and his brother, Ezekiel, had somehow managed to get through Dartmouth. At one point they took turns teaching at Ezekiel's school in Boston and going to college. Then after Daniel Webster had his legal training, he was offered the clerkship of the State of New Hampshire at a salary of $2000 a year. $2000! Webster's father could scarcely believe the news. How wonderful it was that this had happened to him in his old age when he was sick and alone and very poor. If only Daniel's mother had lived to see this wonderful day!

Webster rode over to see his good friend, Judge Christopher Gore. Jubilant, he told the Judge how much it meant to his father to have a son so honored. As for himself, well, he had not yet quite absorbed the fact that such good fortune had come to him.

Webster paused, waiting for congratulations — that did not come.

When Judge Gore finally spoke, it was to tell Daniel Webster that he must not accept the clerkship. To do so would be to sidetrack his career. Instead, he must go to Boston and open a law office to set out on the career that would be denied him if he became the clerk of the State of New Hampshire. There was no doubt whatsoever, Judge Gore said; Daniel must refuse the clerkship. By the end of the afternoon, Webster had made his choice. He would do as Judge Gore advised.

Far harder than making the decision was breaking the news of it to his father. Seated by the fire, his misshapen hands clasped over the head of the cane between his knees, the old man listened in silence while Webster made his explanation and his plea for understanding. After he finished, there was a long pause. Then slowly the old man raised his head.

"Daniel," he said. "You have fulfilled your mother's prophecy. You have come to nothing."

Daniel Webster went to Boston and rented a law office. His rent was $15 a year and for the first two years he was in practice he did not earn enough to pay it.

During his twenty years as Chief Justice of the Supreme Judicial Court of Massachusetts Judge Shaw established himself as one of the most influential men in the history of the American judiciary. In addition, he made a special place for himself in the hearts of Bostonians. His generosity, his warmth, his fondness for children, all of these attributes endeared him to everybody, with the exception of a number of attorneys who had appeared in his court.

Judge Merrick was fond of telling about the January morning he fell on the ice in front of the courthouse. It was a bad fall and he was relieved to have the courthouse custodian come out to help him over to the Parker House.

After the Judge was stretched out on a couch in his rooms at the Parker House, the custodian sighed with relief. "That was a mighty bad fall, sir," he said. "How thankful you must be that it didn't happen to the Chief Justice."

Judge Merrick said that despite the agony of his broken ribs, he could not keep from laughing.

Associated with Judge Shaw on the Court in 1850 were Theron Metcalf (Brown, 1805), Charles A. Dewey (Williams, 1811), and Samuel Wilde (Dartmouth, 1789). Judge Metcalf, the newest member of the court, was from Dedham where he had once taught school and edited the local newspaper. Judge Shaw and he had served together as representatives to the state legislature. A brilliant man, Judge Metcalf was an odd character. He was fond of saying he was taken to fill a gap on the court "as people take an old hat to stop a window." Judge Dewey, at fifty-seven, was by almost ten years the youngest member of the court. A former state senator and a man who had served as a United States district attorney, Judge Dewey was a gentle, quiet man, the least talkative of the four judges.

The oldest judge on the bench was Samuel Wilde. As a young man Judge Wilde resembled the Duke of Wellington. Now, in March, 1850, he was almost eighty, a stooped, white-haired old gentleman with great bushy gray eyebrows. Like his three associates on the court Judge Wilde was a conservative Whig. He was also a very religious man. A friend told about a Sunday morning when, late for services, he had slipped into the pew in front of the Judge. As he sat down, he heard Judge Wilde intoning, "Lord, teach me the statoots." In the opinion of his colleagues that was the only petition Judge Wilde needed to have granted to make him a perfect judge. Of the Lord's common law he was a thorough master.

On Tuesday, March 19, the judges were in their robes, ready to move toward the courtroom well before nine o'clock. Judge Metcalf stood at the window looking down over the crowd.

"The curiosity of human beings is an awesome thing," he said. "It snowed all day yesterday and again last night. Yet this morning the Square is mobbed with people thirsty for details of a tragedy."

During the silence that followed his comment all four judges stood at the windows, observing the crowd.

Then Judge Wilde said, musingly, "I remember Samuel Parkman from our days at the Hartford Convention. He was a Federalist like Harrison Otis and the rest of us. We weren't so stiff and uncompromising as the Essex County men. Pickering, for example." He turned to Judge Shaw. "Did you know Redford Webster?"

Judge Shaw shook his head. "Just as a passing acquaintance. I happened to be in the courthouse the day his widow came in to execute the instrument that made John Webster executor of his father's estate in her place. Her plea was failing health, poor eyesight in particular. I remember somebody giving her instructions to make her mark in place of her signature."

Judge Wilde went on, speaking slowly and reflectively. "I knew Hannah Webster as well as her husband. They were forthright, hard-working people of little education. John Webster was their only child and how proud they were of him." The Judge nodded over that memory. "How proud they were of his marriage to the daughter of the vice consul at St. Michael in the Azores. I recall their pleasure in his appointment as an editor of some professional journal, I don't remember which one. And when he published a book, a chemistry manual, I think it was, their cup was full to overflowing." He paused. "And now he has come to this, a man indicted for the murder of an old friend. It's God's blessing his parents didn't live to see this day."

Abruptly Judge Shaw turned from the window. His glance fell on the desk he stood beside. He seized a pen, inspected it, and threw it back onto the desk.

"Is there a decent pen in this courthouse this morning?" he thundered at the attendant who waited by the door. "What I want is an old-fashioned *quill* pen. Judge Marshall was right. Steel pens are a barbarous invention and no right-minded man should put his hand on one of them!"

CHAPTER X

The Trial:
The Commonwealth's Case
Against Dr. Webster

THE FIRST DAY

As SHERIFF EVELETH looked out over the crowd that jammed
Court House Square on Tuesday morning, March 19, he knew
his elaborate preparations for the trial were justified. He only
hoped they were adequate. At the moment the doors at the
north end of the courthouse were barred. At the back entrance
a police officer stood guard with orders to admit nobody but
those on official business. The general public could get into
the building through only one entrance, the double doors at the
south end. Furthermore, one of those doors was nailed shut and
the two police officers stationed at the other were instructed
to open it just wide enough to admit one person at a time.

Immediately inside the courthouse the Sheriff had set up a
barricade that ran the length of the corridor paralleling the
front of the building. Nobody could get up the stairs at either
end of the corridor except by way of the gate at the center of
the barricade. The officer stationed at the gate interviewed
all persons admitted by the men at the south entrance. Members
of the bar, judges from other courts, law students, professors,
physicians, the Parkman family, Dr. Webster's relatives, all
these had cards issued by the Sheriff and were promptly admitted to the courtroom. People without cards of admission
were sent up the stairs to the gallery. They were instructed that

after they had watched the proceedings for ten minutes,
they would be asked to leave so that others could have a turn.
Gallery spectators were admitted in groups of about thirty.
When it was time to leave, they were directed down two flights
of stairs to the cellar where another police officer sent them out
onto Court Street.

By and large Sheriff Eveleth was pleased with his plans.
During the twelve days of the trial about 60,000 people
saw some part of the proceedings. To manage these huge
crowds at a time when the total police force of the city of
Boston numbered fifty men was no easy assignment. True,
there were problems. One of them was the noise. With gallery
spectators coming and going at ten-minute intervals and as
many as four hundred others on the floor of the courtroom at
any one time, there was bound to be noise. Because Judge Shaw
had strong feelings about quiet courtrooms, Sheriff Eveleth
frequently found himself adding to the din by shouting for
silence. The men stationed at the barricade had a special problem. They were besieged by people trying to bribe their way
into the courtroom. And by the time the trial was over, those
great, heavy doors at the south entrance were so badly scarred
and splintered they had to be replaced. Perhaps that problem
might have been anticipated since, as the *Courier* put it, "No
criminal trial in the United States nor perhaps in any other
country ever excited so intense an interest as that which com-
menced in the Supreme Court of Massachusetts yesterday."

Despite the predictions to the contrary, the courthouse proved
adequate to the demands of the trial. One explanation was
Sheriff Eveleth's skillful management of the crowds. Another
was the fact that the courtroom was large. As a spectator entered that rectangular, high-ceilinged room, he faced the rear
wall with its three small-paned windows, windows similar to
those in Dr. Webster's quarters at the Medical College. High
up on his left was the gallery. Under the gallery was the pris-

oner's dock, an area surrounded by an iron railing. The Bench was on the spectator's right, directly across from the dock. In front of the Bench, their seats at a much lower level, were places for the clerk of the court and his assistant. To the judges' right, at floor level, was the jury box. Between the Bench and the jury box was the witness stand.

Behind the jury box was the space assigned to newspaper reporters. However, on days when the floor of the courtroom was especially crowded, the press ended up over in the corner under the gallery. The reporters, in the manner of newspaper men, did not suffer in silence. They complained that they couldn't see and they couldn't hear. They predicted the prisoner would die a natural death because of lack of ventilation, a fate they would share. But the unhappiness of the press corps reached its peak over the Sheriff's system for handling their dispatches. The Sheriff decreed that all dispatches were to be passed around the room from police officer to police officer until they reached the messengers waiting at the door. Under this system a dispatch intended for one newspaper often ended up in the office of a competitor, a situation that deeply embittered the gentlemen of the press.

At ten minutes to nine on the morning of March 19 Officer E. J. Jones escorted the defendant into the courtroom. Dr. Webster looked fine, although somewhat overweight since he had gained twenty pounds during his months at the Leverett Street jail. He was neatly dressed in a dark suit and he carried gloves. As he walked toward the dock, he smiled warmly and nodded to his many friends in the crowd. His seat in the dock was an armchair furnished with a cushion of Morocco leather and a heart-shaped "leaf," a device Dr. Webster used when he took notes, something he did frequently throughout the trial.

Exactly at nine o'clock the four judges entered the courtroom. While the clerk called the list of traverse jurors summoned for the trial, Dr. Webster sat motionless, his eyes on the Bench. Above, gallery spectators leaned to have a closer look at him. The floor buzzed with talk. The reporter from the Boston *Journal* was on his feet, trying to sketch the scene.

When the clerk had got through the names of the sixty traverse jurors, about a third of that number approached the Bench, requesting to be excused on the basis of age, ill health, or military service. Judge Shaw listened carefully to each request and excused fourteen.

At twelve minutes to ten Attorney General Clifford rose and addressed the Bench. He moved that a jury be impaneled to try Dr. John W. Webster for the murder of Dr. George Parkman, Dr. Webster having been indicted and arraigned on previous occasions.

Before any juror was sworn, Judge Shaw explained at length the statutes governing the selection of jurors. He said the statutes had been enacted for the purpose of excluding from jury duty persons who had formed or expressed an opinion concerning the case in litigation and persons who held opinions that precluded their finding any defendant guilty of an offense punishable with death. Three jurors were set aside on the basis of their convictions against capital punishment. This was one of the aspects of the trial on which Judge Shaw was to be severely criticized in the months ahead despite the fact that he was implementing statutes that were Massachusetts law.

And so the jury of twelve was impaneled. The following day Attorney General Clifford wrote a letter to a close friend in which he said he was surprised not so much that a jury was impaneled so quickly but that it was possible to get one at all. And the Attorney General had a point. Considering the verdict of the coroner's jury and the indictment, both published, plus the spirited defense of Dr. Webster by his very articulate friends, and the plethora of newspaper articles assessing his responsibility for the murder, it is hard to believe that in March, 1850, there were in Boston twelve men who had not formed an opinion on the issue of Dr. Webster's guilt.

Nevertheless, before eleven o'clock on the first day of the trial, twelve men had found seats in the jury box and the Attorney General had risen to make his opening speech. At forty-one, John H. Clifford was a tall, well-built man with light eyes, light hair, and a touch of elegance in his manner. Appointed Attorney General by Governor Briggs less than a year earlier, he was an ambitious man. Understandably he was not unaware of the implications of the case at hand for his political career. The day after Dr. Webster was sentenced, Mr. Clifford wrote to the Hon. Robert Winthrop, "I cannot help feeling this trial to have been a great crisis in my life. A failure in it would have been fatal. A moderate degree of success would have been scarcely less unfortunate." Consequently, Mr. Clifford had given his opening speech much thought. He decided on a simple, factual presentation that raised no issues for the Defense to respond to. Rather, he would put the Defense in the position of making points for him to reply to in due course. He spoke for almost three hours in a quiet, warm tone. Even the Cambridge *Chronicle* remarked on Mr. Clifford's "kindly forebearance."

In his speech Mr. Clifford advanced two major propositions, first, that Dr. George Parkman had been murdered and, second, that Dr. Webster was the murderer. He reviewed the evidence in support of these propositions. He told the story of Dr. Parkman's disappearance, of the search for him, and of Dr. Webster's arrest following the discoveries of human remains at the Medical College. As he named over the parts of the body found in the vault under Dr. Webster's privy, the Reverend Francis Parkman covered his face with his handkerchief. There was a stir in the gallery when Clifford cited the Prosecution's evidence to prove that Dr. Park-

man's skull had been fractured and that his head went into the
fire with his false teeth still in his mouth.

In conclusion, Mr. Clifford said, "If the jury is satisfied that
Dr. Parkman came to his death in any manner by the hand of
Dr. Webster, then law deems it murder unless there is evidence
arising out of the case, furnished by the prisoner, that satis-
fies the jury that there was such provocation that would reduce
it to either manslaughter or self-defense. There must be
provocation reaching to blows. Words alone, no matter how
irritating or exasperating in nature, are not enough. You
are to consider whether it is satisfactorily shown, beyond reasonable doubt, that Dr. Parkman came to his death by the violent hand of the prisoner at the bar. Then, unless he proves
something satisfactory to your minds which, in law, will reduce
the charge below murder, your verdict must be that the indictment is proved."

At the conclusion of the Attorney General's speech, the Prosecution's junior counsel, Mr. George Bemis, called the first of
the witnesses for the Commonwealth. They were Dr. Parkman's agent, Mr. Kingsley, and Mr. Shaw, his brother-in-law.
Both of them laid groundwork for the Prosecution's case by
telling of their participation in events that began with Dr.
Parkman's disappearance and continued through the discovery
of the remains at the Medical College. What their testimony
did *not* do was to serve the Prosecution's objective of establishing the fact that the crime with which the prisoner was charged,
the murder of Dr. Parkman, had actually been committed.
For both Mr. Kingsley and Mr. Shaw testified that had they not
known Dr. Parkman was missing, they would not have recognized the remains as his. This issue was of primary importance in the case of *Commonwealth* v. *Webster*. When it came
time for his charge to the jury, Judge Shaw gave a new interpretation of the law concerning corpus delicti. For this departure
he was to be roundly censured.

THE SECOND DAY

At the Attorney General's request, and over Mr. Sohier's protest, Judge Shaw permitted the jury to visit the Medical College. Early Tuesday morning, March 20, they made the trip to North Grove Street accompanied by Mr. Sohier, Mr. Bemis, and two police officers. They inspected Dr. Webster's lecture room, his private room, the upper and lower laboratories, and the privy. They looked into the furnace where the bones were found, saw the tea chest that had concealed the torso, went down through the trap door, and made their way along the passageway under the building to the place where Littlefield had knocked a hole into the privy vault. One by one they leaned into the vault to see the place where each piece of the body had been found. By 9:30 they had returned to the courthouse, chilled from their ride through a blustery wind and drifted snow.

The Prosecution's first witness of the morning was Marshal Tukey, who brought with him to the witness stand a wooden model of the Medical College. The model, the work of a Boston carpenter by the name of James Hobbs, could be taken apart to show the layout of the rooms at the College, and the Marshal used it for that purpose during his testimony, the story of his part in the developments that followed the discovery of the remains. At Judge Shaw's request Marshal Tukey approached the Bench with the model and for the next few minutes the four judges devoted themselves to the pleasure of examining it. The Marshal then showed the model to the jurors, who went through the same process. By this time the gallery spectators were so eager for a glimpse that the officer in charge had to warn them repeatedly about the dangers of leaning too far out over the railing. The witness who followed Marshal Tukey was Coroner Jabez Pratt, whose lengthy account of his activities relative to the case added nothing signif-

icant to the Marshal's testimony. In describing Dr. Webster's
behavior when he was shown the pieces of the body on the night
of his arrest, the Coroner said Dr. Webster acted "like a
mad creature," a comment that drew no objection from Dr.
Webster's counsel. This puzzled the attorneys among Dr.
Webster's friends. If the jurors were permitted to think of
Dr. Webster as "mad," how could the Defense convince them
that he was a sensitive, warm man, a fine family man and a fine
neighbor?

Tuesday afternoon Dr. Woodbridge Strong electrified the
crowd with his discussion of the best way to burn up human
flesh. He told about his efforts to dispose of the flesh on the
body of a pirate Marshal Tukey once gave him. Dr. Strong
recommended cutting the flesh off the bones, building a roar-
ing fire with wood — pine kindling is fine; coal is not recommended — and allowing plenty of time to get the job done.
Also, anybody setting out to burn up human flesh should be
warned that the odor is so terrible he is bound to get complaints from his neighbors.

The major witnesses for the Prosecution on Tuesday afternoon were the men who served as the Medical Committee for
the jury of inquest, Dr. Winslow Lewis, Jr., Dr. George H.
Gay, and Dr. James W. Stone. Another important witness was
Dr. Frederick S. Ainsworth, the man responsible for the dissection specimens at the Medical College. Through the
testimony of these witnesses the Prosecution made significant
progress toward proving that the pieces of the body found
at the Medical College belonged to a man of Dr. Parkman's
age, height, and build, and there was no evidence that the remains were part of one of the specimens on which students
practiced dissection.

Dr. Lewis acted as spokesman for the Medical Committee.
To illustrate his testimony he used a life-size drawing of a skeleton made by Dr. Jeffries Wyman, in charge of examining the

bones found at the College. In this drawing different colors were used to show which parts of the body discovered at the Medical College were covered with flesh, which were bones, and which were missing. Dr. Lewis described each piece of the body in detail. He said the thorax had an "opening slightly ragged, about one and a half inches in length, under the left nipple, between the sixth and seventh ribs, extending into the cavity of the chest." During his cross-examination Mr. Sohier asked about the hole in the thorax and inquired as to the amount of blood in a body the size of Dr. Parkman's. He elicited from Dr. Lewis the statement that he "could not say the hole in the left side of the body was a stab" and that a body of the size in question might contain two gallons of blood when alive. After death as much as two quarts of blood might be found in the body cavities. Dr. Webster's attorneys asked these questions of other witnesses. Apparently their objective was to establish the fact that the wound in the chest did not kill Dr. Webster. The evidence the Defense relied on was (1) medical testimony concerning the appearance of the wound as indication that it was inflicted after death and (2) medical testimony to the effect that had Dr. Parkman sustained the wound while he was alive, he would have bled a great deal externally. Subsequently their argument was undermined by the physicians' testimony that Dr. Parkman might have died from that wound and bled internally. Also, the chemists testified that ordinary tap water could be used to remove all traces of even a large quantity of blood. The allegation that Dr. Parkman might have died of a stab wound was embodied in the first count of the indictment.

On Tuesday afternoon the Defense did make gains on the question of the corpus delicti, for both Dr. Lewis and Dr. Stone testified that if they had not known Dr. Parkman was missing, they would not have identified the remains discovered at the Medical College as his.

THE THIRD DAY

On Wednesday four major witnesses testified for the Prosecution, Dr. Oliver Wendell Holmes, Dean of the Medical College, Dr. Charles Jackson, who made the chemical examination of the remains, Dr. Jeffries Wyman, who "catalogued" the bones, and Dr. Nathan Keep, Dr. Parkman's dentist.

Before court was in session that morning, Dr. Jackson had a very brief conversation with Dr. Webster.

"Tell me, what kind of work were you doing the last day you used your laboratory before your arrest?"

Dr. Webster answered immediately. "I was getting ready to do Davy's Experiment. That's why the copper sheathing was there."

"Are you *sure?*" Dr. Jackson asked.

"Positive. Absolutely positive," Dr. Webster said as the judges came in and Dr. Jackson hurried off to join the other witnesses.

This conversation was significant because it undermined Dr. Jackson's faith in Dr. Webster's honesty. Dr. Jackson had examined Dr. Webster's laboratory the day after the latter's arrest. He knew for a certainty that Dr. Webster was working with nitric oxide, a fact that Dr. Webster himself verified when he made his speech to the court at the end of the trial.

When Dr. Holmes took the stand for the Prosecution (he later testified for the Defense) he was in the unenviable position of a dean testifying against one of his own faculty members. On this occasion Dr. Holmes handled himself like a man in a hurry to get through a distasteful duty. A little man — Dr. Holmes was scarcely more than five feet tall — he had a clipped, rapid manner of speaking. In response to Mr. Bemis' questions Dr. Holmes said his lecture room was directly above Dr. Webster's and he had never heard any noise from below, granted Dr. Webster's lectures were over by the time his be-

gan. He expressed the opinion that the person who separated
the body knew something about methods of dissection. He
stated that a hole between the sixth and seventh ribs would
not necessarily cause a great effusion of blood externally. That
would depend on the direction of the wound. In concluding
his brief testimony he said that he was familiar with Dr. Parkman's appearance and that he saw nothing about the remains
"dissimilar from it," a backhanded statement to support the
contention that the corpus delicti was yet to be proved.

In contrast to Dr. Holmes, Dr. Wyman testified at length.
He illustrated his careful testimony with the drawing that
Dr. Lewis had used on a previous day. He said his work had
convinced him that all the bone fragments found in the furnace were parts of the head, face, neck, and feet of the same
body. He found no duplicates among all the bits of bone he
examined. Also, in Dr. Wyman's opinion there was evidence
that the skull had been fractured by "mechanical violence"
before it was put into the fire. While the Bench, the jury, and
the spectators watched in horror, Dr. Wyman opened the box
on the table beside him and lifted out a dozen or so bones.
As he talked, he demonstrated how the bones, burned as
they were, could be fitted together to show the outline of
part of the skull or the face or a foot. There was no doubt that
Dr. Wyman's testimony was damaging to the Defense. At the
same time the fundamental question remained unanswered:
there were pieces of a human skeleton found in the furnace
at the Medical College, but whose skeleton was it?

The Prosecution now produced the witness they relied on
to answer that question with unequivocal proof, Dr. Nathan
Keep, Dr. Parkman's dentist. Dr. Keep, a dark-haired, middle-
aged man, was obviously very nervous as he took the witness
stand. Most people in the courtroom knew that he was deeply
grateful to the Webster family for their many kindnesses to
him when he first arrived in Cambridge, a penniless, friend-

less student. Many knew, also, that he had been Dr. Parkman's dentist for twenty years.

Dr. Keep testified that the first time he saw the teeth found in the furnace, he immediately recognized them as teeth he had made for Dr. Parkman. The circumstances under which he made the teeth had impressed them on his memory.

He went on, "In the autumn of eighteen-forty-six Dr. Parkman approached me about making him new teeth. He wanted the teeth for the ceremonies marking the opening of the new Medical College building and if he couldn't have them by that time, he didn't want them. I determined to get the teeth made for him.

"I started as I always do by making an impression of the patient's jaw in soft wax. I use beeswax. Then I oiled the wax impression and poured liquid plaster into it. The plaster hardens and if the wax impression was made properly, it gives an exact impression of the jaw." Here Dr. Keep opened the box he held and took out a plaster cast. At Mr. Bemis' suggestion he handed the cast up to the judges and then showed it to the jury.

He continued, "Here is the cast from which I made Dr. Parkman's teeth. I poured liquid metal into this mold and made a plate. Before I make the gold plates in which the teeth are set, I make a pair in base metal to make sure there are no defects." Here he held up the mold and pointed to the left side. "The irregularity on the left side of Dr. Parkman's jaw was very great so I made the teeth in three blocks and then joined them to the gold plate. I fasten springs on the sides to enable the patient to open his mouth without fear of dislodging his teeth."

Dr. Keep was in the act of pointing out how the springs worked when the city fire bells rang. A moment later the shouting of fire boys and the grating of engines being dragged along the beach stones was audible in the courtroom.

A young man ran into the courtroom and over to the Attorney General's desk. After a few seconds' conversation the Attorney General was on his feet. He said, "Your Honors, the Tremont House is on fire. I request the Court's permission to remove my effects from my apartment which is in the part of the building in danger from the fire."

Judge Shaw declared a recess. Dr. Holmes and Dr. Wyman looked over at the dock where Dr. Webster was smiling and nodding as he talked with the half-dozen friends gathered around him.

Dr. Holmes shook his head. "That man is either innocent or a consummate actor," he said as Mr. Clifford hurried back into the courtroom.

Now court was in session again and Dr. Keep resumed. If anything, he seemed more nervous than when he first took the stand. Hesitatingly he explained that a short time after Dr. Parkman had his teeth, he complained that he didn't have enough room for his tongue. Since the teeth were already on it, the plate had to be ground down with a very small wheel. He paused and looked expectantly at Mr. Bemis who then handed him one of the blocks of teeth recovered from the furnace.

As he pointed to a place on the teeth, Dr. Keep said, "The marks left by the wheel are still visible." He was suddenly quiet. Then he turned to a box on the table beside him. He found the mold from which he had made Dr. Parkman's teeth. From a second box he took the teeth found in the furnace at the Medical College. Slowly he slipped the pieces of plate and the loose teeth in the mold. They fitted perfectly.

Dr. Keep burst into tears. His sobbing was audible throughout the still courtroom.

It was several moments before Dr. Keep could go on. When he did, he showed the Bench and the jury the writing on the side of the mold into which he had fitted the teeth. It read, *Dr. Parkman, Oct. in 1846.*

According to the *Transcript*'s reporter, it was while Dr. Keep

was showing his mold to the Bench that Dr. Webster revealed
emotion for the first time during the trial. There was a twitch-
ing of his facial muscles as he listened to Dr. Keep's testimony,
now and then darting a glance into the crowd on the floor of
the courtroom.

When court adjourned on Thursday, the Prosecution was
confident that the corpus delicti had been established. Mr.
Merrick and Mr. Bemis were now ready to present their star
witness, Ephraim Littlefield. In the opinion of the reporters
and the lawyers who gathered at the Bell in Hand tavern to discuss the trial, Dr. Webster's fate would be determined by the
Defense's handling of the testimony of the janitor at the Medical College.

THE FOURTH AND FIFTH DAYS

By twenty minutes to nine on Friday morning the gallery
was full and the floor of the courtroom was jammed. Ephraim
Littlefield, free on $2000 bail, began his testimony as soon as
court was in session. He was on the stand all day Friday and
until two o'clock Saturday afternoon when Judge Shaw adjourned court until Monday.

Littlefield was a good-looking man in his thirties. Newspaper accounts of his testimony include references to his dark
curly hair and his fine profile. Apparently he was not one to
play down his appearance, for on Friday morning when he
stepped to the witness stand, he wore a blue frock coat, a blue
silk neck scarf, and a standing white collar. In the opinion of
the reporter for the New York *Evening Post,* Littlefield's demeanor was one of quiet confidence. He spoke clearly and force-
fully, giving his answers "with stress and emphasis." His manner was easy. Frequently he directed his explanations to the
Bench and to the jury. A number of times he turned to Dr.
Webster "as if appealing to the prisoner for confirmation of
the truth of his testimony."

Littlefield began his testimony by stating that he had known Dr. Webster for seven years and Dr. Parkman for twenty. He told of the evening of November 19, a Monday, when Dr. Parkman had visited Dr. Webster to demand payment on a debt. He described Dr. Webster's inquiries about the construction of the dissection room vault earlier on that same day. Was it possible to get a light down there, Dr. Webster had asked. Littlefield said no. A few weeks previously Dr. Ainsworth had let a skull down into the vault to macerate and the rope rotted. Littlefield had tried to retrieve the skull but every time he tried to get a light down there, the foul air put it out.

Littlefield gave almost an hour-by-hour account of his activities at the Medical College beginning with Monday the nineteenth of November. Over and over he stressed the difficulty of getting into Dr. Webster's rooms after the Friday when Dr. Parkman disappeared. He told how he had to pound on Dr. Webster's door when Dr. Samuel Parkman came or Mr. Parkman Blake or the police officers arrived. He said that during the week following Dr. Parkman's disappearance, he could hear water running in Dr. Webster's rooms. He heard it hour after hour and this was something out of the ordinary, for in the past Dr. Webster always complained that the sound of running water annoyed him. He told in detail of his conversation with Dr. Webster in front of the Medical College on Sunday evening, November 23. Mr. Trenholm and he were speculating on what might have happened to Dr. Parkman when Dr. Webster approached them. Something in his manner, in his way of speaking, aroused Littlefield's suspicions. That night he told his wife he "was going to watch every step Dr. Webster took."

He certainly did, and he described Dr. Webster's every step for the jury. It was Tuesday that Dr. Webster gave him the order for the turkey, his first gift from the Doctor in the seven years of their acquaintance. It was Tuesday afternoon, also, when Littlefield lay down in the hall, his cheek pressed against the floor so he could look under Dr. Webster's door. He could see Dr. Webster up as far as his knees, walking back and forth across his laboratory. Littlefield testified that the next day, Wednesday, he felt intense heat through the wall of Dr. Webster's laboratory. He was worried for fear the building would catch fire. Dr. Webster's rooms were locked, and Littlefield told how he got into them by inching his way along the brickwork until he reached the big window that looked into Dr. Webster's lower laboratory. To his surprise there didn't seem to be much fire in the furnace. The soapstone cover on the furnace was covered with pots of minerals with an iron cylinder in the middle of them. Littlefield didn't move anything; Dr. Webster had cautioned him about touching anything except what the Doctor put on a special table to be washed.

Littlefield did look into the two hogsheads where water was stored. One of them was more than half empty. Both of them had been full the previous Friday. Both barrels of kindling had been full on Friday, also, and now the kindling was two-thirds gone. Littlefield found that very puzzling. He testified that it was the next day, Thursday, that he decided to break into the privy vault. He was tired of having everybody tell him that if Dr. Parkman was found anywhere, he would be found in the Medical College, and the only place in the College that had not been searched was Dr. Webster's privy vault. He described the moment when he discovered the remains. "I had difficulty in getting a light into the vault because of the draft. When I finally got it in, I saw the pelvis of a man and two pieces of legs. I was violently agitated."

Both attorneys for the Defense worked on Littlefield during the cross-examination. They challenged him about a change in his statement to the coroner's jury as to the day on which Dr. Webster gave him the order for the turkey. They impugned his morals by questioning him about gambling in Dr.

Webster's rooms. They suggested that his sole interest in the tragedy at the Medical College stemmed from the reward. In answer to questions about the reward Littlefield said stoutly, "I never have made or intend to make any claim for either of the rewards that have been offered." (Perhaps Littlefield changed his mind, or maybe it was a matter of his not being willing to *ask* for the reward. In any event, on Saturday, April 6, Littlefield accepted $3000 from Dr. Parkman's brother-in-law, Robert Gould Shaw.)

Throughout the Defense's rough cross-examination, Littlefield retained his composure. He refused to be confused and neither Mr. Merrick nor Mr. Sohier could budge him; his testimony remained unchanged.

The *Transcript*'s reporter wrote that unless Ephraim Littlefield's testimony was broken down by the Defense, things looked black for the prisoner. Well, the Defense did not break down Littlefield's testimony and things did look black for Dr. Webster on Saturday afternoon as, heavily ironed, he rode back to the Leverett Street jail.

THE SIXTH DAY

On Monday morning, Dr. Webster looked refreshed. He had looked tired on Saturday, and the Boston *Journal* had commented that the prisoner appeared to suffer more from the close confinement of the courtroom than he did from Mr. Littlefield's testimony. The jury looked rested, also. On Sunday they were permitted to go to church twice. In the morning they went to Reverend Mr. Huntingdon's church in Washington Street (Old South) and in the afternoon to Reverend Mr. Beecher's church in Salem Street, both times accompanied by the Sheriff and three police officers. The clergymen were requested to make no allusion to the trial, "not even the most distant," in either their sermons or their prayers.

On Monday the crowd was the smallest of any day of the trial,

for the word was out that the Prosecution planned to devote
the day to an examination of Dr. Webster's financial problems.
As usual there were a number of dignitaries present, among
them John Reed, Lieutenant Governor of Massachusetts.

The Prosecution's first important witness was Seth Pettee, a
discount clerk at the New England Bank. Mr. Pettee explained
that it was his duty to sell tickets of admission to the courses
taught by the seven professors at the Medical College. Each
professor had his own tickets. Early in November Professor
Webster had given Mr. Pettee 100 tickets. To date he had
sold 93. Up to November 23, he had disposed of 55. At $15
each, the amount received for that number of tickets was $825.
After November 23, Mr. Pettee disposed of 38 tickets, some of
them on promissory notes from students, a few of them free.

On November 9 the amount due Professor Webster was $510.
Mr. Pettee testified that he had on hand a note signed by Professor Webster, payable to Dr. Jacob Bigelow. The note was
dated April, 1849. The amount due on it, including interest,
was $234.10. This sum was taken out of the money due Pro-
fessor Webster and he was given a check for the balance of
$275.90. The next division of funds was made on November
14 when Professor Webster received $195 for 13 tickets sold.
The next payment of $30 was on November 16 and another of
$90 on November 23, the day of Dr. Parkman's disappearance.
Mr. Pettee said he handed the check to Professor Webster at
the Medical College that morning.

Mr. Pettee stated that Dr. Parkman called on him on November 12, to ask whether Mr. Pettee had funds due Professor Webster. He returned on the fourteenth and was much annoyed
because Mr. Pettee had paid Professor Webster $195 on that
date and had not retained the money to satisfy part of Professor
Webster's debt to Dr. Parkman. Mr. Pettee pointed out that he
had no control over Professor Webster's funds. At that point
Dr. Parkman stated that he would be obliged to distress Dr.

Webster and his family. "Afterwards he made some remarks
the import of which was that Dr. Webster was not an upright
nor an honest man and he asked me to tell Dr. Webster so."
When Mr. Pettee went to the Medical College on November
23 to pay Dr. Webster $90, he told of Dr. Parkman's visits.
Dr. Webster commented that Dr. Parkman was a curious, rather
nervous man, adding, "You will have no further trouble with
Dr. Parkman for I have settled with him."

The Prosecution's next witness was John B. Dana, cashier of
the Charles River Bank. He testified that he had known Dr.
Webster for twenty years. He gave an accounting of Dr.
Webster's deposits and withdrawals from his account at the
Charles River Bank for the period from November 10
through December 21, 1849. Dr. Webster's balance as of November 23 was $139.16. On November 24 he deposited a check
for $90. Drafts on the account during the first few days in
December left a balance of $68.78 as of December 3.

A trustee-process was served and on December 21, the
balance of $68.78 was paid to the trustee.

The Reverend Francis Parkman then took the stand. In a
high, thin voice he told of the Parkmans' long friendship with
the Webster family. The Websters had been members of the
Reverend Mr. Parkman's church for thirty years. As their
pastor he conducted the funeral service when their little son
died, officiated at their daughter's marriage, and in September
of the present year baptized their first grandchild. Those near
Dr. Webster said that the Reverend Mr. Parkman's reference
to his grandson put him in tears. The Reverend Mr. Parkman stated that Dr. Webster's manner was strange when he
called to tell of his appointment with Dr. Parkman at the Medical College. He expressed no concern over the disappearance
of an old friend who had shown him many kindnesses and
neither did he express sympathy for Dr. Parkman's family. The

Reverend Mr. Parkman testified, also, that on the occasion of that call on Sunday afternoon, November 25, Dr. Webster stated that he had paid Dr. Parkman $483 and "some odd cents" when they met at the Medical College on Friday.

By the end of the afternoon most of the spectators in the courtroom were convinced that Dr. Webster had lied when he said he gave Dr. Parkman money. They felt the testimony of the Prosecution's witnesses had made it painfully clear that Dr. Webster had no money to give anybody. Could he have saved up $483.64 in cash to pay Dr. Parkman? Very, very unlikely. But maybe he had, his friends said, and maybe he could *prove* that he had. After all, the Defense had yet to be heard.

It was also clear to everybody in the courtroom that Dr. Webster was in very low spirits. When the wrist irons were on and Officer Jones led him from the dock, he seemed to stagger. The New York *Herald* reporter wrote in his account of the day's events, "Many a sad eye rested on Dr. Webster. I noticed that no one spoke to him as he left the courtroom."

THE SEVENTH DAY

By the middle of the morning on Tuesday, every attorney in the courtroom was aware of Attorney General Clifford's rationale for the management of the Prosecution at that point. It was this: if it can be proved that a man's behavior reflects awareness of guilt then guilt is proved.

The Prosecution's first witness was Officer Samuel Fuller. It was Fuller who found the torso in the tea chest and he testified about that discovery, describing how the trunk was neck-end up in the tea chest and how it felt when he first put his hand down into the tan bark and found it. At that point in his testimony Fuller took away the newspaper wrapping from the package on the table beside him. It was the tea chest, a wooden box two feet square and eighteen inches deep, painted green. Fuller opened the chest and tilted it so the Bench and the jury could see that three sides of it were stained with blood. He went on to tell about the experiments the police made to find out whether all the pieces of the body could have been put down the privy hole. He said the hole measured 9-¾ inches each way and they could get the pelvis through if they tilted it edgewise, but no matter how they tried, they could not find a way to get the trunk through.

Then Mr. Bemis asked Officer Fuller about his visit to Dr. Webster's home on Sunday morning, November 25. The purpose of the visit was to find out whether Dr. Webster had a copy of the mortgage Dr. Parkman was on his way to the bank to satisfy when Dr. Webster last saw him. Officer Fuller testified that Dr. Webster couldn't find the papers. "He seemed to tremble," Fuller said. "He went back to his account book and turned over the leaves two or three times."

There followed a succession of witnesses who described Dr. Webster as exhibiting behavior unusual for him, behavior that supported the Prosecution's allegation that Dr. Webster was guilty of the murder of Dr. Parkman. The first of these witnesses was Dr. Parkman's nephew, Mr. Samuel Parkman Blake.

SAMUEL PARKMAN BLAKE: *Called on Dr. Webster on the Monday following Dr. Parkman's disappearance. Dr. Webster's manner was stiff. It wanted the cordiality usual with him. When I entered the room, he stood still and waited for me to come to him. He expressed no sympathy and made no inquiry for Dr. Parkman's family. As I left, I heard the door bolted behind me.*

OFFICER STARKWEATHER: *Described Dr. Webster's behavior at the jail the night of his arrest. When Dr. Webster and Stark-*

weather were alone after Mr. Clapp left to find Marshal Tukey and Mr. Parker, Dr. Webster was terribly agitated. He asked Starkweather, "Did they find the whole body?" He took something from his vest pocket and slipped it into his mouth. Then he had a spasm or a fit.

NATHANIEL WATERMAN:

Tin dealer in Cornhill Street. Had known Dr. Webster for twelve years. On November 30, the day of his arrest, Dr. Webster ordered a tin box with straight sides. He specified that the handle should be strong. Mr. Waterman offered to solder the lead on the box after it was packed but Dr. Webster said he would do that himself. He wanted the box by Saturday night.

MRS. BETSY B. COLEMAN:

Dr. Webster called on me to talk about Dr. Parkman's disappearance. I told him I had seen Dr. Parkman pass my house late Thursday afternoon. He asked me two or three times if it wasn't on Friday afternoon that I saw him. I said I was sure it was Thursday. When I saw him to the door, he again asked me if it wasn't Friday afternoon that I saw Dr. Parkman.

JOHN M. CUMMINGS:

Turnkey at the Leverett Street jail. Described Dr. Webster's behavior at the jail immediately after his arrest.

	Didn't hear when he was spoken to. Didn't have the use of his limbs. Sweat rolled off his face, which was very red. Acted very frightened. Grabbed Officer Jones around the neck when they were trying to get him upstairs to go to the Medical College.
GUS ANDREWS:	*Jailer at the Leverett Street jail. Read part of a letter Dr. Webster wrote on Monday, December 3. Dr. Webster had written, "Tell Mama not to open the little bundle I gave her the other day but to keep it just as she received it." (The bundle proved to contain the two notes that Dr. Webster said Dr. Parkman had given him after Dr. Webster paid the $483.64.)*

Next, in a further effort to show consciousness of guilt on Dr. Webster's part, the Prosecution introduced into evidence the three anonymous letters.

Mr. Bemis called Mr. Nathaniel Gould, the official penman of the Medical College. Mr. Gould testified that he was familiar with Dr. Webster's handwriting because every professor at the Medical College was required to sign the College's diplomas and he was in the habit of observing handwriting. He had taught penmanship for fifty years. It was his opinion that Dr. Webster had written all three of the letters in question, the Captain of the Darts letter, postmarked November 26, stating that Dr. Parkman was murdered on Brooklyn Heights, the *Civis* letter, dated November 31, making a number of suggestions relative to the search for Dr. Parkman, and the illegible scrawl known as the East Cambridge letter. The Prosecution's second handwriting expert, George Smith, an engraver, said that in his opinion Dr. Webster wrote the *Civis* letter. About the other two he was uncertain.

It happened that two days later, on Friday morning, March 29, Mr. Sohier received a letter dated March 27, postmarked the twenty-eighth, and signed *Civis*. The writer said that he had written the first *Civis* letter and went on to substantiate his statement with a lengthy discussion of his own handwriting. Although Dr. Webster's counsel were at a loss to explain how he had got the letter written and mailed, they were convinced that he was the author of the second *Civis* letter, as well as the first. The second *Civis* letter was not introduced into evidence by either the Prosecution or the Defense.

After the handwriting experts had testified, Mr. Bemis asked the court's permission to call a witness who had just arrived from Grafton, Massachusetts, a physician who testified that he met Dr. Parkman at the entrance to the Medical College between half-past one and two o'clock on Friday afternoon, November 23.

At that point the Attorney-General rose to state that the evidence for the Prosecution was now complete. The Government rested its case.

CHAPTER XI

The Trial:
The Defense

THE EIGHTH DAY

COURT WAS NOT in session until ten o'clock on Wednesday. The rumor was that the four attorneys were in conference, discussing the anonymous letters. While a crowd waited out on School Street on this fine, springlike morning, Dr. Webster's friends besieged the New York *Herald* reporter. They shoved copies of his paper at him.

How dare he write that Starkweather testified that Dr. Webster said at the jail, "Villain that I am, I am a ruined man!" Starkweather never said any such thing and neither did Dr. Webster! They were all in court, too; they heard the testimony. What did the *Herald* mean by printing a statement like that, a lie that could do much damage to Dr. Webster's defense? Wasn't he having a hard enough time already?

The *Herald* reporter was full of apologies. He felt terrible about that error. He wanted Dr. Webster's friends to know he was the last man in the country to do the poor man any harm. He pulled a copy of the *Courier* from his pocket and said he had written the sentence the way it appeared in that paper. He pointed to the line, "Oh, that villain, I am a ruined man." An editor had changed his meaning entirely. The *Herald* deeply regretted the error and in the next day's issue of the paper would say so.

At ten o'clock Mr. Sohier rose to open for the Defense. He was an accomplished speaker. Many in the courtroom were moved by his beginning reference to other years when both they and he were Dr. Webster's students, years when Dr. Webster had earned the respect of the scientific world as well as the world of his family and his friends. He spoke of all that the defendant had at stake in the trial. He told the jury, "It devolves upon you to say whether Professor Webster shall depart hence to his family and there remain the very center of their affections, the very object of their idolatry, or whether he shall depart hence to the scaffold, leaving to that family a name which, if they could, they would bury in the grave with him. Yes, it does devolve upon you to say whether the fire upon his hearth stone shall burn brightly or whether your breath, Mr. Foreman, when you pronounce the verdict, shall extinguish that fire, caus- ing its ashes to be scattered to the winds to be forgotten out of kindness by his friends, out of mercy by his enemies."

Then Mr. Sohier admonished the jury to examine the evi- dence without prejudice. He said he could not believe that every man in the jury box was entirely free from prejudice. "Am I to forget or to suppose that you have forgotten the ex- citement which existed in this city when it was first bruited abroad that George Parkman was missing? How men left their work? How they clustered together on the exchange, in the workshops, at the corners of the streets, in the porches of the churches? Can you or I forget, if we would, that burst of indignation so creditable to the community but so dangerous to the defendant which took place when it was announced that George Parkman's body had been found in the laboratory of the Medical College?"

With this beginning Mr. Sohier went on to build his de- fense around four major points. First, he discussed the rules of evidence as they applied to the indictment. He discussed at length the legal differentiation between homicide and manslaughter, between malice implied and malice expressed. He emphasized the fact that the Government must prove that Dr. Webster killed Dr. Parkman according to the allegations set forth in the indictment. The Government must prove "killing by the means stated."

Next, he stressed the circumstantial nature of the evidence the Government had presented. That evidence, all of it circumstantial, divided into two categories. The first concerned the corpus delicti, the proposition that Dr. Parkman came to his death violently at the hands of a human being. The second category related to the Government's position that Dr. Webster was that human being. Mr. Sohier reiterated his statement that *all* the Government's evidence was circumstantial. Why does the Prosecution say Dr. Webster murdered Dr. Parkman? Because Dr. Webster was the last person known to have seen Dr. Parkman and if he did not kill Dr. Parkman, the Government is at a loss to know who did! But what if Dr. Parkman left the Medical College after his interview with Dr. Webster? If that fact is established, the chain is broken and the Prosecution's case is in pieces. Mr. Sohier went into the question of the corpus delicti. How did the Government hope to convince the jury that the corpus delicti had been established? By the identification of teeth! But what if it is proved that there is no very great peculiarity about those teeth? In that eventuality the Prosecution's proof of identification is not proof: it is nothing. When the evidence for the Defense was in, the jury would see that the Government had not proved their case beyond a reasonable doubt.

In conclusion Mr. Sohier described Dr. Webster as a man incapable of committing the crime with which he was charged. "He is a person of a mild and amiable disposition, remarkable, even, for kindness to all about him. His temperament is nervous and like all nervous men, though occasionally petulant, he has never been known to be violent, but is, in truth, a man of

constitutional timidity." He went on, "We shall present to you
the entire history of Dr. Webster's conduct from Friday, the
twenty-third of November, up to the night of his arrest, from
which it will appear that his demeanor, his words, and his deeds
were all those of an innocent man. Also, if I mistake not, you
will be satisfied that very little, if any, reliance is to be placed
on the testimony of Ephraim Littlefield."

In the opinion of Dr. Webster's friends, Mr. Sohier had made
an able and eloquent speech that was a fine beginning for the
Defense.

His speech concluded, Mr. Sohier introduced the first of the
sixteen witnesses who testified to Dr. Webster's reputation
among the people of Cambridge, the community where he
lived. Judge Shaw instructed them that they could give
only evidence that related to a general estimate as to the defendant's position in the esteem of his community. Individual
and personal opinions were not competent testimony. Consequently their testimony was brief. The men who testified for
Dr. Webster represented all groups in Cambridge. There was
a sprinkling of men in the trades, but the majority of the witnesses were people of demonstrated achievement and of considerable status in the Boston area, if not throughout the state
of Massachusetts. These included James D. Green, former
mayor of Cambridge, George P. Sanger, assistant district attorney for Suffolk County, Francis Bowen, editor of the *North
American Review,* the Reverend Francis Convers, brother of
Lydia Child, the articulate women's rights advocate, and Robert
Apthorp whose forebears had founded Christ Church in Cambridge. The final witness that afternoon was Joseph T. Buckingham, sometime editor of the Boston *Courier* and the "Mr.
Buckinum" of James Russell Lowell's *The Biglow Papers.*

After Court was adjourned at seven minutes to seven, most
of these men and others gathered around Dr. Webster. The
defendant was in fine spirits, shaking hands all round, telling

everybody how pleased he was with Mr. Sohier's speech. Now that the Defense had the helm, the truth would see them all in safe harbor!

THE NINTH DAY

By nine o'clock on this morning the courtroom was packed. The buzz of conversation was the loudest it had been at any time during the eight days of the trial. There was much speculation as to whether the Defense would continue to do as well as it had done Wednesday. Was it true that Dr. Webster's daughters were to testify today? And President Jared Sparks of Harvard. Was *he* to take the stand, too?

Mr. Sohier called Marianne Webster to the witness stand. At seventeen Marianne was a dark-haired girl with her father's round face. She stood very straight, her pallor accentuated by her plain, dark dress. Her nervousness was apparent to everybody in the room. All the same, she managed the situation with poise and with dignity. She spoke in simple sentences in a straightforward manner. While she gave her account of her father's whereabouts from the day of Dr. Parkman's disappearance until the night of his arrest, the courtroom was very quiet. Even the gallery spectators abstained from their usual fussing and scraping of chairs.

Marianne began, "I am a daughter of Dr. Webster. Father was home to tea Friday night, the twenty-third, a little before six. He took tea at home and remained at home till eight, and then went to a neighbor's house with mother, and sisters, and myself. Father left us at the gate. Mother left with him. We were at a small party. When we came home from the party at half-past twelve, he opened the door for me. We all went upstairs at the same time, about one o'clock. It was Father's custom to breakfast at home but I did not breakfast myself Saturday morning so I did not see him again till a little after one o'clock. He dined at home. I did not see him again till dark.

I was not at home myself that afternoon. I don't remember
the *Transcript* being there. One of the neighbors takes it and
Father sometimes borrows it to read. He was at home that evening and read to us and played whist part of the time. I remember he was at home to tea. Before tea, he came into the
parlor with a book.

"I went to bed at ten. Father was at home then. Sunday
morning I don't remember seeing Father until I saw him at
church, at the College chapel. After church he went for a walk
with Mother and sister and returned to dinner at half-past
twelve. We generally dine at one on Sundays but dined
earlier that day in order that Father might go to Boston to tell
Dr. Francis Parkman about having seen his brother on Friday."

Marianne testified that the family kept a journal so they
could inform the married daughter in Fayal about family activities. She used that journal to refresh her memory in preparation for her testimony. She stated that her father frequently
sent things to Fayal, frequently sent plants put up in air-tight
containers. He planned to send some plants this winter, she
knew, but she did not know whether he had made any preparations yet.

The second Webster daughter to testify was Harriet, two
years younger than Marianne. Harriet also conducted herself
with remarkable poise and control considering the situation and
her youth. She held her handkerchief with hands that trembled, but her high, clear voice was audible throughout the courtroom. Her testimony corroborated her sister's, adding a fact
here and there. The Batchelder family had the party the girls
went to the Friday night of Dr. Parkman's disappearance.
Their parents were at Professor Treadwell's home that evening.
The book Dr. Webster read from on Saturday evening was one
he had purchased that afternoon. It was an illustrated edition
of Milton's *L'Allegro* and *Il Penseroso*.

"On Monday I first saw Father at dinner time. I don't remember seeing him in the afternoon of that day. He was home in the evening. Miss Wells and Judge Fay were there and we played whist. On Tuesday I saw him at dinner. I don't recollect seeing him again until tea. In the evening he read aloud part of the time and part of the time we played whist. On Wednesday I breakfasted with him. He spent the morning in the garden. He was home in the afternoon and in the evening he and my two sisters went into Boston. I did not sit up until they came home."

Throughout his daughters' testimony, Dr. Webster leaned his head on the arm that lay on the railing of the dock. It was when his youngest child, Catharine, took the stand that he seemed barely able to control his emotion. He covered his face with both hands and seemed to crouch in his chair. Catharine was visibly frightened. In a voice barely above a whisper she told how she had accompanied her sister Marianne and her father to a party at Mr. Cunningham's house in Boston on the Wednesday evening before Thanksgiving. They took the eleven o'clock omnibus for Cambridge. While they were waiting at the tollhouse, Catharine noticed a poster offering a reward for the discovery of Dr. Parkman. Marianne called their father's attention to the poster and he read it to them "as it was pasted rather high up." Catharine told about the Sunday when she recollected seeing her father, his shoes in his hand, saying he was going to Boston to see Reverend Mr. Parkman. "I heard his voice in the entry about dark and afterwards saw him in his study between nine and ten o'clock." She testified, also, that she had heard her mother say that her father had brought a bundle home from the College on Friday. When Mr. Clifford rose to object to that testimony, doubtless on the ground that it was hearsay, Catharine looked appealingly at Mr. Sohier, whose smile and nod reassured her.

As Catharine joined her sisters in the area set aside for witnesses, the courtroom grew noisy again. Sheriff Eveleth bawled

for silence as Dr. Winslow Lewis, Jr., took the stand, this time
for the Defense. He was followed by Dr. Gay and Dr. Holmes,
both testifying for the second time also. Their eagerness to
help Dr. Webster was apparent. Dr. Lewis said he had been a
student of Dr. Webster's in the days when Dr. Webster was
the almshouse physician and the Medical College was over on
Mason Street. He testified that he frequently had trouble getting into Dr. Webster's rooms because "Dr. Webster locked his
doors against intrusion." Dr. Holmes' contribution to the Defense was to give it the support of the presence of the Dean of
the Medical School. Otherwise his brief testimony contributed nothing significant. He said there were two leading
authorities on the quantity of blood in the body and gave their
opinions. Whether you could tell when a burned bone was
broken — before or after being burned — depended on the
degree to which it was burned.

The next witness was Dr. Eben Horsford, who testified that
flesh and bone could be readily disposed of if they were immersed in separate kettles of nitric acid, "the bone in one vessel,
the flesh in the other," and the heat just below boiling. Dr.
Horsford had tried the experiment with both beef and human
flesh and he found that human flesh dissolved faster. In three or
four hours the flesh was completely dissolved "and the liquid
perfectly clear."

Then Mr. Sohier called Dr. William T. G. Morton to the
stand. Dr. Morton was a sick man. Nevertheless, he handled
himself with characteristic aplomb. He may have been motivated to make the effort to get to the courthouse not only out
of affection for his old chemistry professor but also because he
welcomed an opportunity to refute the testimony of Dr. Nathan
Keep, a man who had betrayed him, he felt, during his struggle
to prove that it was he and not Dr. Charles Jackson, who was
responsible for demonstrating the value of ether as an anes-
thetic. (Dr. Holmes, that incurable punster, said the credit
could go to ether.)

Dr. Morton was a very strong witness for the Defense. When Mr. Sohier handed him the teeth discovered in the furnace, he said there was nothing about them that made them readily identifiable. He could see where the plate had been ground but it was certainly not unusual for a dentist to grind a plate with a small wheel. Dentists did it every day. As he turned the plaster cast of Dr. Parkman's lower jaw in his hands, he said there was nothing particularly unusual about it, either. "If it were placed among a dozen others I could produce, I would not pick it out as different from the others." Dr. Morton said he could identify individuals among his patients whose lower jaw was as prominent as Dr. Parkman's. He commented that the mold was a mold of the gums with the flesh on, a very different thing from the naked bone. Then, while the whole courtroom watched, breathless, Dr. Morton took half a dozen or so loose teeth from his pocket. He fitted them into the mold of Dr. Parkman's plate and, holding the mold up for all to see, he said that the teeth from his pocket fitted it as well as those found in the furnace at the Medical College. As Dr. Morton left the stand, the hubbub grew to such proportions that again Sheriff Eveleth had to shout for silence.

President Sparks took the stand. Tall and handsome, Dr. Sparks was a kind and sensitive man. It bothered him that by an ironic twist of fate, on the very day of Dr. Webster's arrest he had written to the poor man to tell him his salary would be reduced because the course in freshman chemistry had been assigned to a tutor in mathematics. Dr. Sparks knew first hand what it was to worry about money. Born the illegitimate son of a farm girl, he had somehow managed to get through Harvard. Then, in search of a teaching job he had walked three hundred miles into New York, supporting himself by working as a carpenter as he went from town to town.

President Sparks did what he could for Dr. Webster. He testified that Dr. Webster and he had been intimate friends and neighbors for seventeen years. From his own observation he had never known Dr. Webster to be anything but kind and amiable. In reply to the Attorney General, President Sparks said it was true that since Dr. Webster's arrest there had been reports "affecting his character," but President Sparks had never been able to trace these to any reliable source.

The latter part of the afternoon Mr. Sohier examined seven witnesses, all solid citizens of good reputation, who testified that they had seen Dr. Parkman on Friday afternoon. They saw him at different times in a way that showed him moving across the city.

Mr. Sohier's first witness was Mrs. Philena G. B. Hatch, who had known Dr. Parkman for fourteen years. She testified that she saw him Friday, November 23, on Cambridge Street, between Blossom and North Russell, about ten minutes before two. Mrs. Hatch fixed the day because it was early that afternoon that she walked over to the South End to tell her niece that the latter's mother had arrived from Maine for a visit. It was on her way home that she saw Dr. Parkman. As soon as she entered her house, she went to the kitchen to look at the clock and it was ten or twelve minutes to two.

The next witness was Mr. William V. Thompson, clerk of the Registry of Deeds office in East Cambridge. Mr. Thompson had known Dr. Parkman for ten years and saw him frequently. He met Dr. Parkman in Causeway Street on Friday, November 23, at ten or fifteen minutes after two. There was no doubt that it was Friday, the twenty-third, that he saw Dr. Parkman. Mr. Thompson remembered clearly because that was the day he paid for a new coat, and the day on which he made an abstract of a title for a merchant in India Street.

Mr. Samuel A. Wentworth was a Boston merchant who had known Dr. Parkman for two years. He saw Dr. Parkman in Court Street near Sudbury, opposite Mrs. Kidder's medicine store. It was about half-past two and Dr. Parkman was going toward Bowdoin Square. Just after he passed Mr. Wentworth,

Dr. Parkman suddenly faced halfway around, toward the street. His hands were clasped behind him. He seemed to be looking at the tops of the houses on the other side of the street.

Then Mrs. Sarah Greenough testified. She stated she had known Dr. Parkman for many years, "from early life." On Friday afternoon, November 23, she saw Dr. Parkman in Cambridge Street between Belknap and South Russell, about ten minutes to three. She was certain of the time because she had an engagement for tea at three o'clock at her son's home in Temple Street and she had just looked at her watch. "It wanted ten minutes of three."

Next, Samuel Cleland, who had once been a tenant of Dr. Parkman's, testified that he saw the Doctor on the east side of Washington Street between Milk and Franklin at a quarter past three or a few minutes later on Friday afternoon, November 23. They passed so close they almost touched. There was no doubt whatsoever in his mind; he saw Dr. Parkman between a quarter past three and half-past three on the Friday afternoon in question.

Mrs. Abby B. Rhoades and her daughter, Mary, both testified that they had seen Dr. Parkman in Green Street, Bowdoin Square, about a quarter to five on Friday afternoon, November 23. Mrs. Rhoades could not be mistaken as to the identity of the man she saw; she had known Dr. Parkman for twenty-five years. Mrs. Rhoades and Mary had just been to Mr. Hovey's store in Winter Street where they had bought eleven yards of muslin de laine at twenty cents a yard. Dr. Parkman moved so close to them that Mary had to shift the bundle to avoid bumping him with it.

The testimony of these seven witnesses formed the keystone of the case for the Defense. The Prosecution's cross-examination did not shake them. Mrs. Hatch maintained she was positive of the date on which she saw Dr. Parkman during the week of November 19. She had told her visiting sister about the encounter with Dr. Parkman, referring to him as "Old Chin" in an attempt to bring a smile to the ailing woman. Mr. Thompson stated firmly and at length that there was nothing wrong with either his eyesight or his handwriting. Mr. Cleland informed Mr. Bemis that he had not reported seeing Dr. Parkman to Marshal Tukey because Mr. Knapp, the clerk of the Police Court, told him it wasn't necessary for the reason that Dr. Parkman had been seen in the South End later in the afternoon.

By the end of Thursday afternoon the Defense had called to the witness stand an impressive list of men who swore that Dr. Webster was a kind and gentle human being. His daughters' testimony covering the week following Dr. Parkman's disappearance showed Dr. Webster to be a model family man — at a time when he was alleged to be engaged in the terrible work of destroying Dr. Parkman's body. The Defense's response to Dr. Keep's testimony was Dr. Morton, a well-known Boston figure whose position as an expert in all aspects of dentistry could not be challenged. Finally, seven citizens of good repute, all of whom knew Dr. Parkman, had testified that they had seen him Friday afternoon *after* the hour of his appointment with Dr. Webster at the Medical College.

Mr. Sohier rose to tell the court that the evidence for the Defense was now complete. The Defense rested.

CHAPTER XII

The Trial:
The Summing Up

THE TENTH DAY

As SOON AS court was in session on the morning of the tenth day
of trial, Attorney General Clifford called several rebuttal witnesses. John Sanderson, a policeman at Harvard Square, testified that he had seen Dr. Webster get out of the theater omnibus about ten o'clock one night during the week following Dr.
Parkman's disappearance. He wasn't sure of the night, but he
was positive he saw Dr. Webster. Sanderson was standing close
to the horses, facing in the direction of the passengers when they
alighted. He said none of Dr. Webster's family was with him.
Then the Attorney General examined three dentists, all of
whom testified that a dentist could identify his own work just
as an artist would know a portrait he had painted. In the
opinion of Dr. Webster's friends the testimony of those dentists
did little besides make it clear that the Prosecution felt that
Dr. Morton had been successful in rebutting Dr. Keep's testimony.

Then at twenty minutes past eleven Mr. Merrick rose to
begin the closing argument for the Defense. He spoke for six
and a half hours. Dr. Webster listened with rigid attention and
during the final moments of the speech, perspiration fell from
his forehead in great drops. Mr. Merrick held the interest of
the courtroom spectators from the moment he began to speak.

What he did *not* hold was the good opinion of Dr. Webster's friends. Most of them felt strongly that Mr. Merrick's speech was confused and weak when it was not downright inimical to Dr. Webster's best interests.

Mr. Merrick began well enough. He reminded the jury that, in order to prove the allegations set forth in the indictment, the State must prove the death of Dr. Parkman, must prove Dr. Webster was the person who killed Dr. Parkman and, finally, must prove that Dr. Webster acted with malice. If any of these allegations was not proved, Mr. Merrick said the Government could not claim a conviction. If Dr. Parkman left the building after his interview with Dr. Webster, then the Government's case fails. And that is exactly what the Defense had proved, Mr. Merrick stated. Dr. Parkman left the Medical College after his interview with Dr. Webster and since there was no evidence that they ever met again, there could be no proof that Dr. Parkman came to his death violently and at the hands of Dr. Webster.

Mr. Merrick discussed the question as to whether Dr. Parkman was dead. True, human remains were found at the Medical College and Dr. Parkman had not been seen since November 23, but it did not necessarily follow either that Dr. Parkman was dead or that the remains found at the Medical College were his. Here Mr. Merrick commented on Dr. Wyman's testimony. To the dismay of the friends of the Defense, he said that the Medical Committee's report "creates a strong probability that they were the remains of Dr. Parkman." When he referred to Dr. Keep's testimony and said that it was "more precisely to the point and may perhaps be regarded as more conclusive," they looked at each other in amazement. And what did Mr. Merrick mean by saying that Dr. Morton's testimony was not intended to contradict Dr. Keep's?

To the relief of the Webster sympathizers Mr. Merrick began to discuss the fact that the Government had not established the cause of death. "If the cause of death is unknown, can the Government ask a jury to say that death was the result of violence and crime?" Was the cause of death the fracture of the skull? Or did death result from the wound in the left chest? There was no agreement among the medical men, Mr. Merrick told the jury.

Then Mr. Merrick launched into a consideration of the difference between murder and manslaughter, a major mistake in the opinion of most attorneys in the room. Worst of all he prefaced his comments by saying, "In considering this question I must, for the present, assume that the homicide was committed by the prisoner at the bar." Certainly such an awkward expression could jeopardize his client's best interests! Mr. Merrick went on to talk about malice. He pointed out that the fact that Dr. Webster was poor did not constitute evidence of malice. Here he made another unfortunate statement. He said, "Though Dr. Webster asserts that he made the payment to Dr. Parkman, it must be admitted that we have produced no evidence of the source from whence the money was derived. I am free to admit that it is impossible for him to produce such evidence," Mr. Merrick said — and then maintained that Dr. Webster got the money together by saving it up little by little.

The New York *Herald* reporter leaned over to his counterpart on the Boston *Journal*. "He made a mistake in saying that about not having evidence as to where Webster got the money. Wait till tomorrow. Mr. Clifford will rake open that sore place and make it speak with the voice of thunder."

Mr. Merrick was talking about the relationship between Dr. Parkman and Dr. Webster, describing how feeling might have been roused, how Dr. Webster might have got upset. "If Dr. Webster killed Dr. Parkman, it was in the heat of blood. Then horrified by what he had done, thinking of his family and his position in the community, he did his first act of concealment."

Mr. Merrick told the jury that if the Prosecution had convinced
them that the remains at the Medical College were Dr. Parkman's and that he had met his death at the hands of Dr. Webster, the charge must be manslaughter, not murder.

Now Mr. Merrick began his lengthy and severe attack on
Littlefield. Littlefield's behavior was intelligible only on the
basis that he was motivated by something other than suspicion
of Dr. Webster. If he was so suspicious of Dr. Webster, why
didn't he give the police a hint to make a more thorough search
of Dr. Webster's quarters at the Medical College? And when
he got into Dr. Webster's rooms by crawling along the brickwork the day he was concerned about the heat, why didn't he
investigate the privy? Why didn't he look into the furnace
despite Dr. Webster's instructions not to touch anything except what was on a special table? And why did Littlefield tell
Trenholm to come back later when he knew he would be into
the privy vault in a few more minutes? Wasn't it strange that
he didn't want a witness with him when he found whatever
there was in the privy vault?

In conclusion Mr. Merrick referred to the possibility that an
unknown person had murdered Dr. Parkman and then hidden
his body, or parts of it, in the Medical College. He quoted
Dr. Webster as saying the night of his arrest, "I do not believe
that those are the remains of Dr. Parkman, but I am sure I do
not know how in the world they came to the Medical College."
And that is the Defense on which Dr. Webster rests, Mr. Merrick told the jury. "He cannot tell you how they came there;
he cannot unfold to you the deep mystery of circumstances
which have been made to bear so fearfully against him. But
he calls your attention unceasingly to that secret agency, the
reasonable probability of which the circumstantial evidence
of the Government does not exclude."

That night there was discussion of Mr. Merrick's speech in
Boston and in Cambridge. It was the opinion of many that

Mr. Merrick had seriously weakened the Defense by conceding the possibility of manslaughter. Also Mr. Merrick had erred, they felt, in suggesting a number of possible answers to the question of what happened to Dr. Parkman. At one point he suggested that Dr. Parkman was alive, at another that the remains at the Medical College were his — then that they were not his. If Littlefield might be guilty of the murder, as Mr. Merrick strongly urged, then what about his argument that an unknown third person was responsible for the murder? Wouldn't the jury be likely to construe the presentation of so many alternative solutions, particularly *conflicting* alternative solutions, as evidence of a weak case? Or perhaps a manifestation of counsel's feeling about the case? And Defense counsel's attitude was the source of the trouble in the opinion of many. They shared Fanny Longfellow's opinion that Dr. Webster's attorneys had put no real heart or strength into the Defense. She thought they had simply lost interest in Dr. Webster. There were others who said that Judge Merrick's embarrassment — to use the word on everybody's lips — over Dr. Webster's defense was completely understandable. How can you defend — or respect — a client whose word cannot be relied upon, a man who you *know* is withholding facts that are essential to what you are trying to do for him?

THE ELEVENTH DAY

Saturday morning before court was in session the courtroom buzzed with the rumor that both Mrs. Rhoades and Mr. Cleland had revoked their testimony of Thursday afternoon; they had not seen Dr. Parkman after all. However, all was quiet as Attorney General Clifford began his closing speech for the Prosecution. Immaculately dressed and as controlled as usual, Mr. Clifford spoke from nine o'clock until five with the exception of the hour and a half from two to three-thirty when the court recessed for dinner.

Mr. Clifford began with the customary flourish of compli-
ments for the jury. He continued, "I had, if not an expecta-
tion, at least a hope, that the prisoner could furnish some explanation of the terrible circumstances which have weaved
around him a web that seems to be irresistibly contracting to
his doom. I grieve to say to you that after all that has been said
and done, that hope has been utterly disappointed." He discussed the Defense's evidence concerning Dr. Webster's
reputation, his conduct during the week that intervened between Dr. Parkman's disappearance and Dr. Webster's arrest,
the question of Dr. Webster's habits about locking his laboratory, and finally, counsel's attempts to show that Dr. Parkman
was seen in Boston after two o'clock on Friday, November 23.
Mr. Clifford referred to the Defense's discussion of the legal
difference between a charge of manslaughter and a charge of
murder with a careful reference to Mr. Merrick's admission
that it was possible that Dr. Webster might have been guilty
of Dr. Parkman's death. Then he said, "If you find there was
anything of premeditation with regard to this prisoner, that
ends the inquiry of this case. That fixes it, by all authorities,
to be a case of murder." Moreover, the charge of murder must
stand unless there was provocation on the part of the deceased,
provocation manifest in blows — provocation of language is
not sufficient to change a charge of murder to manslaughter.

Then Mr. Clifford asked the jury whether they had a
reasonable doubt that Dr. Parkman was dead. Could the jury
believe that the solemn rites of religion had been performed
over unknown bones, that others had succeeded to Dr. Parkman's large responsibilities with Dr. Parkman in the land of
the living? He argued that the Defense witnesses who thought
they saw Dr. Parkman were mistaken. More important, the
question of whether those people saw Dr. Parkman was im-
material to the jury's verdict. If the jury was satisfied that Dr.
Parkman's remains were found at the Medical College and that

the evidence connected the prisoner with those remains, then what did it matter whether Dr. Parkman was seen at two o'clock on that day or any other day?

Mr. Clifford reviewed the testimony of the physicians and the dentists, particularly the testimony of Dr. Wyman and Dr. Keep. "If Dr. Wyman had produced Dr. Parkman's right hand with the scar on it which every one of his friends would recognize, the evidence of identity could not be more conclusive." He ridiculed the Defense's suggestion that Dr. Parkman might have been brought, dead, to the Medical College, postulating that Dr. Holmes might have been the murderer. He said that a very great number of things happened to Dr. Parkman on Friday, November 23, if he had an interview with Dr. Webster about 1:30, walked the streets of Boston during the afternoon, and that night was murdered and his body concealed in the Medical College. Mr. Clifford asked the jury to remember that the unknown murderer was a tolerably competent dissector as well as something of a chemist. He labeled as absurd the hypothesis that any third person could have concealed the pieces of the body in the College without the knowledge of Dr. Webster and Mr. Littlefield. As far as Mr. Littlefield's involvement in the situation was concerned, this was another absurdity. If Mr. Littlefield had wanted to dispose of the body, he had access to the receptacle for human remains in the dissecting room. If Ephraim Littlefield had been motivated by thoughts of the reward, would he have destroyed the head and the hands, the parts of the body that made it readily identifiable?

Then Mr. Clifford turned to a consideration of the relationship between Dr. Webster and Dr. Parkman, beginning his remarks with the comment that the Defense counsel had given a good description of that relationship in connection with his proposition that if Dr. Webster did kill Dr. Parkman, it was manslaughter, not murder. Mr. Clifford asked the jury to con-

sider how things stood between Dr. Webster and his creditors
in November, 1849. Financially Dr. Webster was stripped
bare. He had no resources left except his household furniture.
Furthermore, his friends' benevolence and their beneficence
were exhausted.

Here Mr. Clifford referred to his papers. After a detailed
review of Dr. Webster's financial situation, he stated that the
Prosecution contended that Dr. Webster's statement about the
money he paid Dr. Parkman, including the statements written
on the slips of paper found in his pockets at the time of his arrest, were all falsehoods. Important evidence was Dr. Webster's
attempt to conceal the two notes he says Dr. Parkman gave him.
In the letter written to Marianne from the Leverett Street jail
on December 3 he asked her to "tell Mama not to open the little bundle I gave her the other day," a bundle that proved to
contain the two notes in question. Yet Dr. Webster said not a
word about *two* notes when he described his interview with
Dr. Parkman. He says Dr. Parkman took the money from him
and, suddenly turning around, dashed his pen through the
signature on *a* note. Yet here in his possession were *two* notes!

Certainly the prisoner and his counsel could not have been
unmindful of the great importance of showing where the
prisoner got the money he says he paid to Dr. Parkman. "He
has had four months during which he could have summoned
to this court every student who ever paid him a dollar. Yet not
one dollar has been accounted for. We come to the unhappy
conclusion that Dr. Webster had no money to pay Dr. Parkman
and, consequently, was compelled to prepare his statement and
his story in the manner I have indicated." And if he did not
have money to give Dr. Parkman, how did he get possession of
those notes? Never in this world would Dr. Parkman have
willingly given up notes involving money owed not only to
himself but to his friends!

The preparation of his story, the false signatures on the

notes, the anonymous letters, all were evidence of a consciousness of guilt. Add to that Dr. Webster's question to Mr. Starkweather when Dr. Webster and he were alone at the jail. "Did
they find *the whole body?*" the prisoner asked Mr. Starkweather. There spoke the guilty conscience, showing a
knowledge that the body of Dr. Parkman was not an entirety
but separated into fragments.

Have you any doubt from all this evidence that Dr. Webster
had an agency in the death of Dr. Parkman, Mr. Clifford asked
the jury. Could you doubt it for even a moment?

He concluded, "I do feel, gentlemen, that upon you rests a
higher responsibility than ever rested on twelve men in
Massachusetts before. With us throughout the trial have been
newspapermen whose work it is to see that all this mass
of proof, unanswered by any explanation on the part of the
defendant, is carried to many lands to be read, gentlemen, as a
testimonial of the degree of flexibility and firmness which you
shall have exhibited in upholding, supreme and paramount,
the law under which human life claims and enjoys protection
in this commonwealth of Massachusetts since its foundation
by the Pilgrims."

As the Attorney General sat down, the hubbub in the courtroom crescendoed, then quickly subsided as Judge Shaw leaned
toward the prisoner. He spoke slowly in his deep, resonant
voice, "John W. Webster, if you have anything to add to the
arguments urged on your behalf by your counsel, anything
which you deem material to your defense by way of explaining
or qualifying the evidence adduced against you, you are at
liberty now to address it to the jury. I feel bound to say to you,
however, that this is a privilege of which you may avail yourself or not at your own discretion."

Dr. Webster's attorneys knew, of course, that Dr. Webster
would have an opportunity to speak in his own defense before
the jury retired to consider their verdict. In preparation for

this moment they had explained at length that they both felt
it would be unwise for him to speak when Judge Shaw offered
the opportunity. Doubtless one of their reasons was the question of the Chief Justice's attitude toward such action on the
part of the defendant. Thirty years earlier when Judge Shaw
was a delegate to the Massachusetts Constitutional Convention
his one speech was against changing the law so that the accused
had the right to testify on his own behalf. How much had his
opinion changed during the intervening decades? Judge Merrick and Mr. Sohier were so thoroughly convinced of the in-
advisability of Dr. Webster's speaking out in court that they
wrote out their opinions, hoping he would study them during
the long evenings at the Leverett Street jail.

Now every eye in the courtroom was on Dr. Webster. Then
the spectators were thrilled and his attorneys dismayed to see
him rise. He braced his arms against the railing of the dock.
Some said he was trembling so much that he needed the support of the railing to stand. Nevertheless, when he spoke his
voice was clear and his words distinct. While he talked, the
courtroom was very still.

Dr. Webster addressed the Bench and the jury. "May it
please your Honors, I am indeed obliged to you for an opportunity to make a statement. I will not enter into any explanation of the complicated network of circumstances which have
been brought to bear against me. It would require many hours
to do so, but if time were granted me, I could without a doubt
explain away nine-tenths of the circumstances which have been
brought to bear against me and in so doing prove my
innocence.

"Acting on the advice of my counsel, I have heretofore
sealed my lips. They, however, have not seen fit to bring forward the evidence that I prepared for them. Their silence has
militated against me to a very serious degree. Consequently at
this time I am compelled to speak.

"I will allude to only one or two of the subjects which have been unexplained by my counsel. The inference from the sentence in that letter to my daughter which led to the examination of my private papers by the police, was different, very different, from what was intended by me. The explanation of that sentence is as follows.

"I had read in one of the daily prints which were distributed at the prison some of the various fabrications which were made respecting me. One of them was that I had purchased a quantity of oxalic acid. It immediately occurred to me that the very parcel referred to could be produced as evidence in my behalf. For several days Mrs. Webster had reminded me of a want of citric acid and laughed at me when I returned home for forgetting to obtain it. On the very day of my arrest, I stopped at Mr. Thayer's apothecary shop in Bowdoin Square, conversed half an hour on various topics and purchased the citric acid. I carried it home and placed it in my wife's hands, saying, 'There is your acid.' I reasoned that the possession of that acid would show it was not oxalic and hence the request about the bundle had no connection with the notes.

"Mr. Cunningham was at my house when the officers came to examine my papers. They broke open a trunk, examined it, and left. Afterwards Mr. Cunningham opened that trunk, and in looking over the papers, found the notes. Thinking the officers might come again, he laid them in sight and made a memorandum about his finding them in the presence of a witness.

"In regard to the nitrate of copper I want to state that either during the lecture preceding my arrest or the one before that, I had occasion to do experiments concerning changes in color in gases. I prepared a large quantity of nitric oxide gas. I did it by placing bits of copper in a two-gallon jug of nitric acid. After it stands a few hours, nitric acid becomes colorless. During my lecture I added oxygen to the jug and the gas became

bright orange in color. When exposed to oxygen, blood is
changed from dark venous blood to florid red. And so I might
go on to explain how many circumstances, described in testimony against me, occurred.

"My very calmness has been brought against me. My trust
has been in my God! I have been advised by my counsel to remain as calm as possible. The money I paid to Dr. Parkman I
laid by from day to day in the little trunk in my home, but no
one saw me. That is the truth but I cannot prove it.

"The following will serve to give the jury an idea as to the
perversions, as I call them, that have been brought forth against
me.

"Every day from the Friday of the disappearance to the following Friday, I was never absent from my home after nine
o'clock at night. Mr. Sanderson is mistaken when he says he
saw me get out of the theatre omnibus about ten o'clock one
night during the week following Dr. Parkman's disappearance. On Wednesday, for example, I went to Munroe's
bookshop and bought a copy of Humboldt's late work. When
I got to Mr. Cunningham's, I found I had left my book at Brigham's. The book was found at Brigham's so I can prove where
I was on Wednesday early evening. Not always, but on most
evenings and on most days I can prove where I was. I will not
detain the court by detailing them."

Dr. Webster sat down but immediately rose again.

"If the Court will allow me to say one word more, I have
felt more distressed by the anonymous letters than by almost
anything else. And I call upon my God to witness while I pos-
itively declare, I never wrote them! My counsel has received
this very day a letter from this very *Civis*. If he is present and
has a spark of humanity, I call upon him to come forward and
acknowledge it!"

Dr. Webster's eyes searched the courtroom. The spectators
sat in frozen stillness. There was barely a sound in the room.
For a moment all life seemed in abeyance.

Dr. Webster repeated his plea. "If he is here, I call upon him to come forward and acknowledge his letters now!"

There was no answer.

When Dr. Webster sat down, Judge Shaw released the tension in the room by declaring a brief recess. The speculation among the spectators was that he would decide to adjourn court since it was already five o'clock. It would take two or three hours anyway for the charge to the jury. Certainly Judge Shaw wouldn't start at this time of day at the end of a long week.

But the spectators guessed wrong. Judge Shaw declared court in session again and it was obvious that he meant to speak. It was also obvious that he was upset. His emotion was apparent in a certain tremulous quality in his voice, in the way he stumbled for a word here and there. Addressing the jury, he was saying, "We feel unwilling, notwithstanding the lateness of the hour, painful, responsible, laborious as it is, not to go on with the cause that you may proceed to consider your verdict.

"The principles of law for which the court is responsible are few, plain, and simple. It will be my duty to consider the rules of law, rather than make an examination of the evidence itself.

"This, gentlemen, is a case in which a person suddenly disappeared, in which evidence has been laid before you to show that he was deprived of life at or about a particular time, under such circumstances as to lead to a strong belief that some person or other has killed him. Now this is to be proved by circumstantial evidence. It would be injurious to the best interests of society to have it so ordered that circumstantial proof cannot avail in such situations. Circumstantial evidence is founded on experience and obvious facts, and coincidences establishing a connection between the known and proved facts, and the facts sought to be proved."

At the conclusion of a discussion of the rules of evidence the Chief Justice asked a rhetorical question. "Then what is necessary to be proved? In the first place it is necessary to establish the corpus delicti, or the offense charged, that the death was effected by violence and that circumstances are such as to exclude accident or suicide. Also, the general rule is that no man shall be held responsible for crime, in any form, until it has been substantially set out in some charge. Therefore, consider the indictment. In the opinion of this court, the indictment is satisfactory."

As Judge Shaw made that statement, the attorneys in the courtroom exchanged glances. Here was a blow to the Defense.

Judge Shaw went on, "Is the crime proved?" He discussed Defense's allegation that Dr. Parkman was seen in Boston after two o'clock on Friday, November 23, 1849, the so-called Parkman alibi. Was Dr. Parkman seen? If he was, that would be a circumstance inconsistent with the allegation that he was last seen entering the Medical College. He told the jury, "When there is a conflict, the conclusion best supported by evidence is the one that stands." He continued, "Gentlemen, perhaps it is somewhat peculiar to our own country that when a great event of this kind arises, the whole community are at once resolved into a body of inquirers. Everybody tells everybody else whom he has seen and what he has seen. Dr. Parkman was a well-known person in Boston. If he was in Cambridge, Court, and Washington streets on Friday afternoon after his interview at the Medical College, would there or would there not have been a great variety of people who would have confirmed the fact that he was seen in those areas? Judge for yourselves."

Again there were glances exchanged among the attorneys. Rufus Choate leaned closer to Franklin Dexter. "Well, there goes another plank out of the raft the Defense sails on."

The Chief Justice addressed himself to the question of the remains. Were those Dr. Parkman's remains that were found at the Medical College? "It is sometimes said by Judges that a jury ought never to convict in a capital case unless the dead body is found. That as a general proposition is true. It some-times happens, however, that the dead body cannot be found even though proof of death is clear, for example a murder at sea when the body is thrown overboard." He discussed the medical testimony. The physicians had established the fact that the pieces were parts of one body and that the remains were not those of a subject used for anatomical dissection. He went on to Dr. Keep's testimony. "You are to determine on the basis of the testimony whether those were Dr. Parkman's teeth and whether they belonged to the same body as the other remains. If so, it has a strong tendency to a proof of death by violence and that the corpus delicti is established."

Again, many raised eyebrows in the courtroom. Mr. Dana whispered to Mr. Loring, "We have just had a new interpreta-tion of the rules of evidence as they relate to the corpus delicti."

"They'll hang him," Loring said.

"Why shouldn't they? He's guilty," Dana whispered back.

The Chief Justice was saying, "With regard to the conduct of the defendant at the time of the arrest and since, it strikes me that not much can be drawn from it. Such are the various temperaments of people, so rare is the occurrence of an arrest for this crime, who can say how a man ought to behave?"

After explaining that unless there was sufficient proof of mitigating circumstances, the crime would be murder, not manslaughter, Judge Shaw instructed the jury concerning character witnesses. "Where it is a question of a great and atrocious crime, so unusual, so out of the ordinary course of things, a man may have been influenced by facts and circum-stances so different, so unique as to make evidences of character far less valuable than such evaluations can be in the case of lesser crimes. Against facts strongly proved, character cannot avail. A person charged with such an atrocious crime as this ought to prove his character by very strong evidence to make it counterbalance strong proof on the other side."

Longfellow looked puzzled. "The burden of proof is on the defendant?" he asked.

Sumner did not reply to Longfellow's inquiry. He was intent on watching the Chief Justice. Judge Shaw's emotion was increasingly apparent. Now he had paused. Would he be able to get through this charge to the jury?

Judge Shaw began again, his voice uneven. "Gentlemen, we commend this case to your serious consideration. Weigh it under the rules of law. And, gentlemen, when it is said that it is possible to err, that is true. It is nothing more than to say that we are human. All we can hope to do — you in your department, we in ours — is to exercise the best faculties of our minds, to give all the weight to the evidence which it deserves, to weigh carefully on both sides. Should we come to a result which at some future time may be proved to be erroneous, a consciousness that we have done our duty will sustain us. I commend this cause to your consideration."

Immediately after Judge Shaw completed his charge, the jury rose in the solemn silence of the courtroom. Mr. Brewster, the foreman, led them toward the jury room.

Then Chief Justice Shaw recessed the court and the Bench retired.

Officer Jones moved toward the prisoner's dock.

CHAPTER XIII

The Trial:
The Verdict

ON WEDNESDAY, APRIL 3, one of the jurors, Mr. Albert Day, wrote a letter to the *Daily Evening Transcript* in which he described what happened in the jury room of the courthouse on the night of March 30, 1850.

The men were locked into the high-ceilinged room with its dark wainscoting at five minutes before eight o'clock. All of them were upset. For more than half an hour they stood in groups, discussing the evidence. "Was there nothing more that could be said in Dr. Webster's defense?" they asked each other. Was this all the evidence — the *only* evidence — on which they were asked to reach a verdict of Not Guilty?

Then the foreman asked them to take their seats. They had a duty to perform, and painful as it might prove to be, they must fulfill their obligation.

Reluctantly the men found their places at the big square table.

They began their deliberations with a prayer for guidance and for the blessings of the Almighty for the prisoner and his afflicted family.

They went over all the evidence. Each of them examined the papers on the table. First, the notes Dr. Webster said Dr. Parkman had given him. In the opinion of all of them there was no reasonable doubt that the signature scrawled across them was in Dr. Webster's handwriting, not Dr. Parkman's. There were the anonymous letters, the report from the Medical Committee, Dr. Wyman's catalogue of the bones, Dr. Webster's bankbook. There was a whole mound of papers.

In about an hour and a half the jury decided that their responsibility was to answer three major questions. They voted on each question separately.

The first question was: Are the remains of a human body found at the Medical College on November 30, 1849, those of the late George Parkman?

When a vote was taken on this question, there was immediate unanimous agreement.

The second question: Did Dr. George Parkman come to his death by the hands of Dr. John W. Webster at the Medical College on November 23, 1849?

There was discussion of this question, but eventually all twelve men voted in the affirmative.

The third question: Is Dr. John W. Webster guilty of the willful murder of Dr. George Parkman as set forth in the indictment?

At that point Mr. Greene, the Boston bookseller who was a close friend of the Websters', cried out, "Can't we stop here? Can't the law be vindicated and justice satisfied if we stop here? Must we take the life of this man?"

While the jury deliberated, a crowd of about two hundred waited. It was a clear, cold night with a full moon and knots of men stood on the courthouse steps discussing the trial.

"Well, Judge Shaw made law tonight," Rufus Choate said. "Beginning tonight all that's required to establish the corpus delicti is a reasonable certainty. No longer is it necessary to prove by direct evidence or actual inspection of the body. That's a major change, I must say."

"And a change that makes the difference between life and death for Dr. Webster, unless I'm much mistaken," Franklin

Dexter said. "And what do you think of Judge Shaw's instructions to the jury to *weigh* the evidence? Obviously the fact that the evidence must be weighed carries with it the assertion that there is doubt. Under these circumstances the existence of doubt always meant acquittal in the past."

"I was not impressed by the precedents Judge Shaw cited, but that's the Chief Justice for you. With him it's the principle that's important, not precedent," Choate said. He added, "Did you notice that in his closing argument, Merrick said Webster's fatal mistake was his decision to conceal the body? If Merrick had based his case on that point — if Webster would have allowed it — in my opinion the verdict would have been different from the one we are about to hear."

"And in my opinion another major mistake was Merrick's decision to argue for a verdict of manslaughter when his client denied any knowledge whatsoever of how the deceased — was he Dr. Parkman? — came to his death," Dexter commented.

A dozen or so reporters and a number of others, Dana, Sumner, and Charles Loring among them, went down to the Bell in Hand. The old tavern, owned originally by Jeremy Wilson, a retired town crier, had stood on Washington Street for half a century. After an hour's discussion of the Webster tragedy, Dana looked around the room in which they stood, at the collection of old theater bills and Hogarth prints on the dark wooden walls.

"It was better in the old days," he said. "I thought about that when the Maxwell youngster testified that Littlefield gave him a message from John Webster to take up to the Parkmans'. When this tavern was built, boys spent their time catching flabby flounders and spiney sculpins of the Neck. In those days there was no occasion to send a boy across the city with a message from a murderer."

Tim worked the beer pumps again and handed around foaming dark pewter mugs.

"I couldn't tell you about the prevalence of murderers fifty years ago although I'll wager there were a few around then, too," Loring said. "But I do know a few things that convince me that the past wasn't so perfect either. I remember Sam Breck's stories of what it was like around here in the late nineties, which was about when this tavern was built. I remember he said he went to a writing school down near the old State House. The town whipping post, painted red, was right under the windows of the school and now and then a huge wooden cart came over to it from the jail on Court Street. Often women were dragged from the cart, tied to the post, and given thirty or forty lashes on their bare backs. Up in the school the teaching came to a standstill because nobody could hear anything above the screams of the women and the uproar of the mob that had gathered to watch the whipping. So I repeat, in my opinion there's much evidence to show that it wasn't all beer and skittles fifty years ago, either."

"But there was much *more* beer and skittles then," Dana persisted. "And since we are arguing beer and skittles, remember the town dinners we used to have? Remember the big celebration for Lafayette when the whole town turned out to welcome him in such generous warm-hearted fashion? Why are there no town dinners anymore, no expression of the civic pride, no — "

Sumner pulled at Dana's sleeve and indicated the watch he held. "We'd better be getting back. It's hard to believe that jury will be out very long and we've been here more than an hour."

About half an hour after they were back on the courthouse steps, the crowd closest to the doors began to move toward the courtroom. The word spread that the jury had sent word to the Chief Justice that they were ready to return their verdict. Inside, a hush pervaded the room as the announcement was made that the jury had agreed. Even from the densely packed gallery there was scarcely a sound.

At twelve minutes to eleven Dr. Webster was led to the dock. He was pale but he was composed. Afterward Officer Jones commented on Dr. Webster's command of himself while the two waited to be summoned back to the courtroom. He said that hard as it was to believe, just as they were to leave for the courtroom to hear the verdict, Dr. Webster said to him, "Tell Parker to send me over some of his best turkey tomorrow, will you, and a handful of cigars, too."

Exactly five minutes after Dr. Webster was in the dock, the jury filed in. They walked slowly and they looked very solemn. There was strain in their faces, in the way they held themselves once they were seated in the jury box.

As the clerk rose to speak, the room was still.

"Gentlemen of the jury, have you agreed on a verdict?" the clerk asked.

"We have," several of the jury replied.

"Who shall speak for you, gentlemen?"

"The foreman."

Then the clerk turned toward the prisoner. "John W. Webster, hold up your right hand. Foreman, look upon the prisoner. What say you, Mr. Foreman? Is John W. Webster, the prisoner at the bar, guilty or not guilty?"

"Guilty!"

As he heard the verdict, Dr. Webster's hand dropped to his side, his eyes closed, and he fell back to his chair, his face buried in his hands. Judge Merrick went to his side. Dr. Webster made no response to Judge Merrick's whispered words. For five minutes he sat as one stunned. The only sign that he was conscious were his tears. Many people in that room were crying. If the Chief Justice was not actually in tears, he was deeply moved. After the verdict Attorney General Clifford approached the Bench to ask that the Chief Justice commend the jury before he dismissed them, but the Chief Justice shook his head.

For moments no one seemed willing to move, to break the

silence that lay over the room. Then the Chief Justice dismissed the jury, remanded the prisoner to jail, and declared court adjourned until Monday morning. The spectators began to leave, but Dr. Webster sat stock-still, as though he were paralyzed.

Then abruptly he jumped to his feet. "Why are you keeping me here to be stared at?" he cried at Officer Jones. "Why don't you take me back to Leverett Street?"

Immediately Officer Jones slipped the wrist irons on and Dr. Webster and he hurried down the stairs to the waiting carriage.

When it was apparent that the verdict would not be handed down until late, the Websters' friends made the decision not to carry the bitter news to Cambridge that night. Accordingly, shortly after nine o'clock on Sunday morning Mrs. Prescott Sr., Mrs. Webster's half-sister, drove slowly up Garden Street. The Websters were watching for her, and the very slowness with which her carriage moved confirmed their deepest fears. When they saw her face as she stood in the doorway, they knew the truth. People on their way to church told how they heard Marianne's screams as they passed the house.

It was Mrs. Prescott who stayed with the family on Monday through those terrible hours when they knew Dr. Webster was awaiting sentence. Dr. Webster was in court at eight minutes to nine o'clock. Anticipating a great crowd the Sheriff had ordered him brought to the courthouse much earlier than usual. This order proved a very wise one, for long before nine o'clock Court House Square was jammed. The crowd was bigger than it was on the first day of the trial.

Dr. Webster came into court followed by a police officer who held his hands out to the prisoner's back, ready to supply support if it was needed. But Dr. Webster managed without that help. His step was almost as firm as usual. Once he was in the dock, he took no notice of the teeming crowd in the courthouse. His eyes were shut and his lips moved as though he were praying.

When the judges came in, Judge Richard Fletcher was with them. A member of the Supreme Judicial Court of the Commonwealth, Judge Fletcher had been occupied with official duties elsewhere. It was in his court that Dr. Webster was arraigned in January.

Court was declared in session and the Attorney General rose.

"Your Honors, the prisoner at the bar was indicted by the grand jury for the crime of willful murder. On that indictment the prisoner was arraigned and pleaded 'not guilty.' Every aid has been rendered him by counsel in his defense that could be rendered. The jury have found him guilty of the charge. It now becomes my most painful duty to move that the sentence which the law of the Commonwealth affixes to this offense be passed upon this prisoner."

The clerk then addressed the prisoner. "John W. Webster, have you anything to say why sentence of death should not be pronounced upon you according to law?"

Dr. Webster rose. Placing his hands against the railing in front of the dock, he seemed about to speak. Instead, he bowed to the Bench and sat down.

Chief Justice Shaw began to speak. He spoke for fifteen minutes. Several times he paused when his emotion made it impossible to continue. Those near him said that there were moments when it was impossible to say who was the more upset, the man on whom sentence was being passed or the man whose responsibility it was to pass that sentence. The Chief Justice said in conclusion, "And now nothing remains but the solemn duty of pronouncing the sentence which the law affixes to the crime of murder, of which you stand convicted."

At this point the Bench, the jury, and everybody else in the courtroom rose.

"Which sentence is that you, John W. Webster, be removed

from this place and detained in close custody in the prison of this county and thence taken, at such time as the Executive Government of this Commonwealth may by their warrant appoint, to the place of execution, and there be hung by the neck until you are dead. And may God in His infinite goodness have mercy on your soul!"

As the Chief Justice concluded the sentence, Dr. Webster slumped down into his chair, covered his face with his handkerchief, and burst into sobs that were audible throughout the courtroom.

Judge Shaw ordered the prisoner removed and declared court adjourned.

Dr. Webster was unable to walk. After he staggered two or three steps, two police officers took him by the arms and helped him out of the courtroom and down the stairs to the carriage.

As the prisoner and the police officers emerged from the courthouse, the cry went up, "There he is! There he is!" Dr. Webster was aware suddenly of the huge crowd gathered in Court House Square and he made a rush for the carriage. As he got in, two little boys standing near the horses called out, "Good-bye, John. Good-bye, John!"

CHAPTER XIV

A Fair Trial?

"DR. WEBSTER is innocent! Dr. Parkman's body has been found! Dr. Webster is innocent!"

The rumor electrified Boston. Once more people left their homes and their shops and gathered on street corners to discuss the murder.

Who had found the body? Where? When? Were they *sure* it was Dr. Parkman?

This was the story. About noon that Saturday two little boys came running up the East Cambridge road as hard as they could go. Their eyes as big as saucers, they told the men at the hay scales that they had found Dr. Parkman's body in the old East Cambridge firehouse. He didn't have any clothes on. He was thin and bony and — and somebody had been cutting at him.

"It was horrible!" The boys burst into tears.

The three men at the hay scales shook their heads. "It can't be," they said. "It simply can't be."

"It is *so* Dr. Parkman!" the boys screamed at them. "We know it's Dr. Parkman!"

The men took off down the East Cambridge road at a run.

But it wasn't Dr. Parkman. A medical student came forward with the explanation. He had got hold of the unclaimed body of an inmate of the East Cambridge House of Correction and

had hidden it in the old East Cambridge firehouse, long abandoned. In his free time he went out there to practice dissection.

The furor over the boys' discovery subsided quickly, but the
incident served to heighten the wave of sympathy for Dr. Webster that spread throughout New England, and indeed the
whole country, after he was sentenced. It was a cruel fate that
dangled vindication within a man's reach only to snatch it
away, leaving him to face the gallows. Maybe Dr. Webster *was*
responsible for Dr. Parkman's death — and most people believed he was guilty — but to *hang* him! That was going too
far!

Furthermore, many were convinced that Dr. Webster's mind
was affected. Consider that incident with Professor Wyman.
Certainly nothing the Prosecution introduced throughout
the whole trial was more damaging to the Defense than
Professor Wyman's testimony about his study of the bits of
bone found in the furnace. It was his testimony that established
the link between the pieces of the body found in the privy vault
and Dr. Parkman, the missing man, for the drawing that Professor Wyman projected from his study of the bones matched
all too well Dr. Keep's cast of Dr. Parkman's lower jaw.

Yet right after Professor Wyman had given that testimony,
Dr. Webster called to him as he passed the prisoner's dock.

"Say, Wyman, that drawing is a fine piece of work! Shouldn't
we have it for the College?" He sounded pleased and excited.

Would a *sane* man have said a thing like that? Would he
have expressed pleasure *in the very testimony that might
hang him?* Certainly not.

And would a *sane* man have attempted to shake hands with a
man at the very place and time he was on trial for the murder
of that man's brother?

Everybody in Boston knew of the Reverend Mr. Parkman's
intense bitterness over his brother's murder. There were

those who said he was "pretty savage for a clergyman," as Fanny
Longfellow put it, but most people thought his feelings were
readily understandable and totally justified. In any event, the
Reverend Mr. Parkman attended every session of the trial and
his bitterness was apparent to everybody in the courtroom.
With one exception. Dr. Webster alone appeared incapable
of assessing the Reverend Mr. Parkman's feelings toward him.
Could any man in his right mind have thought that the Reverend Mr. Parkman would accept the hand Dr. Webster offered
from the prisoner's dock immediately after the Reverend Mr.
Parkman had testified about Dr. Webster's Sunday afternoon
call, the occasion on which Dr. Webster revealed that it was he
with whom Dr. Parkman had his Friday afternoon appointment?

The medical men agreed that in those instances Dr. Webster had indeed exhibited irrational behavior. They agreed,
also, that Dr. Webster had always been a highly excitable
man and very quick to anger. Dr. Blatchford recalled the
time he happened into the barbershop while Dr. Webster
was being shaved. He said to the barber, "Well, this is the
first time I ever saw a man shaving a monkey!" That innocu-
ous comment so enraged Dr. Webster that he seized a knife
and had to be restrained from stabbing Dr. Blatchford. And
Dr. Jarvis told of a summer afternoon years earlier when Dr.
Webster and the other men at the College were making sport
of knocking off each other's tall hats with their canes. Dr.
Webster grew very excited. He lashed about with his cane
and struck Dr. Jarvis on the arm with a blow of such force that
it would have been fatal had he sustained it on his head.

Old Dr. Bigelow commented that under the circumstances,
Dr. Parkman's lifelong interest in the treatment of the insane
was ironic. As a young man just back from Paris, where he had
studied under the great Dr. Philippe Pinel, Dr. Parkman made a
survey in an effort to determine how many insane there were

in Massachusetts. He sent out letters to postmen, clergymen, and physicians, the first survey of its kind in Massachusetts Dr. Bigelow thought. The old man shook his head. The present situation was doubly ironic when you considered that at the time of his disappearance, it was George Parkman who was alleged to be suffering from mental aberration.

Dr. Ware added that there was further irony in the fact that during the last years of his life, Dr. Parkman had had a special interest in the *criminally* insane.

Dr. Bigelow nodded. He talked again of Dr. Parkman's great admiration for Dr. Pinel. In fact, a month or two before his death he had published a biographical sketch of Dr. Pinel in the *Boston Medical Surgical Journal.* Dr. Bigelow smiled, recalling Dr. Parkman's favorite story about the great man.

On some occasion Dr. Pinel was approached by a pompous literary critic, a very religious gentleman who felt that Dr. Pinel's humane treatment of the insane was a blasphemous attempt to deny the will of God.

"Dr. Pinel," he said, "I am writing an encyclopedia of atheists and I intend to find a place in it worthy of you."

Dr. Pinel bowed. "My work on lunatics and idiots is in process — "

Whatever they thought on the subject of his sanity, Dr. Webster's friends were loyal. On Sunday morning, an hour or so after word of the verdict had reached Mrs. Webster and the girls, they received a letter expressing sympathy and avowing continued friendship, a letter written by Edward Everett and signed by Cambridge's leading families. Among the signatures were those of President Sparks, Judge Fay, Andrews Norton, and Henry Longfellow. Many others, like John Sibley, Harvard's librarian, sent in notes and cards.

Two days after Dr. Webster was sentenced, William Appleton received a letter from Franklin Dexter, written from Beverly, suggesting that Appleton approach the Websters' friends for money for them. It was common knowledge that Mrs. Webster and the girls were in dire financial straits.

William Appleton was already at work on such a project when he received that letter. The entry in his journal made on April 2 reads, "Went to Cambridge to see Mr. Everett and Mr. Cushing as to raising some money for Mrs. Webster and daughters."

During the weeks immediately following the sentencing, the country-wide sympathy for Dr. Webster took the form of virulent attacks on Judge Shaw. A Philadelphia paper compared Dr. Webster's sentence to the burning of the witches and head-lined the article, "Judicial Murder in Boston."

In New York the Judge was castigated in a pamphlet written by a Member of the Legal Profession who was Oakey A. Hall, one day to be mayor of New York under Boss Tweed.

"It is scarcely credible that Judge Shaw could have given utterance to the language published in his charge to the jury. From the beginning to the end, it is but an argument against the prisoner," wrote the Member of the Legal Profession. He was amazed that "a judge exists capable of such a performance in the high noon of the 19th century of Christ and in the heart of the Commonwealth of Massachusetts." He called upon the Governor "not in the name of Massachusetts alone but in the name of the whole nation to stand forth in the defense of the common law of the common land . . . Let not this case stand as a precedent upon the record of our country's jurisprudence." He concluded, "We do not hesitate to declare that to find a parallel for such an unscrupulous prostitution of dignity, such an unblushing betrayal of the sanctity of the judicial office, we must go back to the days of Jeffries."

Nearer home, another pamphlet written by the eccentric Boston attorney, Lysander Spooner, gave comfort to Dr. Webster's friends. According to Mr. Spooner, "Dr. Webster was not tried by a legal jury but by a jury packed by the Court

either with a view to a more easy conviction than could otherwise be obtained or with a view to a conviction which otherwise could not be obtained at all." Spooner argued vehemently
that by excluding three persons from the jury on the basis of
their opposition to capital punishment, Judge Shaw had denied
Dr. Webster his right to be tried by a jury drawn from the
mass of the people. "In no event, and for no reason whatsoever,
can the jury be packed in the manner it was done in Dr. Webster's case *for that is destroying the trial by jury itself,*" wrote
Lysander Spooner. "In Dr. Webster's case three persons, equal
to one fourth of the jury, were excluded from the panel on
account of their opposition to the death penalty. Thus one
fourth of 'the country' were virtually disfranchised of their
constitutional right to be heard both on the question of the
guilt and the question of the punishment of one of their fellow
men. Will so large a portion of the community acquiesce
in such a disfranchisement?"

The Massachusetts periodical *The Monthly Law Reporter*
was also among the publications that printed articles critical
of Judge Shaw. In its May issue the *Reporter*'s subscribers
read, "We cannot escape the thought that Professor Webster
had been tried before the bar of public opinion and that it was
the strength of the public conviction of his guilt rather than
the perfectness of the case against him which secured the verdict . . . The government fortified itself by a stealthy and in-
quisitional process worthy of Louis XI . . . The Attorney
General pressed before the jury numerous facts and circumstances which might properly enough have great weight upon
public opinion but which clearly do not constitute evidence
upon which a man is capitally convicted." In the opinion of the
writer, "the embarrassment of the counsel for the defense more
than anything else tended to injure the prisoner's case with the
public and the jury."

There were many who were sharply critical of Judge Merrick and Mr. Sohier. One of their colleagues at the bar was heard to say that whatever the professional strengths and personal merits of Merrick and Sohier, if both those gentlemen lived to be as old as Methuselah, never again would either of them be retained by a citizen facing a murder charge.

Over at the Harvard Law School, Joel Parker thought otherwise. In his opinion Dr. Webster was defended by able counsel and from him that was high praise. Judge Parker was interested in other aspects of the case. The question of the kind of evidence from which malice is to be implied, for example. If it was only necessary for the Goverment to show that Dr. Parkman came to his death at the hands of Dr. Webster in order to make a prima facie case of willful murder through the implication of malice, that was one thing. But if malice is to be implied only from a voluntary and intentional killing, that is something else. In other words, if express malice is not shown, from what kind of evidence is malice to be implied so that the charge of murder is to be regarded as proved, prima facie, at least?

Physicians as well as attorneys had much to say about the trial. In its April tenth issue, published eight days after Dr. Webster was sentenced, the *Boston Medical and Surgical Journal* carried on article in which Dr. A. C. Castle of New York attacked the testimony of both Professor Wyman and Dr. Keep. Dr. Castle's article made it clear that whatever his competence in evaluating medical testimony, he had a confused picture of the construction of the Medical College building on North Grove Street and erroneous information as to some of the events that led up to the murder. He wrote of Littlefield's "digging a hole in the sink" and after reference to Littlefield's trouble with stifling and suffocating gases, raised question as to how his candle "burned vividly in this hole of non-combustion sufficiently brilliant to enable him to discover the remains of a human being." The facts were that Littlefield had no occa-

sion to dig a hole in any sink and that it was his efforts to get
a light down into the dissecting room vault — not the privy
vault — that were defeated by the gases.

The following issue of the *Journal* included a peppery reply
to Dr. Castle's article which was signed, "A Medical Witness."
The Medical Witness was none other than the Dean of the
Medical College, Dr. Oliver Wendell Holmes.

"Mr. Editor," wrote A Medical Witness, "let me advise those
who live at a distance from the scene of this dreadful murder
not to meddle with facts they have but a very imperfect knowledge of. They do not help Dr. Webster's case by their lucubra-
tions but only make it worse. Dr. Webster has friends here
who will do all for him that it is in their power to do, and everyone would be delighted to learn any fact that would tend to
mitigate the crime of which he is convicted. This I believe is
the general wish of all the medical witnesses who were anxious
that evidence should be discovered that would exculpate him
from the dreadful charge made against him."

Was Dr. Webster's trial a fair trial? Or had the Commonwealth of Massachusetts spent eleven days and almost $3000
on a trial that would be a blemish on the record of a court as
highly regarded as the United States Supreme Court itself —
to say nothing of the terrible consequences for Dr. Webster!
Had Dr. Webster suffered grievous injustice in Judge Shaw's
court? That question was a popular topic of conversation
throughout the country in the spring of 1850. In Cambridge
Dr. Webster's friends talked of little else during those first
weeks after the trial.

"Was there enough evidence to justify a *legal* conviction?"
the Cambridge *Chronicle* asked editorially.

Certainly not, Dr. Webster's friends answered. The jury
should not have bowed to Judge Shaw's charge, a "hanging
charge" if ever there was one. John Adams had said it was not

only a juror's right but his obligation to act on his own convictions when those convictions ran counter to the court's instruction. Alexander Hamilton had said specifically that in a criminal case a jury was bound to acquit if they were convinced that the court's direction to them was wrong.

Dr. Webster was deeply moved by his friends' loyalty. What more did a man need when he was sustained by his family's love and the loyalty of his friends? In good spirits again he set to work on an appeal to Governor Briggs. He felt confident that the Governor would look kindly on his petition. The eleventh child of a blacksmith, Governor Briggs knew firsthand what poverty can mean to a man with a family. Furthermore, the Governor was a very religious man and a just man.

In his petition, carefully written in his own hand, Dr. Webster declared that he was entirely innocent of this awful crime and that he had never entertained any but the kindest feelings toward Dr. Parkman. Never had he felt any inducement to injure, in any way, a man whom he had numbered among his best friends.

He wrote, "To Him who seeth in secret, and before Whom I may ere long be called to appear, would I appeal for the truth of what I now declare, as also for the truth of the solemn declaration that I had no agency in placing the remains of a human body in or under my rooms in the Medical College or do I know by whom they were so placed."

While Dr. Webster was at work on his petition for a full pardon, his attorneys were preparing to petition for a writ of error on the bases that the court by which Dr. Webster was tried did not have jurisdiction over "either the cause or the person" of the defendant and that neither the judgment rendered nor the sentence pronounced was in conformity with the laws of Massachusetts. Dr. Webster knew about his attorneys' petition but he was pleased that at last he had spoken out for

himself. He was sorry he had not published the declaration of
innocence he had written shortly after his arrest. He had made
a mistake when he accepted his counsel's recommendation
to keep silent. He said as much in his petition to the Governor.

As the days passed, Dr. Webster turned more and more to the
pleasures he had enjoyed over the years. Food had always been
a source of both pleasure and consolation for him. Now he
enjoyed in a special way the treats the girls brought over from
Cambridge, the custard tarts, the brown bread with raisins.
He looked over each piece of fruit Charles Cunningham
brought him, commenting on the size of the oranges, the texture and the flavor of the peaches. When Ned Sohier asked
what he could do, Dr. Webster suggested a supply of his favorite cigars. The messages he sent over to Parker's grew longer
and more frequent. He counted it as one of his blessings
that he did not have to survive on the food the Commonwealth
of Massachusetts provided for the jail inmates at a weekly per
capita outlay of sixty-three cents.

And Dr. Webster hungered, also, for news of Boston. Ned
Sohier stopped in to see him often now. The sight of him in
his funny-looking cap and his green eyeshade always lifted
Dr. Webster's spirits. And Sohier was always good for a story
or two about what was going on around the courthouse. On
one of his visits he reported that Herman Melville was in Boston, and the rumor around town was that he had come to borrow money from Judge Shaw to buy himself an old farmhouse
up around Pittsfield. Handy thing, having a father-in-law with
plenty of money. Melville was halfway through a novel about
whaling days in New England. He said he felt like a frigate
crowded with a thousand souls. There was a lot of writing going on around Pittsfield this spring, Sohier commented. Holmes
was up at his farm, working on a poem for the Phi Beta Kappa
meeting at Yale in August.

And it was Ned Sohier who supplied Dr. Webster with an

eyewitness account of Daniel Webster's arrival in Boston the last of April. Benjamin Curtis met him at the station and they rode over to the Revere House in an open carriage. Bowdoin Square was crowded that day, Sohier said, but the next day when Webster made a speech from the steps of the hotel, it was packed solid. Webster looked fine in his blue coat with the brass buttons. He sounded fine, too. Maybe he could deliver Massachusetts to the Whigs after all, James Russell Lowell and his crowd to the contrary.

In May Dr. Webster read the announcement of Catherine Bigelow's marriage to Francis Parkman, the Reverend Dr. Parkman's son. He understood young Parkman was having less trouble with his eyes these days, which was splendid. That boy had had more than his share of health problems. Dr. Webster remembered Catherine Bigelow as a tall, willowy child, a great favorite of her father's. He thought then of his own marriage on a May afternoon thirty-two years earlier, May 16 it was. The day was fine and there was never a lovelier setting for a wedding than his father-in-law's home, a handsome old house, its Spanish garden fragrant with roses and lemon trees. That year he spent in the Azores was a time in his life when the future looked as sunny as the mornings he spent collecting the mineral specimens he wrote about in his first book.

By chance — or so he thought at first — Mr. Prescott came to see him on the afternoon he was ruminating about St. Michael — Mr. Prescott, the one man in Boston who knew the island as well as he. Indeed, many an afternoon they had spent together, exploring the island's ruined monasteries and its ancient castellated Spanish houses. Mr. Prescott's readers wondered how he could write about Spain so vividly when he had never been there. Well, Dr. Webster could have told them. It was the year he, too, spent on St. Michael, at his grandfather Hickling's house in Ponta Delgada, the very house where Dr. Webster was married.

After they had talked awhile about the old days, it was apparent that Mr. Prescott had called at Leverett Street for a purpose. He had come to tell Dr. Webster that he was leaving for England, sailing from New York on May 22. He said he would be away until autumn. When they parted, Mr. Prescott straining to see Dr. Webster in the shadowy cell, neither of them said what both were thinking — that it was possible, if not probable, they would never meet again on earth.

Perhaps it was no coincidence that Dr. Webster talked much more freely than usual when Dr. Putnam called on him the morning of May 23, the day after Mr. Prescott had sailed for England. Since the trial Dr. Putnam had made a practice of stopping at the jail for short visits two or three times a week. On the twenty-third he stayed until they brought Dr. Webster's dinner over from Parker's. When he left the jail, he walked slowly up Belknap Street and down across the Common, thinking. When he was opposite West Street, he saw a hearse turning into Tremont. It was followed by the Parkman carriage. Then he remembered Dr. Peabody's telling him that on Thursday, May 23, Dr. Parkman's body was to be moved from the vault under Trinity to the family plot at Mt. Auburn. Hat in hand, Dr. Putnam stood looking after the carriage as it followed the hearse along Tremont Street.

Throughout June Dr. Putnam visited Dr. Webster daily. Every morning they worked over large sheets of foolscap, writing and rewriting, talking endlessly. Toward the end of the month Judge Merrick joined them occasionally. More often it was Ned Sohier who took part in their discussions. It was he who brought Dr. Webster the news that the petition for a writ of error had been denied. Dr. Webster gave no outward sign of being upset. He was still confident that things would turn out well for him. His family said he was as cheerful as always. He wanted to hear all about the girls' activities, their gardening and their sewing. Were they keeping up with their music? He looked at Marianne over his glasses. Was she taking proper

care of her cello now that he was not at home to keep an eye
on it — and her?

In June Dr. Webster read in the *Transcript* that Rufus Choate
was going to England for a vacation. Rufus Choate, who always said a lawyer's vacation was the time between the question he put to a witness and the latter's answer. Choate was a
fixture around Boston: he was always in town. Three or four
times a week you met him on Court Street or saw him emerging
from the Bell in Hand or some other tavern. When he was
trying a case, Boston was invariably inundated with stories of
his courtroom antics. To have him away, even temporarily,
made it seem that one of the town's most solid supports had
worked loose. Choate never came over to the Leverett Street
jail to visit. Nevertheless, sitting alone in his cell, thinking
back over all the years he had known Rufus Choate, Dr. Webster felt a sense of loss.

Then at the very end of the month the most appalling rumors
about Dr. Webster began to circulate in Boston. His Cambridge friends were incensed. Nonsense. Idle talk. Gossip.
Those rumors simply were not true.

CHAPTER XV

The Committee on Pardons

THE RUMORS were true.

On July 2 Dr. Putnam delivered to the Governor a second petition from Dr. Webster. The brief document read as follows:

> John White Webster, a convict under sentence of death in Boston jail, in behalf of himself and of his wife and his children, respectfully petitions that the sentence awarded against him by the law may be commuted to such other less horrible and ignominious punishment as your honorable body may mercifully decree.
>
> Your petitioner fully admits that he was tried before a fair and impartial tribunal, and that, under the law, as it exists, his jury composed as it was of honorable and high-minded men, could have returned no verdict other than they did. But he respectfully reminds your honorable body that the two great moral ingredients of the crime of murder, malice and premeditation, have never been found against him by a jury, but have been necessarily inferred by the arbitrary rules of the law from certain general facts which your petitioner will not deny, but the extenuating details of which no man, in your prisoner's situation, can ever possess legal evidence to prove. These details your petitioner has confided to the friend who presents his petition, with authority to state them to your honorable body, in the hope that you will find therein reason to extend to your petitioner and his family that mercy of which the law has made you the dispensers.
>
> J. W. WEBSTER

Boston, June, 1850

At noon on the same day on which he delivered the petition to the Governor, Dr. Putnam appeared before the Committee on Pardons at his own request. The Lieutenant Governor, John Reed, was the chairman. The four other members were the Honorable Samuel Wood, the Honorable Charles M. Owen, John Tenney, a Boston merchant, and Dr. Luther Bell, retired superintendent of the McLean Asylum and a close friend of the Governor.

The July morning was hot and the courthouse windows were open. When Dr. Putnam rose to speak, the sounds of Boston were audible in the chamber where the committee met, snatches of conversation from passersby, the squawks of the parrots owned by the silversmiths across the way, the hammering from Frost's carriage shop. On this occasion Dr. Putnam showed far more feeling than was ever apparent in his very intellectual sermons. His hands grasping the back of a chair, he told the men at the long oval table that he appeared before them not as an advocate but as a man expressing his own beliefs. Speaking with great solemnity he said it was his deep conviction that the homicide of which Dr. Webster was guilty took place in a moment of passion and under great provocation.

As he looked from one to the other of the five committee members, Dr. Putnam said he firmly believed there was no premeditation on Dr. Webster's part and no murderous intent. Although Dr. Webster was guilty of homicide, he had not committed a crime for which death was the punishment under the usual interpretation of the law in Massachusetts. Dr. Putnam took papers from an inner pocket to give the committee a statement of the facts concerning Dr. Parkman's death from Dr. Webster's own lips. But first, he wished to explain how Dr. Webster came to make the statement that Dr. Putnam would shortly read.

Dr. Putnam began by saying that he had known Dr. Webster only slightly before the trial. However, when Dr. Webster asked that Dr. Putnam serve as his spiritual adviser, Dr. Putnam felt he had received a request no clergyman had a right to refuse.

"I had followed the reports of the trial and I believed the verdict to be a just one. I was of the opinion that the sentence passed upon Dr. Webster should be carried into execution. I felt that Dr. Webster was guilty despite his pleas of innocence. However, I did not make any attempt to draw a confession from him during the first weeks that I visited him. I did not lead him to commit himself one way or the other on the question of his guilt or innocence. I carefully avoided any remark or inquiry that might tempt him to make a false declaration. He seemed to understand me and neither denied nor declared his guilt. I expected he would finally be induced to communicate to me whatever he knew about the disappearance of Dr. Parkman and about the remains found at the College. But I was in no hurry about this. I thought I should be more likely to obtain from him the exact truth by waiting till a favorable time. Accordingly, it was my object for the first weeks to become acquainted with him, to win his confidence and attachment by attention and sympathy and to give him the spiritual guidance suited to his situation."

Here Dr. Putnam paused while a wagon rattled over the beach stones of School Street.

Then he told the committee that on the way over to the jail on Friday, May 23, he decided that the time had come to demand a full statement of the facts from Dr. Webster. Consequently, as soon as he entered Dr. Webster's cell, he said he had something of extreme importance to discuss. He asked Dr. Webster to listen to what he had to say until he had finished and not to interrupt.

He began by saying that during the past weeks Dr. Webster must have felt, as Dr. Putnam did, that there was one barrier between them, one point on which they did not understand each other. It was Dr. Putnam's conviction that this barrier went far to negate the satisfaction and the profit that Dr. Webster had a right to expect from their discussions.

"I said that he must certainly have some knowledge respecting the fate of Dr. Parkman which he had not shared with me and that the unshared secret must be an oppressive and intolerable burden to him. I told him the time had come when he ought to share that secret with someone. Under the circumstances I felt I was that person. I pointed out that hitherto I had scrupulously foreborne to press him on this point. I urged it now only because it would be for his relief and peace of mind. Furthermore, by this time he must feel he owed me the truth. I told him he need not fear to tell me the whole truth for I was not there to reproach him nor to judge him but to try to comfort him in his distress and to help him make peace with God. I told him I wanted to assist him to live while he lived and to die when he should die with the humility of a sinner, the firmness of a man, and the hope of a Christian. I told him it was my conviction that if I were to be of any real service to him, there must be truth and true relations between us."

Dr. Putnam said he cautioned Dr. Webster not to answer hastily and not to speak till he was prepared to tell the whole and absolute truth. Perhaps Dr. Webster wished to take a day or two to consider whether he wanted to take Dr. Putnam's advice about making a full disclosure.

Dr. Webster shook his head. He seemed very moved. He said, "I am ready to tell you all. It will be a great relief to me."

Dr. Putnam gestured toward the papers on the table. He said that it was at this point that Dr. Webster began the description of the circumstances surrounding Dr. Parkman's death contained in the statement Dr. Putnam had brought to the committee. He added that he questioned Dr. Webster closely during his narrative of the events that took place at the Medical College on the afternoon of November 23 and that Dr. Webster answered all questions readily and with every appearance of honesty.

Also, Dr. Putnam felt it was important for the committee to bear in mind that when Dr. Webster gave the information embodied in his statement, his petition for a full pardon was in the Governor's hands. Dr. Webster was well aware that his family and his friends were making every effort to find facts to support that petition. Dr. Putnam was convinced beyond any doubt that when Dr. Webster made his confession, he had no thought of making changes in his petition to the Governor. Also, in the course of telling his story he showed considerable anxiety for fear Dr. Putnam might have to testify against him if he were granted a new trial. The petition for a writ of error that his attorneys had filed in May was still pending.

"If there is a new trial, won't you be summoned and compelled to reveal all I have told you?" Dr. Webster asked apprehensively.

Dr. Putnam answered that while Dr. Webster lived, Dr. Putnam would not disclose his revelations without his consent. If Dr. Putnam survived Dr. Webster, Dr. Webster must leave this matter to Dr. Putnam's discretion. Dr. Putnam was certain it never crossed Dr. Webster's mind that his statement might be used to his own advantage. "He seemed to me to make his disclosures simply because he was unwilling to deny my earnest request and wished to manifest his confidence in me."

In Dr. Putnam's opinion all this was evidence that confirmed his conviction that Dr. Webster spoke the truth in the document Dr. Putnam would now read to the committee.

"On Tuesday, November 20, I asked Littlefield to deliver a note to Dr. Parkman, a note he apparently gave to the Maxwell boy to take over to Walnut Street. The note was unsealed. I wrote to ask Dr. Parkman to call on me on Friday, November 23, after my lecture.

"Of late Dr. Parkman had pressed me hard for the money I owed him. He had threatened to sue me and to drive me from my position on the College faculty if I did not pay him. In the note I only asked for a conference. I did not say what I would do or could do about paying my debt. My objective in asking for the appointment was to gain at least a few days' respite from the very disagreeable and alarming threats to which I was daily subjected by him. I did not expect to pay him on Friday. My plan was to explain my financial difficulties and to apologize for conduct of mine that had offended him. I knew he was upset because I had offered Mr. Robert Shaw my mineral cabinet as security for a loan I desperately needed, property Dr. Parkman looked upon as already mortgaged to him. I meant to throw myself on Dr. Parkman's mercy, to beg for further time to repay my debt for the sake of my family. I meant to make as good promises to him as I had any hope of keeping.

"The note was dispatched on Tuesday and I did not hear from Dr. Parkman that day or the next. On Thursday I learned he had been looking for me in Cambridge. I was afraid he had either forgotten the appointment or did not mean to keep it. Consequently I called at his home Friday morning to remind him that I hoped to see him at the College at half-past one that afternoon. I did not stop to talk with him then because I expected the conversation to be a long one and I had my lecture to prepare for. Also, I did not want to get involved in an upsetting conversation when I had a lecture ahead of me. Dr. Parkman agreed to call on me as I requested.

"When he came into my lecture room, I was busy removing equipment from my lecture table to the upper laboratory at the rear of my lecture room.

"Walking rapidly, as was his custom, he followed me into the laboratory.

" 'Are you ready for me?' he demanded. 'Have you got the money?'

"I replied, 'No, Dr. Parkman,' and I began to explain my situation.

"But Dr. Parkman would not hear me. He called me a liar and a scoundrel and heaped on me the most opprobrious epithets and taunts. As he shouted at me, he drew from his pocket

the two notes for the money I owed him and an old letter from
Dr. Hosack, a letter in which Dr. Hosack congratulated Dr.
Parkman on getting me appointed as a professor of chemistry
on the Medical College faculty.

" 'I got you into your position and now I will get you out of
it!' Dr. Parkman thundered at me.

"I cannot tell how long the torrent of threats and invectives
continued. I cannot begin to recall all that Dr. Parkman said to
me in those moments. At first I kept trying to interject comments in the hope of pacifying him, but I could not stop him
and soon my own anger was aroused. At that point I felt nothing
but the sting of his words. I grew furious.

"While he was speaking and gesturing in the most violent
and menacing manner — thrusting Dr. Hosack's letter in my
face — I seized whatever thing was nearest me, a stick of wood,
and dealt him a blow with all the force that passion could sum-
mon. I did not know, nor think, nor care where I should hit
him, nor how hard, nor what the effect should be.

"He fell to the floor instantly. He did not move.

"I knelt beside him. Blood flowed from his mouth and I got
a sponge and wiped it away. I got some ammonia and held it
to his nose. I spent perhaps ten minutes in attempts to resusci-
tate him, but he was dead.

"In my horror I ran to the doors and bolted them. A terrible,
awful panic engulfed me. What should I do?

"It never occurred to me to go for help, to tell what had happened. All I could see was the need to conceal Dr. Parkman's
body in order to avoid the blackest disgrace.

"Consequently, the first thing I did, when I could do anything, was to drag the body into the private room adjoining my
upper laboratory. There I stripped Dr. Parkman of his clothes,
putting all the clothes in the fire burning in the upper laboratory. They were all consumed that afternoon, papers, pocketbook, and everything else Dr. Parkman carried with him. I

did not examine the contents of his pockets nor remove anything from them except his watch. I put his watch in my own
pocket and threw it over the bridge as I went home to Cambridge that night.

"My next action was to get the body up in the sink in the
small private room off my upper laboratory. By propping it
against the wall in a sitting position and getting up into the
sink myself, I was able to draw the body up into the sink. There
I dismembered it. This work was done quickly and with a terrible sense of urgency. The knife I used was the one found in the
tea chest. I made no use of the Turkish knife, as it was called
at the trial. I kept that knife as an ornament on a mantel in my
house in Cambridge. My daughters cleaned it frequently, a
fact that accounts for the marks of oil and whiting found on it.
I had brought it over to Boston to get its silver sheath mended.

"While I dismembered the body, I kept a stream of water
running in the sink, carrying off the blood through a pipe that
passed down through the lower laboratory. I had the furnace
going in the lower laboratory and I put the head and the viscera
and some of the extremities into the fire before I left the College that afternoon. The pelvis, the thorax, and the remaining
limbs were put into the lead-lined wells in my lecture table.
Those pieces of the body remained there until after the police
officers visited me on Monday.

"Then I set about cleaning up all traces of what had been
done. During that process I took up the stick with which the
fatal blow had been struck. It was a stump of a large grapevine
about two inches in diameter and about two feet long. I had
brought it over from Cambridge for the purpose of showing the
effect of certain chemical fluids in coloring wood. The grapevine is well suited to this purpose since it is very porous. That
afternoon before I left the College, I put the grapevine stump
into the fire.

"From either the floor or that table — I think it was the

table — I picked up the two notes showing my indebtedness to
Dr. Parkman. For a reason that is not clear to me, I seized an
old metal pen lying on the table, dashed it across the face of the
notes, and then put them into my pocket. I do not know why
I did this rather than put them in the fire, for I had not considered for a moment what effect either mode of disposing of
them would have on my indebtedness to Dr. Parkman and the
others. Neither had I given a single thought to the question as
to what account I should give of the object or the results of my
interview with Dr. Parkman.

"I then collected myself as well as I could so that I might
meet my family and others with composure. At six o'clock I left
the College to go home.

"Saturday evening I read the notice in the *Transcript* respecting Dr. Parkman's disappearance. At that time I felt deeply the
necessity of immediately taking a position as to the nature of my
interview with Dr. Parkman, for I saw that it must become
known that I had had such an interview with him. I had arranged the interview by an unsealed note on Tuesday and then
on Friday had myself called at Dr. Parkman's house in broad
daylight and confirmed the arrangement. I had probably been
seen by Dr. Parkman's manservant and perhaps he overheard
our conversation. Moreover, I knew not how many persons
Dr. Parkman might have told about his appointment with me
or how many had seen him entering my rooms. In all probability it was known that Dr. Parkman had an appointment
with me. Therefore I must be ready to explain it.

"This problem caused me great anxiety. However, by Sunday I had decided on my course of action. I would go into Boston and be the first to declare myself the person, as yet unknown,
with whom Dr. Parkman had had an appointment at half-past
one on Friday afternoon. I would take the ground that I had
invited him to the College to pay him the money and that I
had paid him the money. I fixed upon the sum by taking the

small note and adding the interest. It appears that I did not do this correctly. If I had thought of this course earlier, I should not have deposited Pettee's check for $90 in the Charles River Bank on Saturday. I should have kept it and said it was part of the sum I paid to Dr. Parkman. Pettee knew that at the time of the interview I had money from the sale of tickets to students. He himself had given me the money earlier that morning. It had not occurred to me that I should ever show the canceled notes in proof of payment. If it had, I should have destroyed the large note and let it be inferred that it was gone with the missing man. I should have kept only the small one, which was all that I could pretend to have paid. As it was, my single thought was concealment and safety. Everything else was incidental to that. I was in no state to consider my ulterior pecuniary interests. Money, though I needed it so much, was of no account with me in that condition of mind.

"If I had designed and premeditated the homicide of Dr. Parkman in order to get possession of the notes with the objective of canceling my debt, I not only should not have deposited Pettee's check, I should have drawn my money from the bank and taken occasion to mention to the cashier that I had a sum to take out for Dr. Parkman. I should have said the same to Henchman when I borrowed $10 of him. I should have remarked to him that I was that much short of a large sum I was to pay to Dr. Parkman the following day. I borrowed the $10 from Henchman in order to have pocket money for the day.

"If I had planned and intended the homicide of Dr. Parkman, I should not have made the appointment with him twice, each time in so open a manner that other persons would certainly know of it. I sent word to him by an unsealed note; I went myself in the broad light of day to confirm our appointment. And I should not have invited him to my rooms at an hour when the College would have been full of students and others for the hour I suggested, for our meeting was the hour — just after the

lecture — at which persons having business with me were always directed to call.

"I acted on my decision to visit the Reverend Francis Parkman on Sunday afternoon. On that occasion I told him that I
was the person with whom Dr. Parkman had had an appointment on Friday afternoon. I said that I had asked Dr. Parkman
to come to the College to see me so that I could pay him money
I owed him. I told the Reverend Mr. Parkman that I paid
Dr. Parkman the money and that he went away immediately
after I had done so.

"After my interview with the Reverend Mr. Parkman, I
stopped in at my rooms at the College but I did nothing with
the remains. It was not until after the visit of the officers on
Monday that I took the pelvis and some of the limbs from the
lead-lined wells and threw them into the privy vault. I thought
I did not pack the thorax into the tea chest until after the officers' second visit on Tuesday, but Kingsley's testimony shows
that I must have done it sooner. The perforation of the thorax
which was given so much consideration during the trial was
made by the knife at the time of the removal of the viscera.

"On Wednesday I made a fire in the furnace in the lower
laboratory. Some of the limbs, I cannot remember which ones,
were consumed at that time. This was the last I had to do with
the remains. I ordered the tin box for the purpose of disposing
of the thorax, although I had not concluded how I should get
rid of it. The fish hooks, tied up as grapples, were to be used
for drawing up the parts in the vault when I had decided what
to do with them.

"When the officers called for me on Friday, the thirtieth, I
was in doubt as to whether I was under arrest or whether
there was to be another, more careful search of my rooms. The
latter hypothesis was hardly less appalling than the former.
When we went into Boston by way of Craigie's bridge, I
thought the arrest was probable. When we stopped at the jail,

I was sure of my fate and before I got out of the carriage, I took a dose of strychnine from my pocket and swallowed it. I had prepared it in the shape of a pill before I left my laboratory on the twenty-third. I thought I could not bear to survive detection. I thought I had taken a large dose, but the state of my nervous system probably defeated its action, at least partially. The effects of the poison were terrible beyond description. It took effect at the College but was much worse afterwards.

"The 'little bundle' referred to in the letter to my family that was detained by the jailer contained only a bottle of citric acid for domestic use. I had seen it stated in the papers that I had purchased a quantity of *oxalic* acid which it was presumed I meant to use for the removal of blood stains. I wished the parcel to be kept untouched so that if the occasion should arise, I could show what it really was that I had purchased.

"I wrote only one of the anonymous letters produced at the trial, the one mailed from East Cambridge."

Dr. Webster's statement concluded, Dr. Putnam returned papers to the table. He told the committee that when Dr. Webster finished his account of Dr. Parkman's death and of subsequent events, Dr. Putnam challenged him abruptly.

"Dr. Webster," he said, "in all probability your days are numbered. You cannot, you dare not, speak falsely to me now. You must not die with a lie in your mouth and so prove to yourself that your repentance for your sins is insincere and ineffectual. Tell me the truth in a confidence to be kept sacred during your lifetime and as much longer as my regard for the happiness of your family shall seem to me to require and the interest of truth and justice to permit. Search to the bottom of your heart for the history of your motives and tell me, before God, did it never occur to you before the death of Dr. Parkman that his death, if you could bring it to pass, would be of great advantage to you? As a dying man, I charge you to answer me truthfully or else be silent. Had you not such a thought?"

Dr. Webster answered with great feeling. "No, never!" he cried. "As I live and as God is my witness, never! I was no more capable of such a thought than one of my innocent children. I never had the remotest idea of injuring Dr. Parkman until the moment the blow was struck. Dr. Parkman was extremely severe and sharp-tongued, the most provoking of men, and I am irritable and passionate. A quickness and violence of temper has been the besetting sin of my life. I was an only child, much indulged, and I have never acquired the control over my passions that I should have acquired early, and the consequence of it is all this."

"But you notified Dr. Parkman to meet you at a certain hour and told him you would pay him when you knew you did not have the means to do so," Dr. Putnam said.

Dr. Webster shook his head. "I did not tell him I should pay him and there is no evidence that I told him so except my own words spoken after his disappearance. Those words were part of the miserable tissue of falsehoods to which I was committed from the moment I began to conceal the homicide. No, I never had a thought of injuring Dr. Parkman."

As he concluded his comments on his discussion with Dr. Webster, Dr. Putnam again took up the papers from the table. At Dr. Webster's request he would now read additional material Dr. Webster had written to explain certain incidents testified to at the time of the trial.

In what he called his Supplementary Explanations, Dr. Webster was at pains to show that Littlefield was mistaken when he said the blood he was asked to procure from the hospital was to be used during Dr. Webster's lecture on the day of Dr. Parkman's disappearance. At great length Dr. Webster explained that every year he revised all his lectures and he wanted the blood for the purpose of trying experiments he was considering adding to his already prepared lecture.

He wrote, "One of the experiments which I determined to try was to make a pile of pieces of pasteboard and animal muscle, the pasteboard being soaked in blood. I had read that with such an arrangement, currents of electricity would be set in motion between the blood and the muscle. This I was desirous of putting to the test and of introducing into the lectures on Animal Chemistry."

Dr. Webster was at pains, also, to explain that he was interested in the dissecting room vault only because of the offensive odors that were a problem to everyone in the building. He had advised the janitor to dissolve twenty-five pounds of sulphate and throw it into the vault as a way of dispelling the odors. Moreover, Dr. Webster was curious to find out what gases were evolved from the animal matter in a vault to which sea water gained admission.

He wrote, "I was the more desirous of examining this mixture of gases as the attention of medical men and the public has recently turned to the consideration of the effects of the gases from cemeteries upon health and many startling statements have been made, especially in London. It was one object with me to make experiments upon the gases with various chemical agents for the purpose of arriving at the cheapest and simplest method or material for neutralizing their injurious effects. To ascertain if the bases would support combustion, I suggested putting a lighted candle down into the vault. In order to collect the gases, I wanted to get a bottle filled with water into the vault. When the bottle was inverted, the gases would take the place of the water and could then be subjected to experiment."

Dr. Webster told how it happened that there were spots of nitric acid on the stairs. In his lecture on chemical affinity it was his object to show the changes in the appearance and properties of chemicals that can result from their action on each other. "To show this it was my practice to prepare a quantity of nitric

oxide gas by the action of nitric acid upon copper. Great heat
is developed during the action and the glass retort containing
the materials is very liable to crack. The action of the acid upon
the copper gives rise to a green liquid; viz., nitrate of copper.
Whenever the retort cracked from the heat, I always took it
quickly out of the room on account of its unpleasant odor and
its injurious effects upon any brass or other metal. As I ran
down the stairs to the lower laboratory where I threw the
cracked retort into the sink, the nitrate dropping from it made
the spots of green liquid that were seen on the stairs and the
wall."

Then Dr. Webster made a statement about the grapevine
stump. He said he had the grapevines sent over from Cambridge solely for the purpose of burning them to have their
ashes for use in his garden at home. He said that the year before he had saved all the trimmings from his vines and burned
them in a small stove in his garden. "I left the stove to cool and
on my return found that an Irishman who worked in the garden had cleared out the stove and thrown away the ashes. To
avoid a similar accident I decided to burn the vines in a stove
in my laboratory. For this purpose they were sent over from
Cambridge."

As he refolded the papers on which Dr. Webster's supplementary statement was written, Dr. Putnam looked at the men
seated at the oval table. Something in their expressions
prompted him to say that if the committee's response to the pe-
titioner was not favorable at this time, he hoped their report
would not be made until they had heard additional arguments
at another sitting.

Three days later Dr. Putnam again appeared before the
Committee on Pardons. This time Mrs. Webster and the Webster girls were with him. Except for her visits to the Leverett
Street jail, this was Mrs. Webster's first venture outside her
home since Dr. Webster's arrest. She handled her appearance

before the committee with great dignity and considerable composure. Later Dr. Putnam said that when he had the heart-rending duty of telling Mrs. Webster of her husband's confession, he found that she had long suspected the truth. The three Webster girls made their pleas for commutation of their father's sentence with courage and in a manner that made apparent their desperate eagerness to help him. There was no doubt that the committee was moved by their appeals.

At half-past ten on the morning of July 8 the committee heard others who wished to speak in support of Dr. Webster's petition. Dr. Charles M. Winship of Roxbury told how even a slight blow on the temple might cause death. A man could die from striking his temple during a fall. The Reverend James Ritchie, also of Roxbury, knew of a case where death resulted from the blow of a ruler on a man's temple. Dr. Jeffries Wyman told the committee that on the basis of his examination of the bones, he judged that Dr. Parkman's skull was slightly below average in thickness and, as was often true of older people, his skull was brittle.

Professor Francis Bowen, who taught philosophy at Harvard College, presented a petition for commutation of sentence signed by thirty-eight Cambridge families. The Reverend Charles Spear, a leader in the movement for the abolition of capital punishment, presented a number of other petitions, one of them from Manchester, New Hampshire, signed by seventy-nine *women*. He asked that the committee grant Dr. Webster's friends more time to collect other petitions circulating through the country. His request was granted and another hearing was scheduled for July 18.

Lieutenant Governor Reed commented that many petitions had been received from women "whose sympathies were excited by the case." He added that most of the petitions had been signed before Dr. Webster made his confession. Holding up a petition with "Thou shalt not Kill" written on it, the Lieutenant Governor said he understood that the more accurate translation of that passage was "Thou shalt not Murder." Before he adjourned the hearing, he reported that the committee had received a letter from one of the jurors, Benjamin H. Greene of Cambridge, supporting Dr. Webster's petition for commutation of sentence. He reported, also, that during the previous day three men had claimed to have murdered Dr. Parkman.

Dr. Webster's friends were deeply disappointed in the number of petitions they had accumulated by July 18. They had scarcely 1500 names to present to the committee that morning. To their dismay and their amazement Boston people had been most apathetic about circulating petitions. Could it be that President Zachary Taylor's death on the ninth had channeled public sympathy away from Dr. Webster? For days half the people in town were busy shrouding their front doors in black, and now nobody seemed to talk about anything but Dr. Luther Bell's eulogy at Boston's own funeral service for the late President of the United States.

At the conclusion of the hearing the Reverend J. M. Usher rose to urge a stay of execution for Dr. Webster until after the next election. He felt that before another hanging took place in Massachusetts, the people themselves should have an opportunity to express themselves on the question of the death penalty.

However, on July 19, the committee presented its recommendation to Governor Briggs. After the most careful deliberation it had concluded that "the palliating facts and circumstances set forth in the confession have not been so confirmed by other evidence and circumstances as to form a proper and sufficient basis for Executive interference." The committee named Friday, August 30, as the day of the execution.

The Governor's Council accepted the committee's recommendation, one man, Benjamin F. Copeland, a member of Dr. Putnam's congregation, voting in the negative on the basis that there was insufficient evidence to warrant the committee's recommendation.

The committee's report came as no surprise to most Bostonians. Notwithstanding Dr. Putnam's statements — and certainly there was no question whatsoever of that gentleman's integrity — many felt that Dr. Webster's confession was a contrived piece of writing that smacked of a desperate man's frantic efforts to escape the gallows. A man who had lied for months might very well lie again especially when he had nothing to lose by lying. Witness his statement in his first petition to the Governor. "To Him who seeth in secret, and before whom I may ere long be called to appear, would I appeal for the truth of which I now declare, as also for the truth of the solemn declaration that I had no agency in placing the remains of a human body in or under my rooms in the Medical College. I am wholly innocent of this charge to the truth of which the Searcher of all hearts is a witness." Could a man capable of such blasphemy ever again be trusted?

The consensus was that the answer was no. Consider Dr. Webster's conflicting statements about the grapevine stump, the weapon with which the fatal blow was struck. In his Confessional Statement, so called, he said he had brought the stump over to the laboratory to show his students the action of certain chemicals on porous wood. But in his Supplementary Explanations he told the committee he had the grapevines sent over from Cambridge solely for the purpose of burning them in his laboratory furnace so he could have the ashes for his garden. Well, did Dr. Webster have the stump in his laboratory to use in a demonstration during a lecture or did he have it sent over from Cambridge to burn for ashes for his garden? *Which?* Or was there another explanation, the true explanation? Did he have the stump on hand because he planned to use it to murder Dr. Parkman?

There were those who said that Dr. Webster's petition for

commutation of sentence would have been granted if he had
not submitted that supplementary material to the Committee
on Pardons. Others were of the opinion that Dr. Webster still
would escape the gallows — if the Parkman family decided to
intercede on his behalf. Most people thought that if the
decision were Mrs. George Parkman's, the family would approach the Governor. However, it was common knowledge
that Mrs. Parkman's views were not dominant in her family.
Everybody knew of George Parkman Jr.'s exchange of letters
with Dr. Putnam over certain statements the latter had made
to the Committee on Pardons, statements young Parkman considered insulting to his father's memory. And certainly all
Boston was aware of the Reverend Mr. Parkman's feeling over
the loss of his one remaining brother under such terrible circumstances and at the hands of a man the Parkman family had
befriended for years. Also, the younger Francis Parkman, who
very rarely agreed with his father on any subject, shared his
feeling about Dr. Webster. He wrote a friend that Dr. Webster had murdered Dr. Parkman "in order to prevent the ex-
posure of numerous frauds and swindling transactions of
which he, Webster, was guilty . . . the feeling of satisfaction
at the result of the trial is, I believe, universal."

The consensus was that the Parkman family would not inter-
vene in Dr. Webster's behalf. He would hang. And he *should*
hang, Richard Henry Dana said. In a man of social and academic position the behavior of which Dr. Webster was guilty
was appalling. In a word, John Webster had committed the
unpardonable sin: he had betrayed his class.

CHAPTER XVI

The Hanging

MONDAY MORNING, July 22, Sheriff Eveleth walked slowly but resolutely toward the Leverett Street jail. A warm-hearted man, he would have given much to avoid the official responsibility that weighed heavily on him this fine summer morning. He pondered the conversation he was to have with Dr. Webster. Was there any kind way to tell a man that within six weeks he would swing from a scaffold in the yard of the Leverett Street jail?

Sitting opposite Sheriff Eveleth, a bouquet from his own garden on the table beside him, Dr. Webster did all he could to ease the situation. He said he welcomed an opportunity to tell the Sheriff that he felt the Governor's decision, of which his attorneys had already informed him, was a just decision. Then Dr. Webster made a statement he was to repeat many times during the remaining weeks of his life. He said, "If by giving my life, I can atone even in part for the wrong I have done, I am glad to die on the scaffold."

He added that he had no fear of dying. Dr. Putnam had helped him achieve true repentance and he had firm faith in the Almighty's willingness to forgive a truly repentant sinner, even a man whose sins were as black as his own. Littlefield and his wife had come to see him at his request and he had begged — and received — their forgiveness. To the others,

the Reverend Mr. Parkman among them, he had written letters to be delivered after his death. Now he felt at peace; he
was ready to atone for the terrible thing he had done. When
at the end of their interview the Sheriff said it was his duty to
ask for Dr. Webster's razor and his belt, Dr. Webster surren-
dered them readily. Shaking his head he said he had no
thought of suicide: he was too much of a Christian for that.

Then Dr. Webster's expression changed. His face grew very
grave. Leaning forward, he said he had one request to make
of the Sheriff, by far the most important request of his entire
life. After a pause he said he could bear whatever lay ahead
of him — the crowd, the scaffold, the hangman — if only he
could spare his family the agony of knowing that his last hour
on earth was at hand. He did not want his wife and his
daughters to know the time of his execution until that time
had passed.

As far as anybody knows, Mrs. Webster and the girls visited
Dr. Webster on Thursday, August 29, unaware that they were
seeing him for the last time. They stayed about four hours,
the usual length of their visit, and their conversation with him,
as well as their comments to Gus Andrews, the jailer, gave Dr.
Webster every reason to believe they knew nothing of the
event scheduled for the following day.

Before his family arrived that afternoon, Dr. Webster was
tense and anxious for fear something in his manner or some
comment that escaped him would betray his secret. He did
have a few moments of terrible anxiety. Just as Mrs. Webster
and the girls were leaving, Gus Andrews appeared unexpectedly and told a long story about how the jail yard was noisy
with men unloading wood, fuel for the winter, and he was sure
it would be much pleasanter for the ladies if they left by a door
that opened on Lowell Street. They could easily do that by
walking through Andrews' quarters. He had taken the liberty

of directing their carriage over to Lowell Street, where it was now waiting.

Later when Andrews came back to see him after Mrs. Webster and the girls had gone, Dr. Webster knew his panic was justified. Andrews told him that during the afternoon a crowd had gathered on Leverett Street. On other occasions there had been a dozen or so people waiting to see Dr. Webster's family leave the jail but never a crowd of this size. Andrews was worried for fear word had leaked out about Friday and alarmed that somebody in the crowd would cry out the information to Mrs. Webster and the girls. Hence the story about the winter wood. Dr. Webster grasped Andrews' hand. In tears he said there was no possible way he could show the depth of his gratitude for Andrews' kindness and his compassion.

Dr. Putnam came at half-past seven that evening, his third visit of the day. Dr. Webster was never alone now, the Sheriff's orders, and Officers Jones and Leighton were with him when Dr. Putnam arrived. Because Dr. Putnam insisted on more privacy, Gus Andrews took their place, so it was he who was with Dr. Webster and Dr. Putnam during the last evening they spent together. During those hours Dr. Webster said again and again that he was reconciled to death on the scaffold. If he faltered during the execution, it would not be from fear of dying nor because of the terrible conditions under which he was to face death. If he faltered it would be because of his misgivings about his repentance. Was his repentance sufficient to save him from a fate that could be his throughout all eternity?

Then he told how in the last reading of the Bible they would ever share, his wife and his daughters and he had come to the fifteenth chapter of Saint Paul's letter to the Corinthians. He said that they had begun to read the New Testament together months earlier. They had taken each book in its proper order, skipping none. And now on the last afternoon they would be

together in this life, they reached the passage which for Dr.
Webster had always been the most comforting in all the New
Testament. He could not help but feel that this was a sign of
forgiveness from the Almighty. Nothing, *nothing*, that could
have happened on that afternoon would have given him more
comfort.

He read the passage aloud. When he reached the concluding
lines, he was in tears. "O death, where is thy sting? O grave,
where is thy victory? The sting of death is sin; and the strength
of sin is the law. But thanks be to God, which giveth us the
victory through our Lord Jesus Christ."

Dr. Putnam and Dr. Webster talked a long time of Saint
Paul's promises of resurrection, Dr. Webster returning again
and again to the passage from Corinthians. He repeated that
he was not afraid to die. He knew in detail how the execution
would be managed and, strange as it might seem, that made it
easier. Sheriff Eveleth had been to see him earlier in the week
and explained exactly what would happen, so he knew what
to expect. He trusted his faith in Almighty God to provide
the strength he would need to get through the events of the
morning.

It was nine o'clock when Dr. Putnam left the jail. As he
crossed the prison yard, he saw the wagons with the lumber for
the scaffold entering the gates.

When Dr. Putnam had gone, Officers Jones and Leighton
returned to Dr. Webster's cell. Afterward they reported he appeared calm throughout the remaining hours of the evening.
He spent part of the time looking through his books, selecting
some he wanted sent as gifts. He wrote an inscription in each
volume and as he did, he commented on how much he
treasured his friends. Ned Sohier had come to see him that
morning and Dr. Webster was deeply grateful. It would have
been understandable if Sohier had chosen to avoid a meeting
that was not easy for either of them. He was grateful, also, for

Professor Treadwell's visits, and Professor Horsford's, for the calls he had from Lowell and Sumner. A man who had such friends was truly blessed. He gestured toward a pile of correspondence on his table. But during these last weeks he had had no interest in seeing strangers. He had lost count of the number of requests for interviews he had received, almost all of them from clergymen. Some of the letters admonished him; others attempted to console him. In any event, he had granted no interviews to strangers, a decision in which Dr. Putnam concurred.

Some of the evening he devoted to cleaning and polishing a large shell which he gave to one of the men at the jail. He said he had always had a hankering after the unusual. His interest in spiritualism was a manifestation of this inclination. He was convinced that one day we on earth would find ways — better ways, rather — to be in touch with the Departed. As he worked on the shell, he told of the experiment he had once done on the body of a pirate who had been hanged. Using a special piece of equipment, a galvanic battery, he had tried to restore life to the dead man. He remembered how excited he was about that experiment. The Sheriff had given him the body the very minute it was cut down.

As the hour grew late, he began to talk of his firm faith in the Almighty's compassion even for a sinner such as he. He read the Bible for an hour or so. About midnight he lay down on his cot and was soon asleep.

Dr. Webster was awakened about six o'clock by the hammering of the carpenters building the scaffold. He ate breakfast, including two mugs of tea, and finished with a cigar. He divided his remaining cigars between Officers Jones and Leighton.

By seven o'clock the Sheriff and his deputies had arrived at the jail. They were in full-dress uniform, the handles of their swords tied with black crepe. The Sheriff had issued 250 tickets of admission to the execution and before eight o'clock about 150 men were assembled in the jail yard. There were twenty newspapermen, most of them from Boston and New York papers. Twenty-five others were the official witnesses summoned by the Sheriff. Among these were Osmyn Brewster and Pearl Martin, both of whom had served on Coroner Pratt's Jury of Inquest, William Barnicoat, Chief of the Boston Fire Department, Peter Harvey, Daniel Webster's close friend, and William Schouler, editor of the *Atlas*. The Sheriff had sent tickets to the families of both the deceased and the prisoner, as the law stipulated, but there was no member of either family present at the execution.

The jail yard was visible from the second floor windows of the houses on Leverett, Wall, and Lowell streets. Three houses on Leverett were closed and placarded with signs that read WE DO NOT BELIEVE IN CAPITAL PUNISHMENT. At the other houses, about seventeen in all, places were to be had at the upper windows for a fee of a dollar a person. Long before nine o'clock, the hour set for the execution, all the windows were crowded. People stood on the roofs of the sheds and the other outbuildings in the neighborhood. Boys climbed the trees near the wall that enclosed the yard. More than a thousand people watched Dr. Webster die at the Leverett Street jail on that Friday morning in August.

Dr. Putnam arrived at a quarter to eight. For an hour Dr. Webster and he prayed together. Again and again they spoke of the consolation and the comfort the Scriptures offer the dying and the sinful. At the end of the hour Dr. Webster asked to see Sheriff Eveleth. There was much affection in their leavetaking, Dr. Webster speaking at length of the Sheriff's kindnesses to him.

The Sheriff left Dr. Webster to return a few minutes later

accompanied by the official witnesses and a number of newspapermen. When he opened the cell door, Dr. Webster was on his knees before a chair, his head bowed over his clasped hands.

Dr. Putnam, standing in the doorway of the cell, offered a prayer. For seven minutes he prayed for God's forgiveness for the condemned man. He prayed that Dr. Webster's repentance be accepted. He prayed for those who had been bereaved by the transgressions of the man who was about to die. "We commit Thy child to Thee. Behold him an humble supplicant to the throne of Him who tempereth justice with mercy and receiveth the contrite heart! Open the doors of Thy mansion that he may enter!"

At the conclusion of the prayer Sheriff Eveleth turned to Dr. Webster. He said that the purpose of his visit was to inform the prisoner officially that within a few minutes he would be escorted to the scaffold.

Then the Sheriff returned to the jail yard to make his official inspection of the scaffold. Crossing to the center of the yard, he mounted the scaffold, paying particular attention to the drop. The construction of this scaffold was different from those in common use in New England. The drop on which the prisoner was to stand would be released by a spring, not in the old way, by the cutting of a rope. His inspection finished, the Sheriff came down from the scaffold and went directly to the prisoner's cell.

As Dr. Webster had requested, his arms were pinioned with a strap, not with cords. The strap was looped over his arms just above the elbows and taken around his body. Then his crossed hands were tied together at the wrists over his abdomen. He had on a dark frock coat, buttoned, and dark trousers. He wore no stock and the neck of his white shirt was visible.

At twenty minutes after nine the procession toward the scaffold began.

Immediately behind Sheriff Eveleth were Gus Andrews, the jailer, and Officer Jones, the turnkey at the jail.

Next came Dr. Webster with Dr. Putnam beside him. Dr. Webster's step was firm. He appeared calm and controlled.

Following Dr. Webster and Dr. Putnam were two constables, Officers Dexter and Easterbrook.

At twenty-nine minutes to ten the procession reached the scaffold. The Sheriff ascended and Dr. Webster was directed to follow. Dr. Putnam was behind him.

The Sheriff motioned to Dr. Webster to stand under the rope.

At twenty-five minutes to ten Deputy Sheriff Coburn stepped forward to announce that Sheriff Eveleth would read the Executive death warrant. He called upon the official witnesses to take note of the reading of the warrant.

As the Sheriff stood on the scaffold, the warrant in his hand, a light breeze fluttered the black crepe on his sword handle. The voices of children were audible above the subdued murmur of the crowds watching from the houses.

The Sheriff read the warrant in full voice.

"To Joseph Eveleth, Sheriff of our County of Suffolk,
"Greetings:

"Whereas, at the term of the Supreme Judicial Court, begun and holden at Boston, within the county of Suffolk, and for the counties of Suffolk and Nantucket, on the first Tuesday of March, being the fifth day of said month, in the year of our Lord one thousand eight hundred and fifty, John W. Webster, of Cambridge, in the county of Middlesex, was convicted of the crime of murder, and was thereupon, by our said Court sentenced to suffer the pains of death, by being hanged by the neck, until he shall be dead; all which, by an exemplification of the record of the said Court, which we have caused to be hereunto annexed, doth to us fully appear:

"We therefore command you, that, upon Friday the thirtieth day of August, one thousand eight hundred and fifty, between the hours of eight and eleven o'clock before noon of the same day, within the walls of the prison of the said County, or within the inclosed yard of the prison of the said County of Suffolk, agreeably to the provisions of the one hundred and thirty-ninth chapter of the Revised Statutes, you cause execution of the said sentence of our said Court, in all respects to be done and performed upon him the said John W. Webster; for which this shall be your sufficient warrant.

"Whereof fail not at your peril, and make return of this warrant, with your doings thereon, into our Secretary's office, within twenty days after you shall have executed the same.

"Witness His Excellency, George N. Briggs, our Governor, with the advice and consent of our Council, and our seal hereunto affixed, the nineteenth day of July, in the year of our Lord one thousand eight hundred and fifty, and of the Independence of the United States of America the Seventh-fifth.

"By His Excellency the Governor, by and with the advice of the Council.

W. B. Calhoun
Secretary of the Commonwealth"

Brief as the document was, the Sheriff had to stop twice during his reading of it to silence the boys in the trees nearest the jail yard.

While the Sheriff read the warrant, Dr. Webster and Dr. Putnam talked together, their voices very low. When Dr. Putnam spoke, Dr. Webster nodded vigorously. When the Sheriff had finished, Dr. Webster and Dr. Putnam shook hands for the last time.

Then Gus Andrews placed a chair behind Dr. Webster. When Dr. Webster was seated, Andrews pinioned his legs with a strap. As Dr. Webster rose, the Sheriff stepped forward and extended his hand. Dr. Webster shook the Sheriff's hand convulsively and seemed loath to let it go. He did not speak.

Now the rope was placed around Dr. Webster's neck, the knot behind his right ear. By accident it was pulled too tight. Dr. Webster's pale face flushed and his eyes filled.

At nineteen minutes to ten the black cap was in position. As it was lowered over his face, the rope held Dr. Webster's head rigid but his eyes were turned to the left, straining to see Dr. Putnam who, sobbing, leaned against the scaffold railing.

The Sheriff faced the assembled spectators. In a loud voice he said, "In the name of the Commonwealth of Massachusetts I will now do execution on the body of John W. Webster."

He turned and took one step forward. It was eighteen minutes to ten.

The platform on which Dr. Webster was standing dropped. He plunged seven and a half feet.

In the first seconds after the fall Dr. Webster's legs jerked spasmodically twice. There was no other outward sign of struggle. The official report of the execution states that "Within four minutes all signs of life were extinct."

The body hung for thirty minutes. Then Dr. Henry G. Clark, the city physician, and Dr. Charles H. Stedman, superintendent of the Boston Lunatic Asylum, examined it. They informed Sheriff Eveleth that Dr. Webster was dead.

Sheriff Eveleth made that announcement and dismissed the official witnesses.

At twelve minutes past ten o'clock the body was lowered into a black coffin and the rope was cut. A funeral director, John Peak, arranged the body in the coffin and nailed the lid shut. The coffin was taken to Dr. Webster's cell.

According to the newspapers the body was to remain in the cell until evening when Dr. Webster's friends would call for it. The papers further stated that a funeral service would be held at the Webster residence. Then, in accordance with Dr. Webster's wishes, he was to be interred in the family vault at Mt. Auburn Cemetery.

But that was not what happened. The Websters' closest friends had decided on a different plan — a secret plan they felt was far wiser, all the circumstances considered.

About eleven o'clock on the night of the execution a wagon pulled into the yard of the Leverett Street jail. The driver, Ned Sohier, threw the reins to the half-grown boy beside him and jumped down off the seat.

Gus Andrews was waiting inside the door of the jail. On the floor beside him was the coffin.

"I got Jones to help me bring it up. I thought it would save time."

Sohier looked at him questioningly.

"He didn't think it was anything out of the ordinary. The papers all say the body would be taken out to Cambridge at some time or other."

Sohier looked relieved. "Let's get it out to the wagon," he said. "I brought plenty of robes to cover it, though I don't think we'll be bothered by many inquiries this time of night."

The two men hoisted the coffin onto the bed of the wagon and covered it with the carriage robes Sohier had brought.

Then they climbed up onto the seat.

"This is my son, Will," Sohier said to Gus Andrews by way of introduction. He turned to the boy. "You may as well drive, Will. We'll go over to Commercial and then up Charter Street."

It was a clear summer night with a warm breeze off the river. As they drove along Commercial Street, scattered lights from the wharves on their left dotted the blackness. The houses they passed on their way up Charter Street were dark.

There was no sound except the shifting of the coffin in the
wagon bed as Copp's Hill grew steeper.

"Here," Ned Sohier said, and the boy drew on the reins.

"The lanterns in back?" Andrews asked.

"Under the seat with the shovels," Ned Sohier told him.

The two men got the lanterns and the shovels from under
the wagon seat. Then Ned Sohier said to his boy, "There's a
big willow tree about ten yards ahead. You can tie up there."
As he gestured toward the willow, he added, "And that's no
ordinary willow, son. It once grew on Napoleon's grave at St.
Helena."

Gus Andrews had one of the lanterns lit. Its rays found the
headstones of the Copp's Hill Burying Ground. He looked
over his shoulder at Sohier, busy with the wick of the second
lantern.

"Where?"

Sohier straightened and pulled a pair of gloves from his
coat pockets. "Over to your left. There's a place just off the
path about fifteen, twenty feet from where you're standing."

"I'll be glad when this job's done," Andrews said.

By the time the men were back in the wagon the sky had
begun to lighten and birds were stirring in the willow tree.

"We didn't finish any too soon," Ned Sohier said as they
went back down Charter Street.

From the hill they could see farm wagons moving toward
Faneuil Hall for the Saturday markets.

They rode in silence almost to Lowell Street.

Then Will turned to his father. He looked puzzled. "Won't
even Mrs. Webster know?" he asked.

Ned Sohier shook his head. "Not even Mrs. Webster," he
said quietly.

According to the four men who knew where Dr. Webster
was buried — Professor Treadwell, Gus Andrews, Ned Sohier,
and his law partner, Charles Welch — the Webster family

never knew the location of his grave. One reason for the secrecy, they said, was their fear of body-snatchers. They believed that the notoriety of Dr. Webster's trial would inevitably make him a target for such ghouls. Perhaps there were other reasons. In any event, Dr. Webster's wishes were disregarded. He was never interred in the Webster family tomb on Narcissus Path in Mt. Auburn Cemetery.

CHAPTER XVII

"The Long Agony Is Over"

IMMEDIATELY AFTER THE HANGING, the Reverend Mr. Putnam went from the jail yard to Cambridge to see the Webster family. He drove out Massachusetts Avenue under the hot noon sun. Harvard Square was quiet. On Garden Street the elms showed the dust of a long, dry summer.

Dr. Putnam was a very self-confident man but at the door of the Websters' comfortable, clapboard house he hesitated. Nothing in his long experience with sorrow had prepared him for an occasion like this. How could he help this family bear the terrible news he brought? What could he say to console them?

Mrs. Webster heard him in silence, her suffering all too apparent in her thin face, her youngest daughter, Catharine, sobbing in her arms. It was Marianne who screamed uncontrollably; it was she whom he seemed unable to reach with any prayer, any word of comfort. Gradually, as the afternoon wore on, her grief was made endurable by the memory of that last afternoon with her father. Now she understood why he was in tears when she read from Paul's Epistle to the Corinthians. From the deep religious convictions that had sustained her father, she herself was now able to draw strength.

Dr. Putnam left the Websters to go to Edward Everett. Much to his disappointment Dr. Everett was not at home. That evening Dr. Putnam wrote to Dr. Everett "to discharge faithfully the commissions intrusted to me by the late Dr. Webster." He told of Dr. Webster's gratitude to the Everett family for their continuing concern for Mrs. Webster and the girls. In the message he left Dr. Webster said he realized he had forfeited all claim to Dr. Everett's esteem. All the same, he hoped to be remembered with charity, compassion, and forgiveness.

From the Everetts' house on Summer Street Dr. Putnam went over to the old Parkman mansion in Bowdoin Square. There he delivered to Dr. Francis Parkman a letter Dr. Webster had written to him early in August. During the following two or three days Dr. Putnam and Dr. Parkman must have discussed that letter. Although Dr. Webster had specifically requested that the letter be kept private, Dr. Putnam wished to see it published, and the week after the execution it appeared in the *Daily Evening Transcript*. It was published with Dr. Parkman's consent. It read in part:

> I had never, until the two or three last interviews with your brother, felt towards him anything but gratitude for his many acts of kindness and friendship. That I should have allowed the feelings excited on those occasions to have overpowered me so as to involve the life of your brother and my own temporal and eternal welfare, I can, even now, hardly realize.
>
> I may not receive from you foregiveness in this world, yet I cannot but hope and believe that you will think of me with compassion, and remember me in your prayers to Him who will not turn away from the humble and the repentant. Had I many lives, with what joy would I lay them all down could I in the least atone for the injury I have done or alleviate the affliction I have caused, but I can now only pray for foregiveness for myself and for every consolation and blessing upon every member of your family.
>
> In justice to those dearest to me, I beg to assure you, and I intreat you to believe me, no one of my family had the slightest doubt of my entire innocence up to the moment when the contrary was communicated to them by Dr. Putnam. That they have your sincere pity and sympathy, I feel assured.

On the Sundays during September clergymen throughout the country preached on the Webster tragedy. Many of the clergy — and many others — saw the paragraph in Dr. Webster's letter that began "I had never until the two or three last interviews with your brother" as evidence that Dr. Webster had indeed committed deliberate, premeditated murder with malice aforethought. They said the letter proved that Dr. Webster had lied in the statement Dr. Putnam had taken before the Committee on Pardons as he had lied on so many other occasions. In other sermons Dr. Webster's professional training was advanced as the explanation of his callousness and his cruelty. The attitude of the English toward butchers was cited as a case in point. Was it not because their work was known to generate insensitivity that butchers were disqualified from jury service in England? And there was the matter of Dr. Webster's lifelong interest in fine food and fine wines. Did not that preoccupation with fleshly pleasures predispose him toward evil? Paul in his letter to the Philippians wrote of those "whose end is destruction, whose God is their belly." Among clergy and laymen alike the consensus was that Dr. Webster's lack of personal discipline was a major factor in his tragedy. An only child whose every whim was indulged by wealthy parents, he had never learned to accept any kind of restriction. As he himself said, "My passions have been my besetting sins."

The press as well as the pulpit had much to say about Dr. Webster at the time of his execution. In New York Horace Greeley was concerned that a man suffered death on the basis of purely circumstantial evidence. At the same time he was reassured that in the United States social position and education did not shield a man from the law's vigilance or its penalties. At home the Cambridge *Chronicle,* so staunchly loyal to Dr. Webster up to the day of his confession, deplored the fact that "over-wrought philanthropy spent its ill-timed and injudicious eloquence to over-turn the law and give the violator of its most solemn injunctions acquittance." But there were people in both Cambridge and Boston who nodded reflectively when they read the *Daily Times* the morning after the execution. The *Times* asked its readers, "Who can say which will stand best before that Tribune, which will be the most ready to meet the other, the murderer hounded to madness or the murdered who dogged him like a shadow?"

Whatever their opinions about Dr. Webster's fate, Mrs. Webster and her children had a circle of generous, compassionate friends. On the second Sunday after the execution many of those friends saw the Websters in their pew at the New North Church, all three heavily veiled in black. On that September Sunday the family did not risk facing the Reverend Francis Parkman, for he had resigned his pastorate at the New North the previous December. But in the opinion of those who knew her best Mrs. Webster would have been equal to such a meeting. Her courage had sustained her family throughout their ordeal, but the impact of her suffering had seriously undermined her health. She was never again a well woman and in October, 1853, she died. After her death Marianne and Catharine joined their sisters in Fayal.

Now, in September, 1850, the Websters' friends discussed the family's financial plight. They all knew that Mrs. Webster had neither income nor other resources. True, Marianne could continue to teach drawing, but she would earn no more than a pittance. The decision was that the family's friends would again be approached for financial help for them, so once more William Appleton set about collecting the money. It was easy work. On September 28 he noted in his journal, "Engaged in getting subscriptions for Mrs. Dr. Webster. Got $4000 in a small part of a day."

In all, Mr. Appleton collected $20,000. And legend has it that the first contribution, a check for $500, was made by another recent widow. Mrs. George Parkman.

Notes and Sources
Index

Notes and Sources

Chapter I. November 23, 1849

1 My main source for the description of Boston's waterfront in 1849 is Samuel Eliot Morison, *The Maritime History of Massachusetts, 1783–1860*, Boston, 1921.

1 Oscar Handlin, *Boston's Immigrants*, Cambridge, 1959, provided information about the Boston Irish in the late 1840's.

2 William H. Prescott's letters to his son are among his papers at the Massachusetts Historical Society. The letter dated December 2, 1849, is one in which he describes the Boston parties of that Thanksgiving season.

2 Dr. Parkman rented 8 Walnut Street. Subsequently the Parkman family bought the property and it was to this house that Francis Parkman, the historian, returned in 1859 after a winter spent in Paris in an attempt to recover from the blow of his wife's death. The house still stands.

2 The clothes Dr. Parkman wore on the day of his murder are described on the posters (28,000 of them) circulated after his disappearance. His posture and his walk are described in Howard Doughty, *Francis Parkman*, New York, 1962.

2 Fisher Ames' comment about the importance of Thanksgiving to Bostonians is found in many sources. One of them is *Bulfinch's Boston* by Harold and James Kirker, New York, 1964.

3 The lilacs in Governor Hancock's yard are included in most descriptions of his mansion. See Henry Cabot Lodge, *Early Memories*, New York, 1913.

page

3 Dr. Parkman's route from 8 Walnut Street to the Medical College was established at the trial. See George Bemis, *Report of the Case of John W. Webster,* Boston, 1850. Mr. Bemis was involved in the trial as a counsel for the Commonwealth. There are a number of accounts of the trial but the Bemis report is the most complete. The copy of the *Report* that I worked from was once owned by Pliny Merrick, chief counsel for the defense.

3 The location of the old almshouse at the corner of Beacon and Park is recorded by a number of writers. See Samuel Adams Drake, *Old Landmarks and Historic Personages of Boston,* Boston, 1873.

4 Dr. Parkman's training at La Salpêtrière, his admiration for Dr. Pinel, and his attitudes toward the insane are discussed by Oliver Wendell Holmes in *The Benefactors of the Medical School of Harvard University with a Biographical Sketch of the Late Dr. George Parkman,* Boston, 1850.

4 The story about Sam Eliot and his practice of standing during church service is from George Tyack, *George Ticknor and the Boston Brahmins,* Cambridge, 1967.

4 Many authors have written about the problem that developed during the Reverend Peter Thatcher's installation at North Church. One of them is George F. Weston, Jr., *Boston Ways: High, By, and Folk,* Boston, 1957.

5 The fact that Cornhill was the only Boston street with a sidewalk during Dr. Parkman's childhood is corroborated by Walter M. Whitehill, *A Topographical History of Boston,* Cambridge, 1959.

5 Daniel Webster's penchant for long canes is mentioned in *Reminiscences and Anecdotes of Daniel Webster,* Peter Harvey, Boston, 1877.

5–6 The incident about Dr. Parkman and the Irish widow with the sick child is based on Lucius M. Sargent, *Dealings With the Dead,* Boston, 1856.

7 The book referred to on the subject of Boston's rich men is *Our Rich Men,* published anonymously in Boston in 1846.

7 Harriette Parkman's name is spelled "Harriet" in the trial proceedings, but I have used the other spelling because her brother, George, so spelled the name in his will.

8 The description of the old Bulfinch homestead and the fact that Charles Bulfinch watched the battle of Bunker Hill from the roof of that house are from Charles A. Place's biography of Bulfinch published in Boston in 1925.

page

9 The story about Cornelius Coolidge and the State House privies has been told many times. See Samuel Eliot Morison, *Life and Letters of Harrison Gray Otis*, Boston, 1913, two volumes.

9 President Kirkland's unsuccessful attempt to get the hour of the Harvard chapel services changed is described in Howard Doughty, *Francis Parkman*, New York, 1962.

10 Samuel Eliot Morison tells the story of Salem Towne in his *Life and Letters of Harrison Gray Otis*.

10–11 Dr. Parkman's conversation with the boys, their mother, and with Elias Fuller is quoted from the trial proceedings as recorded by Bemis. Dr. Parkman's purchases at the grocery store and his arrangements about the lettuce are from the same source.

12 The location of Sam Prince's sail loft is from William S. Rossiter, ed., *Days and Ways in Old Boston*, Boston, 1915.

12–13 The Joseph Barrell story is from Charles A. Place's biography of Charles Bulfinch.

13 Dr. Holmes purposefully kept his students amused. He said that was the only way he could keep them awake in a lecture room that was poorly ventilated at an hour right after dinner. See Catherine Drinker Bowen, *Yankee from Olympus*, Boston, 1943.

Chapter II. Saturday Morning

page

14 Patrick McGowan's visit to Robert Gould Shaw's home early on Saturday morning was established by his testimony and by Mr. Shaw's testimony during the trial. See George Bemis, *Report of the Case of John W. Webster*, Boston, 1850.

15 Robert Gould Shaw's personal history is from *Famous Families of Massachusetts* by Mary Caroline Crawford, Boston, 1930. The pictures referred to are shown opposite page 244 in Volume 1 of Miss Crawford's work.

16 The family's concern over the unidentified visitor who called on Dr. Parkman on the morning of the day he was murdered was brought out during the trial.

17 The story about Dr. Frothingham and the glass roof on the First Church is from "Old Summer Street, Boston," Henry F. Bond, *The New England Magazine*, Vol. XIX, November, 1899.

18 The source for the story about John Gardner's talent for making

page

money is a footnote in the chapter on the Gardner family in Mary
Caroline Crawford, *Famous Families of Massachusetts.*

19 *The New England Historical and Genealogical Register,* Vol. 48,
Boston, 1894, is the source of the story about Dr. Parkman's tutoring
of David Clapp. John Audubon's gratitude to Dr. Parkman and Dr.
Parkman's interest in Audubon's work are discussed in Francis
Hobart Herrick, *Audubon the Naturalist,* New York, 1938, and in
Audubon and His Journals edited by Maria R. Audubon and Elliot
Coues, New York, 1897. The story of Audubon's naming a wren for
Dr. Parkman is told by G. E. Gifford, Jr., in an article entitled
"Parkman's Wren" in the *Harvard Medical Alumni Bulletin,* Vol. 36,
1962, pp. 26–29.

23 The story of Governor Hancock's dinner at the Green Dragon Inn is
from Samuel Adams Drake, *Old Landmarks and Historic Personages
of Boston,* Boston, 1873. The feast in celebration of the French
Revolution is described by M. A. DeWolfe Howe in *Boston, the
Place and the People,* New York, 1903.

23 The fact that Samuel Parkman bought the *Columbia's* cargo of tea is
from Samuel Eliot Morison, *The Maritime History of Massachusetts,
1785–1860,* Boston, 1921.

24 The material on the Bulfinch family is primarily from Charles A.
Place, *Charles Bulfinch,* Boston, 1925; Harold and James Kirker,
Bulfinch's Boston, New York, 1964; and Morison, *Maritime History.*

25 The principal source concerning the Reverend Francis Parkman's
difficult relationship with his son is Howard Doughty, *Francis Parkman,* New York, 1962.

25 The description of the Reverend William Ellery Channing's appearance is based on David Donald, *Charles Sumner,* New York, 1960.
Josiah Quincy recalled Channing in *Figures of the Past,* Boston, 1883.
He commented that Channing's many gifts did not include the capacity for making small talk, and told of an afternoon Channing spent
sailing with a family who were his parishioners. The family included
a shy young girl with whom Channing felt he should converse. He
addressed the young lady as follows: "Do these waves look to you as
though they were moved by the wind or as though each wave was
propelled by the impulse it receives from the one following it?"

26 Information concerning Samuel Parkman's divorce and his financial
problems is from Howard Doughty, *Francis Parkman,* New York,
1962.

page

26–27 Bronson Alcott moved back to Boston on November 17, 1849, and began circulating the information that cards for his Conversation Series to be held in a room on West Street were for sale at $5 each. The source for this material is Odell Shepard's *Pedlar's Progress, the Life of Bronson Alcott,* Boston, 1937.

27 The story about Henry Clay and the four aces is from Samuel Adams Drake, *Old Landmarks and Historic Personages of Boston.*

27 Dr. Parkman's interest in the Boston Lunatic Asylum and his gift of the organ for the institution's chapel is discussed by Dr. Oliver Wendell Holmes in *Benefactors of the Medical School of Harvard University with a Biographical Sketch of the Late Dr. George Parkman,* Boston, 1850. The Boston Lunatic Asylum later changed its name to the Boston State Hospital.

27–28 Dr. Parkman wrote two pamphlets on the treatment of the insane. Both were printed by John Eliot at his shop on Cornhill Street, Boston. Here I refer to the second pamphlet, which was entitled *Management of Lunatics with Illustrations of Insanity,* printed in 1817.

28 The paper Dr. Parkman read before the Medical Society was entitled "Remarks on Insanity" and appeared in the *New England Journal of Medicine,* Vol. 7, pp. 117–130, and was reprinted in the *London Medical Physicians Journal.*

28 The description of the Magee place, together with the fact that it was once Governor Shirley's mansion, is from Francis S. Drake, *The Town of Roxbury,* Boston, 1905.

28 Nathaniel I. Bowditch discusses Dr. Parkman's failure to get the McLean appointment in his *History of the Massachusetts General Hospital,* Boston, 1851.

29 The source for the story about Louis XVI and the chamber pots is Sanche de Gramont, *Epitaph for Kings,* New York, 1967.

30 The story about Dr. John Jeffries and the identification of General Warren's body is from Esther Forbes, *Paul Revere and the World He Lived In,* Boston, 1942.

30 John Collins Warren's comparison of Edinburgh and Paris as centers of medical training is to be found in L. K. Eaton, *New England Hospitals,* Ann Arbor, 1957.

31 Samuel Parkman's friendship with Count Rumford is mentioned by Dr. Oliver Wendell Holmes in *Benefactors of the Medical School of Harvard University with a Biographical Sketch of the Late Dr. George*

page

> *Parkman.* Their apprenticeship to the same dry goods merchant in Union Street is mentioned in Samuel Adams Drake, *Old Landmarks and Historic Fields in Middlesex,* Boston, 1876.

31 Dr. Parkman's pleasure in Count Rumford's hospitality could not have extended to the social philosophy the Count developed in later years. In his efforts to help the King of Bavaria industrialize that country, he took part in manhunts to drive the poor into workhouses. "It is necessary to punish those who give alms; the poor must be forced to work," he said. He used his studies in nutrition to develop the cheapest possible diet for workers. Even his most sympathetic biographers describe the Count as a cold, obstinate, egotistical man. See Dirk J. Struik, *The Origins of American Science,* New York, 1948. Autueil was once the home of Lavoisier, to whose widow Count Rumford was unhappily married.

32 The Boston Street Directory shows that Edward Blake and Charles Loring had their law offices at 39 Court Street. Loring and Charles Sumner were closely associated in the abolition movement.

Chapter III. The Search

page

36–37 The facts about the Saturday night search and the Parkmans' Sunday visitors, including Dr. John Webster's visit — and the Reverend Mr. Parkman's reaction to his visit — were brought out during the trial.

37 The Franklin mansion had an aura of romance about it at the time Redford Webster bought it. The story is that Sir Charles Franklin fell in love with a beautiful maid-of-all-work at a Marblehead inn where he was a guest. As the weeks went by it became obvious to the maid, Agnes Surriage, that Sir Charles' intentions were not honorable. However, Agnes was able to live with this fact, so to speak, and things went well until the couple arrived in London in the autumn of 1755 to visit Sir Charles' relatives. The latter treated Agnes so miserably that Sir Charles took her off to Lisbon. It so happened that there was an earthquake in Lisbon in November, 1755, and in the course of this calamity, Sir Charles was "overwhelmed" by falling rock. Agnes saved his life by extricating him from the rock, and to reward her for her efforts he married her. *Old Landmarks and Historic Personages of Boston* by Samuel Adams Drake, published in Boston in 1873.

page

38 The Reverend Francis Parkman lists the baptisms, burials, and marriage ceremonies at which he officiated for the Webster family in a journal that is among the holdings of the Massachusetts Historical Society.

38–39 Dr. Webster's financial problems were discussed at great length during the trial.

39 President Everett's letter to Dr. Webster refusing him permission to take the job of Weigher of Drugs for Boston on the basis that such work would be undignified for a Harvard professor is dated July 30, 1848, and is in the Harvard Archives.

39 My source for President Kirkland's statement that Edward Everett's looks compared favorably with Apollo's is from Van Wyck Brooks, *The Flowering of New England*, New York, 1936.

40 The information that Dr. Webster spent a considerable part of his inheritance on his mineral collection is from H. B. Irving, *A Book of Remarkable Criminals*, New York, 1918.

41 Mr. Shaw's testimony included a statement that Dr. Parkman and he had passed Dr. Webster in Mt. Vernon Street on an afternoon early in November, that they had had a lengthy discussion of Dr. Webster's financial difficulties, and that Dr. Parkman was furious when he learned that Dr. Webster had offered his mineral cabinet as security for the money Mr. Shaw loaned him.

42 Dr. Holmes testified that he noticed Dr. Parkman's new teeth on the occasion of the dedication of the new Medical College building.

44 Dr. Webster's Sunday afternoon visit to the Medical College was established during the trial. So were his inquiry to Littlefield as to how the dissecting room vault was built and his request for blood from the hospital for experimental purposes.

45 The Monday visit to the Medical College by Kingsley and Starkweather and the Tuesday visit by Clapp, Rice, Fuller, and Kingsley are described in the testimony these men gave at the trial.

48 Marshal Tukey produced the letter in the yellow envelope during the trial.

49 Dr. Jacob Bigelow was a man of many talents. He was an excellent physician, a pioneer in the public health movement, and a gifted botanist. He died at the age of ninety, blind and senile. During his last years he was to be seen tottering into Mt. Auburn Cemetery, reaching up to feel the statue he had erected to the Civil War dead.

54 Dr. Webster's gift of the turkey was established during the trial. So were Littlefield's attempts to see under the door of the lower labora-

page

tory, his alarm about the possibility of fire at the Medical College, and his trip to Mr. Hoppin's wharf to fulfill Dr. Webster's request for a lump of lime "as big as your head." Littlefield testified that he went to a dance at the Odd Fellows Lodge on Thanksgiving night and danced eighteen out of the twenty dances on the program.

Chapter IV. The Discovery

page

60 Eli Kinsley's trial testimony describes his visit to Marshal Tukey's office. The letter in the red envelope was produced at the trial.

60 Information about the Boston police force and the question of Marshal Tukey's deteriorated status is found in E. H. Savage, *A Chronological History of the Boston Watch and Police,* Boston, 1865.

62 The fact that Dr. Webster was in the Union Street area at the time Eli Kinsley was in Bowdoin Square is substantiated by testimony given at the trial by William Mead, a hardware merchant in Union Street from whom Dr. Webster bought fish hooks and cord on Friday morning, November 30.

62 Dr. Daniel Treadwell, also of the Harvard faculty, testified that Dr. Webster was at a party at his house on the evening of the day during which he was alleged to have murdered Dr. Parkman.

63–64 The description of Dr. Webster's visit to Littlefield's kitchen is based on the trial proceedings. So are Littlefield's discussions with Dr. Jackson and Dr. Bigelow.

64 This Dr. Jackson was neither the Dr. Charles Jackson who had the controversy with Dr. Morton over the latter's discovery of anesthesia nor Dr. James Jackson, the man primarily responsible for the founding of the Massachusetts General Hospital. This Dr. Jackson is Dr. John Barnard Swett Jackson, nephew of Dr. James Jackson, and the man who was teaching anatomy at the Medical College at the time of the murder.

64 Dr. Holmes' feeling about cruelty is discussed by his biographers. See Eleanor M. Tilton, *Amiable Autocrat,* New York, 1947, and also Thomas F. Harrington, *The Harvard Medical School,* Boston, 1905.

69 Littlefield described his discovery of the pieces of the body at the time of the trial.

Chapter V. Saturday Morning at the Medical College

The narrative of this chapter was developed from testimony given at the time of the trial. I made use of four different versions of the trial proceedings, but for the most part I relied on George Bemis' *The Report of the Case of John W. Webster*, Boston, 1850.

page

89 My interpretation of Marshal Tukey's personality is mainly from two sources, Justin Winsor's *Memorial History of Boston*, Vol. III, Boston, 1881, and Edward H. Savage's *A Chronological History of the Boston Watch and Police from 1631 to 1865*, Boston, 1865.

91 The bulletin *This Month at Goodspeed's* for June, 1937, describes the note in which Dr. Webster expressed his objections to Littlefield's making money by renting out rooms to college students. The note, written in pencil and possibly a draft, was found in a copy of the trial proceedings acquired by Goodspeed's. It was dated a few weeks before the murder.

96 Dr. Webster's preference for candles rather than lamps is in Littlefield's testimony on page 104 of the Bemis version of the trial proceedings.

Chapter VI. Dr. Webster in Jail

page

110 Dr. Webster's letter to Marianne is in the trial proceedings. In the Bemis version (*Report of the Case of John W. Webster*, Boston, 1850) it is on pages 195–196.

111 The description of Dr. Webster's appearance in Judge Luther Cushing's court is from the Boston *Transcript* for Tuesday, December 4, 1849.

111 The story about Timothy Dexter and his punctuation is from Agnes Edwards, *The Romantic Shore*, Salem, Massachusetts, 1915.

112 The list of Dr. Webster's visitors is compiled from a number of sources, among them Dr. Webster's letter to Marianne referred to above, William H. Prescott's papers at the Massachusetts Historical Society, Longfellow's journals at Houghton Library, and John Sibley's journals in the Harvard University Archives.

112–113 The information about the Reverend Charles Lowell's ministry at West Church, about Mrs. Lowell's depression during her last years, et cetera, is from Mary Caroline Crawford, *Famous Families of Massachusetts*, Boston, 1930.

113 The stories about Thomas Amory's mansion and Christopher Gore's orange coach are from *Bulfinch's Boston* by Harold and James Kirker, published in New York in 1964.

114 A letter to William Prescott, Jr., written by his brother and dated December 16, 1849, states that William Hickling Prescott had ar-

page

ranged to have Dr. Webster's meals sent down from Parker's. The letter is among the Prescott papers at the Massachusetts Historical Society. The prisoners' diet at the Leverett Street jail is discussed in Abel Bowen, *Bowen's Picture of Boston,* Boston, 1829. Dr. Webster's service to the sick inmates at the Leverett Street jail is discussed in a pamphlet entitled *Inspector of State Prisons, Fifth Annual Report,* dated September 30, 1832. The pamphlet is in Widener Library, Harvard University.

115 The description of Dr. Webster's cell is from a sketch in the pamphlet issued by the Boston *Daily Mail* during the trial in March, 1850. There is a copy of the pamphlet in the Boston Medical Library. Longfellow commented on Dr. Webster's cell in the January 12, 1850, entry in his journal when he mentioned his visit to Dr. Webster. Houghton Library, Harvard University. *The Children's Mission Reports, 1832–1850,* in pamphlet form in Widener Library, cite the noise at Leverett prison as a problem.

115–116 Dr. Howard B. Sprague tells of the Websters' visit to the Treadwells' home on the evening of Dr. Parkman's disappearance in "The Murder of the Penultimate Puritan," *Transactions of the Association of American Physicians,* Vol. LXXI, 1958.

116 Caroline Gardiner Curtis tells of the Thanksgiving party at the Charles Cunninghams' home on Winter Street, Boston, in *Memories of Fifty Years,* Boston, 1947.

116–117 John Sibley's journal tells of his visit to Dr. Cornelius Felton's house the day after Dr. Webster was arrested.

117–118 Julia Ward Howe's comment on Boston's Charitable Eye and Ear Hospital is from Laura E. Richards and Maud Howe Elliot, *Julia Ward Howe,* Boston, 1915.

118 A letter in the Boston Medical Library written by Dr. F. William Marlow, who as a young man had known the son of Edward D. Sohier, one of Dr. Webster's defense attorneys, mentions the fact that Dr. Webster's heavy smoking was a strike against him in the eyes of many Bostonians. K. A. Shenstone discusses Henry Ward Beecher's fondness for peanuts in *Anecdotes of Henry Ward Beecher,* 1887.

118 Redford Webster's will, probated on September 9, 1833, is to be seen in the office of the Register of Wills, Suffolk County Courthouse. The will includes a bequest of one dollar a week to be paid toward the support of Mary Bagley of Amesbury, Massachusetts. Miss Olive R. Carter, librarian, Amesbury Public Library, and James H. Gillespie,

page

Town Clerk, Amesbury, both kindly searched the Amesbury town records for me. There is no record of a Mary Bagley as a resident of Amesbury in 1833. During those years the practice in Amesbury was to destroy all records showing that a resident of Amesbury was an inmate of the almshouse at the time of his death. There is no record of the death of a Mary Bagley at the Amesbury Town Hall.

119 The description of Colonel Perkins' house and of the Colonel himself is largely based on Mary Caroline Crawford, *Famous Families of Massachusetts*. The curl paper story is from Louise Hall Tharp, *The Peabody Sisters of Salem*, Boston, 1950. The old Perkins mansion, much altered, of course, still stands on Temple Place, Boston, and houses the Provident Institution for Savings.

120 The story about Epes Sargent and the fancy quotation relating to President Polk's visit to Boston is from Joseph Edgar Chamberlin, *The Boston Transcript*, Boston, 1930.

120 A map in the Winsor Memorial Map Room of the Harvard College Library shows that the house that Dr. Webster built stood on Ware Street (formerly Concord Street) near Harvard Street.

121 John Sibley recalls his conversation with Dr. Parkman about Brahms in the entry in his journal dated December 6, 1849.

122 The minute books of the Medical School faculty meetings are in the Boston Medical Library. The faculty met on December 1, 3, 5, and 8. The minutes, signed by Dr. Oliver Wendell Holmes, the dean, are a bare record of the action voted by the faculty in relation to finding a substitute for Dr. Webster, suspending classes at the Medical College, et cetera. Understandably and appropriately, the minutes show nothing of the discussions that must have absorbed the men who met in Dr. Bigelow's library those four afternoons during the week following Dr. Webster's arrest. Dr. Webster's letter to Dr. Holmes, formally requesting the faculty to find a substitute for him, "someone fully competent whose services will be acceptable to the Corporation," is at the Boston Medical Library. It is dated December 10, 1849. Dr. Holmes' letter to President Jared Sparks recommending Dr. Eben Horsford, Dr. Webster's close friend, as a substitute lecturer for Dr. Webster is among President Sparks' correspondence in the Harvard Archives. In a postscript to his letter Dr. Holmes stresses the fact that "it is of course understood that nothing more than a temporary substitute is wished for in the emergency of the present situation." The letter is dated December 12, 1849.

page

123 The Boston *Transcript* for Tuesday, December 4, 1849, gives the content of Dr. Jacob Bigelow's speech to the medical students.

123–129 I developed the narrative of the activity at the Medical College on Monday from the testimony of the men who were there on that date as recorded in the trial proceedings.

125 The letter written to William Prescott, Jr., by his brother and dated December 16, 1849, tells about the markings on Dr. Parkman's body that enabled Mrs. Parkman to identify the remains. The letter is at the Massachusetts Historical Society.

125 Longfellow records his conversation with Mrs. John Farrar at the Dante lecture in the December 1, 1849, entry in his journal. Mrs. Farrar, the wife of a wealthy Harvard professor, was one of Cambridge's foremost hostesses of the era.

Chapter VII. Wanted: Counsel for Dr. Webster

page

130 John Sibley, the librarian of Harvard College in 1849, tells in an entry in his journal dated December 6, 1849, how Dr. Parkman's remains were prepared for burial. The journal is in the Harvard Archives.

130–134 My interpretation of George Ticknor's personality and my description of his house are based on David B. Tyack, *George Ticknor and the Boston Brahmins,* Cambridge, 1967. Mr. Tyack was kind enough to answer my questions about Ticknor's attitude toward Dr. Webster and the murder.

130 My source for the fact that 5000 people had visited the Medical College by the second day it was open to the public is Thomas Francis Harrington, *The Harvard Medical School,* Vol. II, Boston, 1905.

131 Julia Ward Howe was the Ticknors' chilly guest. The story is from Laura E. Richards and Maud Howe Elliot, *Julia Ward Howe,* Boston, 1915.

132 The Reverend Ephraim Peabody's interest in Frederick Douglass is discussed in Mary Caroline Crawford, *Famous Families of Massachusetts,* Boston, 1930.

In 1849, the Reverend Mr. Ephraim Peabody, a blacksmith's son from New Hampshire, was dying of tuberculosis. His wife was Mary Jane Derby, one of the wealthiest young women in New England. When the Reverend Mr. Peabody had proposed marriage, Miss Derby

page

was totally unperturbed by the prospect of life as the wife of a clergy-man with an income of only $1000 a year. However, the capacity to accept financial deprivation has its limits; Miss Derby insisted on an engagement ring.

133 Henry Thoreau's criticism of Harvard is found in David B. Tyack, *George Ticknor and the Boston Brahmins.*

133 The story about Hawthorne and the Brook Farm pigs is from Donald C. Seitz, *Horace Greeley,* Indianapolis, 1926. Hawthorne was notoriously absent-minded. When he wrote to ask the Reverend James Freeman Clarke to perform their marriage ceremony he forgot to mention either the date or the place where he and Sophia Peabody planned to be married.

133 Under the date of December 9, 1849, Longfellow wrote in his journal about Charles Sumner and the suit involving the Negro youngster, Sarah Roberts. Longfellow's journals are in the Houghton Library.

134 Charles Francis Adams records his conversation with Henry Clay about the murder in his diary, the entry of December 5, 1849. His diaries are at the Massachusetts Historical Society.

134 Franklin Dexter tells of his approach to Daniel Webster regarding Dr. Webster's defense in a letter to Edward Everett dated December 25, 1849. The letter is among the Everett Papers at the Massachusetts Historical Society.

135 The deaths of Daniel Webster's children are, of course, discussed in many Webster biographies. One of them is *Reminiscences and Anecdotes of Daniel Webster* by Webster's close friend, Peter Harvey, published in Boston, 1877. The only subject on which Daniel Webster and Ralph Waldo Emerson saw eye to eye was the subject of trees. Emerson's daughter, Edith, wrote that when she was eight or nine her father took her out to their orchard and introduced her to every tree. George Ticknor and Emerson agreed on nothing.

135 Several writers have reported the confusion in the British press as to which Webster murdered whom. See Richard B. Morris, *Fair Trial,* New York, 1952, and David Donald, *Charles Sumner,* New York, 1960.

136 The description of Rufus Choate's idiosyncrasies is from several sources, among them Claude M. Fuess, *Rufus Choate, The Wizard of the Law,* New York, 1928, and Joseph Neilson, *Memories of Rufus Choate,* Boston, 1884.

137 Wendell Phillips' description of Choate's courtroom behavior is from the Fuess biography of Choate.

page

137 The story about Choate, Webster, and the $500 is from "Old Summer Street, Boston" by Henry F. Bond in *New England Magazine*, Vol. XIX, November, 1898.

138 The fact that Rufus Choate discussed Dr. Webster's defense with Daniel Webster is from Richard B. Morris, *Fair Trial*. Rufus Choate's discussion of the strategy for Dr. Webster's defense is taken with few changes from Joseph Neilson, *Memories of Rufus Choate*. Choate and Webster, the closest of friends for so many years, both thought of ships as they lay dying. In his last hours, Choate said, "If a schooner or a sloop goes by, don't disturb me, but if there's a square-rigged vessel, wake me up." When Webster knew he was dying, he said to his long-time Negro servant, William, "Hang a lantern at the shallop's mast-head and raise her colors. I want to keep my colors flying and my light burning till I die."

140 A letter written by Edward Everett on December 26, 1849, establishes the fact that both Charles Loring and Benjamin Curtis had declined to defend Dr. Webster. The letter is in the Everett correspondence at the Massachusetts Historical Society. The reason both men gave for their refusal, their connection with the Harvard Corporation, may not have been the real reason for their unwillingness to help Webster. Benjamin Curtis was related to the Ticknors — George Ticknor's mother was a Curtis — and shared their attitudes regarding class betrayal. By 1849 Charles Loring was deeply involved in the abolition movement.

140 Charles Francis Adams tells about Sumner's visit to him on the afternoon of December 21, 1849, to discuss the letter Sumner had received from Webster. Adams' journals are at the Massachusetts Historical Society.

140 It was Henry Adams who wrote about Dr. Parkman's afternoon visits to his grandfather in *The Education of Henry Adams*, Boston, 1918. The story about John Quincy Adams' pronouncements on Shakespeare to Fanny Kemble at the Parkman dinner party is from Mary Caroline Crawford, *Famous Families of Massachusetts*.

142 The Boston *Transcript* for December 31, 1849, reports Dr. Webster's writing of his defense and discusses the arguments he was said to be planning to use.

143 The source for Rufus Choate's conversation with the Reverend George Putnam is Claude M. Fuess' biography of Rufus Choate.

Chapter VIII. The Indictment

page

144 Franklin Dexter's statement that it would be impossible to identify the remains found at the Medical College is from a letter written by William Hickling Prescott and dated December 2, 1849. The letter is at the Massachusetts Historical Society.

148–149 The Faculty Record Books, Vol. VIII, in the Harvard Archives record John Webster's misdemeanors as an undergraduate.

149 George F. Hoar tells about Dr. Webster's interest in sky rockets in his *Autobiography of Seventy Years,* New York, 1903.

149 The story about Dr. Webster's dinner party and the bowl of phosphorus has been told by a number of people. One of them is Annie Fields in *Memories of a Hostess,* Boston, 1922.

150 Joseph A. Willard describes Dr. Webster's abuse of a dog in *Half a Century with Judges and Lawyers,* Boston, 1895.

154 The main source for biographical material on Judge Pliny Merrick is the memorial to him in the April, 1867, issue of the *American Law Review.*

154 Joseph A. Willard gives a biographical sketch of Edward Sohier in *Half a Century with Judges and Lawyers.* The story about the Police Court motto is from that source.

156 The material on Fanny Kemble is from Margaret Armstrong's *The Passionate Victorian,* New York, 1938.

156 Hawthorne's desperate financial plight before the success of *The Scarlet Letter* has been told by a number of authors. David Donald includes the story in his *Charles Sumner,* New York, 1960.

156 John C. Calhoun's comment to Edward Everett about selling slaves at the foot of Bunker Hill is from Vincent I. Bowditch, *Life and Correspondence of Henry Ingersoll Bowditch,* Boston, 1902.

157 The story about the gift of the silver pitcher to Samuel Parkman is told by the Reverend Chandler Robbins in his *History of the Second Church,* Boston, 1852.

157–158 Samuel Appleton's earnings as a teacher are reported in Mary Caroline Crawford, *Social Life in Old New England,* Boston, 1914.

158 The indictment returned against Dr. Webster by the grand jury is in George Bemis, *Report of the Case of John W. Webster,* Boston, 1850, beginning on page 1. I have made a slight omission in the section quoted at the end of this chapter.

159 Dr. Webster's letter to President Sparks, written on pale blue station-

page

ery and dated January 27, 1850, is among the Sparks papers in the Harvard Archives. The letter is quoted with the permission of the Harvard University Archives.

Chapter IX. The Weeks of Waiting

page

160 Fanny Longfellow was one of those who felt the Reverend Mr. Parkman was "very savage for a clergyman." Edward Wagenknecht, *Mrs. Longfellow: Selected Letters and Journals of Fanny Appleton Longfellow (1817–1861),* New York, 1956.

160 The Reverend Francis Parkman's journals are at the Massachusetts Historical Society. The entry of February 9, 1850, is quoted with the permission of the Society.

162 Fanny Longfellow tells of the Webster family's efforts to make ends meet in a letter to Mary Longfellow Greenleaf dated February 14, 1850. Wagenknecht, *Mrs. Longfellow.*

163 The legend about Mme. Vassall and the slaves is from Newton Arvin's *Longfellow; His Life and Work,* Boston, 1963.

163 The source for the statement that *Two Years Before the Mast* was the only book in print that provided a description of California is Carl Bode, *The Anatomy of American Popular Culture,* Berkeley, 1949.

164–165 Judge Merrick's and Edward Sohier's problems with their client are commented on in the memorial to Judge Merrick in the *American Law Review,* April, 1867. Their pessimism about the outcome of his trial is mentioned in a letter in the Boston Medical Library dated March 11, 1961. The letter was written by Dr. F. William Marlow, Jr., who knew Edward Sohier's son, William.

165 Biographical material on Lemuel Shaw is from a number of sources. Among them are Leonard W. Levy, *The Law of the Commonwealth and Chief Justice Shaw,* New York, 1957, and Claude Fuess, *Rufus Choate: The Wizard of the Law,* New York, 1928.

166 The story about Judge Emory Washburn and the railroad track is from George F. Hoar, *Autobiography of Seventy Years,* New York, 1903. The stories about Judge Merrick's fall on the ice and about Judge Wilde and the "statoots" are from the same source.

167 The biographical material on Daniel Webster is from a number of sources, including Peter Harvey, *Reminiscences and Anecdotes of Daniel Webster,* Boston, 1877.

page

169 Judge Richard Fletcher was also one of the associate judges on the Supreme Judicial Court of Massachusetts in 1850. He was not on the bench when the court heard *Commonwealth* v. *Webster* because he was "otherwise occupied with official duties." He was present when the court, serving as the appellate court, denied the application for a writ of error, action it took after the verdict. Judge Fletcher, a bachelor, was a Whig and a very religious man. After one term as a Whig representative from Massachusetts, he refused to return to Washington on the basis that he could not live in a town that was so shockingly immoral.

170 The document in which Hannah Webster requested that Dr. Webster be made executor of her husband's estate is dated September 3, 1833, and is in the Suffolk County Court House. It begins, "Whereas by reason of infirmity and loss of sight, I am unable to attend to the business that may devolve upon the execution of administration of the estate of my late husband, Redford Webster, I hereby decline the office and request that my son, John W. Webster, be appointed to transact all necessary business." Hannah Webster's mark is at the bottom of the document.

Chapters X, XI, XII, and XIII — The Trial Chapters

page

The general sources I have used for these chapters are as follows: George Bemis, *The Report of the Case of John W. Webster*, Boston, 1850; Luther S. Cushing, *Reports of Cases Argued and Determined by the Supreme Judicial Court of Massachusetts*, Vol. V, Boston, 1852; J. D. Lawson, *American State Trials*, Vol. IV, St. Louis, 1915; James W. Stone, *Report of the Trial of Professor John W. Webster*, Boston, 1850. *Newspapers:* Boston *Atlas*, Boston *Courier*, Boston *Daily Herald*, Boston *Daily Mail*, Boston *Journal*, Cambridge *Chronicle*, Boston *Evening Transcript*, New York *Evening Post*, New York *Daily Tribune*, New York *Herald*, Salem *Gazette*.

In these chapters on the trial, the speeches of the attorneys, the witnesses, and Dr. Webster are all based on the report of the trial by Bemis. However, in all instances I have shortened the speeches and otherwise changed them when by doing so I thought I could make the material more readable.

175 The letters in which John H. Clifford tells the Hon. Robert Winthrop

page

about his plans for managing his case against Dr. Webster and his feeling about the importance of the trial for his career are among his papers at the Massachusetts Historical Society and are dated March 20, 1850, and April 2, 1850.

180 In an undated letter to his sisters, written after Dr. Webster's conviction, Dr. Charles Jackson said that he examined Dr. Webster's lecture room and concluded beyond any doubt that Dr. Webster had been lecturing on the expansion of air by heat when he met his classes for the last time before the Thanksgiving recess. This is contrary to statements Dr. Webster made to Dr. Jackson and to other friends at the time of the trial. The letter is in the Boston Medical Library.

203 The letter in which President Jared Sparks notified Dr. Webster of a reduction in his salary is among his papers in the Harvard Archives and is dated November 30, 1849.

211 The letter in which Fanny Longfellow expresses her feelings about Dr. Webster's attorneys is dated April 8, 1850, and is included in *Mrs. Longfellow: Selected Letters and Journals of Fanny Appleton Longfellow (1817–1861)* by Edward Wagenknecht, New York, 1956.

230 The story about the little boys bidding good-bye to Dr. Webster is from the Boston *Transcript,* April 1, 1850.

Chapter XIV. A Fair Trial?

page

231 The story about the body in the abandoned East Cambridge firehouse is from the New York *Herald,* April 2, 1850.

232 The source for Dr. Webster's comments to Professor Jeffries Wyman and his attempt to shake hands with the Reverend Francis Parkman during the trial is Edward Wagenknecht, *Mrs. Longfellow: Selected Letters and Journals of Fanny Appleton Longfellow (1817–1861)*, New York, 1956.

233–234 Dr. Oliver Wendell Holmes tells about Dr. Parkman's survey to determine the number of persons in Massachusetts who were mentally ill in *The Benefactors of the Medical School of Harvard University with a Biographical Sketch of the Late Dr. George Parkman,* Boston, 1850.

234 Dr. George Parkman's biographical sketch of Dr. Philippe Pinel was published in the *Boston Medical and Surgical Journal,* Vol. 41, 1850.

page

235 William Appleton's journals are at the Massachusetts Historical Society. The "Mr. Cushing" referred to is doubtless Dr. Webster's friend Levi Cushing, a Cambridge bookseller.

237 Judge Joel Parker discussed the trial at length in his unsigned review of George Bemis' report on the trial in the January, 1851, issue of the *North American Review*.

238 Catherine Drinker Bowen identifies Oliver Wendell Holmes as the "Medical Witness" who wrote to the editor of the *Boston Medical and Surgical Journal* in response to the article on the trial written by a New York physician. See *Yankee from Olympus*, Boston, 1943.

239 Dr. Webster's petitions to Governor George Briggs are reprinted in George Bemis' *Report of the Case of John W. Webster*, Boston, 1850.

Chapter XV. The Committee on Pardons

page

246 Dr. Putnam's discussion of his relationship with Dr. Webster and his comments on Dr. Webster's confession are to be found in George Bemis, *Report of the Case of John W. Webster*, Boston, 1850. I have shortened Dr. Putnam's presentation and have made a number of other changes in it, all minor, in the interest of easier reading.

248 Dr. Webster's confession and his supplementary explanations are also to be found in George Bemis' report of the trial. I have shortened both of these documents considerably for use in this chapter. Understandably, Dr. Webster's eagerness to influence the Committee on Pardons made him long-winded at times. I omitted some of his explanations. For example, I did not include any of his lengthy discussions of how he came into possession of the bunch of rusted keys found in his private room off the upper laboratory. I decided that the keys were not important enough to justify the use of the space. By and large, Dr. Webster wrote in a simple, straightforward, and very readable style, something that cannot be said of his spiritual adviser, the Reverend George Putnam.

253 In his confession Dr. Webster refers to borrowing $10 from Daniel Henchman, a druggist, on the day of Dr. Parkman's murder. At the trial Mr. Henchman testified that Dr. Webster gave him a check for $10 on the Charles River Bank, a check returned by the bank "for want of funds."

258 Information relative to the hearings held by the Committee on

page

Pardons on July 5, 8, and 18 is from newspapers, mainly the Boston *Transcript*.

260 The report made to the Governor and his Council by the Committee on Pardons is to be found in George Bemis' book on the trial.

262 The letters exchanged between George Parkman, Jr., and Dr. Putnam on the subject of Dr. Parkman's personality are at the Massachusetts Historical Society.

262 The letter in which Francis Parkman, Jr., expresses his feeling about Dr. Webster is dated April 2, 1850, the day after Dr. Webster was sentenced, and was written to E. G. Squier. It is to be found in *The Journals of Francis Parkman*, Wilbur R. Jacobs, editor, Norman, Oklahoma, 1960.

262 Material on Richard Henry Dana's attitude toward Dr. Webster is to be found in Samuel Shapiro, *Richard Henry Dana, Jr., 1815–1882*, East Lansing, Michigan, 1961, and in *The Journals of Richard Henry Dana, Jr.*, Robert L. Lucid, editor, Cambridge, 1968.

In *Famous Families of Massachusetts*, Boston, 1930, Mary Caroline Crawford tells the story that Dr. Webster confessed to his old friend Judge P. P. Fay on the night of the murder and asked the judge to defend him, a request Judge Fay is alleged to have refused on the basis that the burning of parts of the body made the defense a lost cause. According to this story, the source for which is Christina Hopkinson Baker's *The Story of Fay House*, Cambridge, 1929, Dr. Webster called at Judge Fay's home Friday evening, November 23. In my opinion, this information is suspect for a number of reasons. According to the testimony at the trial, Dr. and Mrs. Webster were together throughout the evening of the twenty-third at a party at Professor Treadwell's home where Judge Fay was among the guests. In Mrs. Baker's story, Judge Fay and his daughter, Maria, were waiting outside their house for Dr. Webster when he arrived "wearing a long cloak and looking like an assassin." Consequently, there is no implication in this story that Dr. Webster called on Judge Fay late at night, after the party at Treadwell's.

Chapter XVI. The Hanging

page

264 Dr. Webster's letter to the Reverend Mr. Parkman, dated August 6 and later published in the Boston *Transcript* with the latter's consent,

page

is included in the appendix of George Bemis, *Report of the Case of John W. Webster,* Boston, 1850. The second paragraph of this letter is believed by some to be a confession that the murder was premeditated. The paragraph reads as follows:

> I had never, until the two or three last interviews with your brother, felt towards him anything but gratitude for his many acts of kindness and friendship. That I should have allowed the feelings excited on those occasions to have overpowered me so as to involve the life of your brother, and my own temporal and eternal welfare, I can, even now, hardly realize.

Dr. Webster's letter to Judge Pliny Merrick in which he apologizes for statements made in court attacking his counsel is in the appendix of George Bemis' book. The letter is dated July 18. Bemis includes, also, the part of Dr. Webster's letter to Ned Sohier that Mr. Sohier felt he could make public. That letter is dated July 19.

264–267 The material on Dr. Webster's final visit with his family and his activities the night before his execution is from two sources: George Bemis' report on the trial and Joseph A. Willard's *Half a Century with Judges and Lawyers,* Boston, 1895. Willard was one of the deputy sheriffs present at the execution. It was to him that Dr. Webster gave the shell he worked on the night before he was hanged.

268–272 The account of the execution is based on the descriptions of the event in newspapers, mainly the Boston *Transcript,* Boston *Daily Times,* New York *Herald,* and New York *Evening Post.* The newspaper accounts differ slightly on matters of detail.

273–275 The description of Dr. Webster's burial is based on a letter to Dr. C. Sidney Burwell written by Dr. F. William Marlow of Brookline, Massachusetts. The letter is dated March 11, 1961, and is in the Boston Medical Library. In this letter Dr. Marlow explains that his mother was a close friend of Louisa Sohier, the daughter of Will Sohier, the young man who drove the hearse the night Dr. Webster was buried. As a young man, Dr. Marlow was a frequent visitor at the Sohier home and on a number of occasions heard Mr. Sohier tell of the night Dr. Webster was buried.

274 The statement as to the names of the men who knew the location of Dr. Webster's grave is based on two sources. In an entry in his journal made in 1876 John Sibley says, "Professor Treadwell told me that only three persons knew what became of Dr. Webster's body and he was one of them. The family on making inquiries were bluffed off or

page

discouraged from pursuing their inquiry." Sibley's journals are in the Harvard Archives. In a biographical sketch of Charles A. Welch in Vol. 63 of the *New England Historical and Genealogical Register,* Boston, 1909, the statement is made that Mr. Welch "took with him to the grave the secret of Dr. Webster's burial place."

Chapter XVII. *"The Long Agony Is Over"*

page

276 The title of this chapter is from the opening line of the letter that John H. Clifford, the Attorney General, wrote to the Hon. Robert Winthrop the day after Dr. Webster was sentenced. "The long agony is over and I am once more by my own hearthstone trying to restore the equilibrium which two weeks' straining of my entire being had deranged and disturbed." The letter is among the Clifford papers at the Massachusetts Historical Society and is quoted with the permission of the Society.

276–277 Dr. George Putnam's letter to Edward Everett telling of his disappointment at not finding Dr. Everett at home on the afternoon of August 30 is among Dr. Putnam's papers at the Massachusetts Historical Society.

277 The appendix of George Bemis' *Report of the Case of John W. Webster,* Boston, 1850, includes a paragraph of a letter Dr. Webster wrote to Mr. Edward Sohier on July 19, 1850. In the brief paragraph quoted, Dr. Webster expressed his thanks for Mr. Sohier's kindnesses and asked forgiveness for any offense he had given. Mr. Sohier did not give permission to publish the letter in full on the basis that the content was personal in nature. In his letter to Mr. Sohier, Dr. Webster asked that Sohier deliver to Judge Merrick a brief letter — reprinted in full in the Bemis book — in which Judge Merrick is asked to pardon Dr. Webster's criticisms of his counsel. "Accept my sincere gratitude and thanks for your exertions on my behalf."

277 Dr. Webster's letter to Dr. Francis Parkman is quoted in full in George Bemis' report on the trial.

279 John Sibley's journals in the Harvard Archives record the date when Mrs. Webster died and the fact that Marianne and Catherine went to Fayal after her death.

279 The quotation from William Appleton's journal is from *Selections from the Diaries of William Appleton,* Susan M. Loring, Boston, 1922.

Index

Bigelow, Dr. Jacob (*contd.*)
nances, 40, 121, 188; kindliness of,
49–51, 114; and cancellation of
Medical College classes, 121–124,
126, 127; and evidence against
Dr. Webster, 124–126; at coroner's
investigation, 126–129; visits
Dr. Webster in prison, 157–158;
and question of Webster's sanity,
233–234
Bigelow, Mrs. Jacob, 69
Bigelow, John Prescott, 109
Blake, Edward, 32–34; and Little-
field's discovery of the "body,"
70–73; and Dr. Webster's arrest,
81, 86
Blake (Samuel) Parkman, 32, 86,
95, 185; as witness, 191
Blatchford, Dr., 233
Boott (Kirk) mansion, *see* Revere
House
Boston *Courier*, 160, 172, 195, 198
Boston *Daily Times*, 279
Boston *Journal*, 174, 187, 209
Boston *Post*, 42
Boston *Standard*, 162
Boston *Transcript*, 120, 145, 183–
184, 187, 200, 223, 243, 252, 277
Boussais, Dr. François, 31
Bowdoin Square, 8, 15, 18, 21, 23,
27, 36, 137, 241, 277; Reverend
Dr. Parkman's residence in, 24,
25
Bowen, Professor Francis, 198, 259
Breck, Sam, 226
Brewster, Osmyn, jury foreman, 95,
148, 152, 221; witness to hanging,
268
Briggs, Governor George Nixon,
175; Webster petitions, 239; and
Committee on Pardons' recom-
mendations, 260
Brook Farm, 133

Brooks, Charlotte, 39
Brown, Dr., 27
Buckingham, Joseph T., 198
Bulfinch, Charles, 8, 9; and Barrell
mansion, 12; and the Parkman
family, 24; and Leverett Street
jail, 113
Bunker Hill, 8, 30
Butler, Benjamin, 165
Butman, Officer, 106, 107, 109; and
search of Medical College, 89,
93–95, 103; and discovery of bone
fragments, 99, 101

Calhoun, Mr., foundry worker, 42
Calhoun, John C., 156
California, 153, 156
Cambridge *Chronicle*, 152, 175, 278–
279; questions fairness of trial,
238
Cary, Lizzie, 119
Castle, Dr. A. C., 237–238
Channing, Ellery, 132–133
Channing, Dr. Walter, 46, 122
Channing, Reverend William El-
lery, 25, 131, 132
Charitable Eye and Ear Hospital,
117
Charles River, 12, 13, 97, 126
Charles River Bridge, 24
Charlestown, 30
Charlestown Bridge, 13
Child, Lydia, 198
Choate, Rufus, 133, 134, 141–143,
220, 224–225, 243; refuses to be
Dr. Webster's defense counsel,
135–139; described, 136–137; and
Judge Shaw, 166
City Hall, 34
Clapp, David, 19
Clapp, Officer Derastus, 49–51, 71–
73, 126, 192; and search of Dr.
Webster's laboratory, 51–53, 58,

Lafayette, Marquis de, 3, 31, 119, 226

Lawrence, Abbott, 133

Lawrence Scientific School, 112

Leighton, Mr., jail clerk, 85, 86, 88; with Dr. Webster before hanging, 265, 266, 267

Leverett Street almshouse, 112

Leverett Street jail, 74, 76, 110–113, 140; removal of Dr. Webster's body from, 273

Lewis, Dr. Winslow, Jr., 95, 101, 126–128; and Medical Committee, 146; Prosecution witness, 178–179, 181; Defense witness, 202

Lincoln, Governor Levi, 114

Littlefield, Ephraim, custodian at Medical College, 42, 62–64, 128, 141, 198, 225; his suspicions about Dr. Webster, 43–44, 54–58, 64–66, 185; and search of Medical College, 45–54, 66–67; spies on Dr. Webster, 54–58, 64–66, 185–186; and reward for information about Dr. Parkman, 55; his search of Dr. Webster's privy vault, 57, 58, 63–69; discovers pieces of body, 69–73; as suspect, 81, 88; and Tukey's examination of the privy, 85–88, 92; at final examination of Medical College, 91, 94, 96–98, 100–103; and evidence against Dr. Webster, 97, 124, 127; at discovery of human torso, 106–108; Choate discusses murder with, 138; and coroner's jury, 147–148, 152; witness for Prosecution, 184–187; described, 184; Defense's cross-examination of, 186–187; Merrick's attack on, 210, 211; in Clifford's summation, 213; post-trial criticism of, 237–238; in Dr. Webster's confession, 242, 256;

seeks Dr. Webster's forgiveness, 263

Littlefield, Mrs. Ephraim, 54, 57–59, 65, 67, 69, 71, 93; seeks Webster's forgiveness, 263

Long Wharf, 51

Longfellow, Fanny Appleton, 39, 162, 211, 233

Longfellow, Henry Wadsworth, 39, 125, 149, 156; visits Dr. Webster in jail, 162–163; puzzled by Shaw's charge to jury, 222; loyalty to Webster family, 234

Loring, Charles, 33, 140, 221, 225–226

Lowell, Blanche, 161

Lowell, Reverend Charles, 112, 113, 157

Lowell, James Russell, 112n, 113, 132, 156, 157, 198, 241; visits Dr. Webster in jail, 161; and slavery issue, 162; concern for Webster family, 162; visits Dr. Webster before hanging, 267

Lowell, Judge John Amory, 132

Lowell, Maria, 113

Lowell, Rose, 161

McDonough, Thomas, father of Mrs. Parkman, 19

McLean Asylum, 9–10, 13, 245; and Dr. Parkman, 27–30, 157

McGowen, Patrick, Parkmans' manservant, 14–21, 37

Mallory, Tim, 44–45

Martin, Pearl, coroner's juror, 95; witness to hanging, 268

Mason, Mary, 83

Massachusetts General Hospital, 10, 12, 27, 29, 123; and Dr. Holmes, 65

Massachusetts Medical College (Harvard University), 5, 13, 18, 31, 157, 182; Dr. Webster's appointment